WHAT'S IN STYLE
WINDOW
TREATMENTS

WHAT'S IN STYLE
WINDOW
TREATMENTS

Megan Connelly

CREATIVE HOMEOWNER®, Upper Saddle River, New Jersey

CRE▲**TIVE**
HOMEOWNER®

A Division of Federal Marketing Corp.
Upper Saddle River, NJ

Publisher: Natalie Chapman
Editorial Director: Timothy O. Bakke
Production Manager: Kimberly H. Vivas

Senior Editor, Home Decorating: Kathie Robitz
Editor, Home Decorating: Therese Hoehlein Cerbie
Associate Editor: Linda Stonehill
Photo Editor: Stanley Sudol
Copy Editor: Ellie Sweeney
Editorial Assistants: Dan Houghtaling, Sharon Ranftle
Indexer: Schroeder Indexing Services

Senior Designer: Glee Barre
Book Designer: Stephanie Phelan
Associate Book Designers: Virginia Rubel, Nancy Stamatopoulos
Cover Design: Glee Barre, Robert Strauch
Front Cover Photography: Robert Harding Picture Library
Back Cover Photography: (left and upper right) Giammarino and Dworkin; (lower right) Jessie Walker

Manufactured in the United States of America

Current Printing (last digit)
10 9 8 7 6 5 4 3 2 1

What's in Style—Window Treatments
Library of Congress Control Number: 2001090770
ISBN: 1-58011-111-4

CREATIVE HOMEOWNER®
A Division of Federal Marketing Corp.
24 Park Way, Upper Saddle River, NJ 07458
Web site: **www.creativehomeowner.com**

dedication

For Ray Connelly, my father and rock.

contents

introduction

Windows are key **components** of a room, and selecting the most **appropriate** treatments for them will **enrich** the **design** of both the windows and the **room.**

Window treatments serve decorative and practical functions, both of which should hold equal sway when you're budgeting your decorating dollars. Ignoring one or the other will mean spending more money and time to remedy or replace a mistake. How does a professional decorator walk into a room and quickly determine the best way to dress a window, while the rest of us can spend months being unable to make a decision about a curtain, blind, or hardware? The answer is that a designer knows how to size up a window as well as the best available options.

While you don't always need a decorator's help to choose attractive and functional window treatments, you do need information and inspiration. *What's in Style—Window Treatments* offers plenty of both. It presents the latest window fashions with advice for using them to your home's best advantage. Turning these pages, you'll be motivated by an array of designs, clearly described and beautifully photographed in various settings. And whether you're buying custom- or ready-mades, or making your own, you'll find what you need to fit your style and budget.

The opening chapters demystify and showcase various styles of "soft" and "hard" window treatments. Chapter One covers all types of curtain and drapery styles, from café curtains to floor-length panels puddled on the floor, with plain, gathered, pleated, or tabbed headings, and ends with advice on which fabrics will work best. Because these treatments are made from fabric, they are often referred to as "soft" window dressings. Chapter Two explains the differences between shades, blinds, and shutters, often designated as "hard" window treatments. Although many

times a shade, blind, or shutter sits below a soft treatment, each can stand alone. This chapter also explains how to take accurate measurements so that all of your window treatments will fit properly. Chapters Three and Four cover valances, cornices, swags, and jabots, otherwise known as top treatments. Sometimes a top treatment alone is enough window dressing. At other times a valance or swag is the crowning touch over panels or a shade or blind.

Need help in selecting the best drapery rod, pole and finials, or curtain holdbacks? Chapter Five gives the inside track on the latest decorative hardware that will fit and enhance your window treatment. Chapter Six presents the various ways that the additional flourishes and trims— rosettes, tassels, and tiebacks, to name a few—can give your window treatment a special finishing touch that sets it apart from all the rest.

Do you have a window—a bay, casement, or dormer, for example—that's a challenge to treat? Chapter Seven offers solutions that will not only dress the window with style but also enhance it. Or perhaps your room calls for a window treatment that minimizes fuss. In Chapter Eight you'll find ideas that emphasize the texture, lines, and space in the room, steering clear of unnecessary trims and embellishments.

What's in Style—Window Treatments covers both the decorative and practical aspects of window treatments right down to choosing the best hardware and the perfect tiebacks and trimmings. Whether your taste is formal or casual, traditional or contemporary, armed with the facts and this portfolio of styles and ideas, you'll find just what you're looking for to make your windows dramatic focal points and important supporting elements in your home's interior design.

1

curtains & draperies

Curtain and drapery **treatments** offer many **options** for decorating all **styles** and types of windows.

tylish and effective window treatments are no longer limited to off-the-rack, formal pinch-pleated draperies for the living room and to de rigueur frilly cotton tieback curtains for the kitchen and bathroom. A look at the latest curtain and drapery fashions will convince you that there is an enormous variety of brilliant choices for dressing windows in all the rooms of your home. Not only can you can choose from exciting adaptations on traditional window treatment styles, but for a completely personalized look you can also combine custom-ordered and ready-made components.

Although the terms "curtain" and "drapery" are often used interchangeably, drapery typically refers to heavier, formal lined panels, while curtains may be comparatively lightweight, unlined, and less formal. The style of the room and your needs for privacy, light control, and insulation will affect your choice. For a bright, airy look, sheer panels might suffice. But if you prefer a formal treatment, draperies drawn closed with a cord system can make the outside world all but disappear. Think about your objectives as you review the types of panels and fabrics available.

When choosing a curtain or drapery, also consider the style of its heading. The heading is the top part of a curtain or drapery, constructed in one of many ways to accommodate a pole or rod. In a sense, it turns a simple run of fabric into a curtain or drapery panel and gives it a particular style. For this reason, choosing the right type of heading for your panel is just as important as selecting the appropriate fabric or color.

PANELS

The basic unit of all curtains and draperies is the panel. Panels vary in length and heading style and come in virtually any kind of material, from velvet to voile. You can buy ready-made single panels, but most conventional treatments require two panels per window opening.

Lined panels fall under the drapery category. A lining enhances a panel's light-blocking and insulating ability and helps to define its shape. Although you'll often see white or beige linings, a patterned lining or one in a contrasting color can be pretty—especially when the curtain is pulled back. But remember that sunlight shining through a lightweight fabric can affect the color. An interlining is often used to separate two patterned layers and to prevent either design from showing through to the opposite side.

Panel Length

Although there are no set rules concerning the length of curtain or drapery panels, remember that the longer the treatment, the more formal it will look. But unless you're pulling together a traditional or period setting, you can determine the length to suit yourself, the style of the room, and the activity around the window. For instance, you don't want to block heat vents with heavy panels that fall to the floor.

The most common lengths for curtains and draperies are sill, below-sill, floor, and puddled.

Sill Length. These panels just graze the top of the windowsill. Windows that benefit from short, sill-length curtains or draperies include those arranged in a horizontal series, bay and bow windows, and windows that are frequently opened.

Tab-top striped drapery panels sport buttons to match the vibrant green lining. Sunlight passing through the floor-length panels projects the lining's color to the front of the draperies, adding depth to the overall look.

Below-Sill Length. Curtains and draperies should fall at least 4 inches below the window frame to conceal the apron. But if they fall too low, they may look awkward or unfinished. Below-sill-length treatments look great on picture windows and over window seats.

Floor Length. A treatment this long can dress a room with the elegance of an evening gown. Be sure it falls to exactly ½ inch from the floor, and when using layered panels, keep the back panels ¼ to ½ inch shorter than the front panels. If you'll need to open and close these long treatments, install the proper hardware, such as a traverse rod or a pole with rings.

Puddled. This highly dramatic effect is particularly appropriate for floor-to-ceiling treatments in formal rooms. It requires an extra 6 to 8 inches of fabric because you'll be turning the hem under and arranging the rest in gentle poufs on the floor. Unless you want to rearrange the curtains frequently, restrict this treatment to low-traffic areas; don't puddle panels that you plan to open and close frequently.

Café and Tiered Curtains

Café curtain panels cover just the lower part of a window. Whether alone or paired with a simple valance, café curtains look casual. And because they leave the upper portion of the window mostly bare, café curtains allow natural light to enter a room while offering partial privacy. Tiered curtains, or tiers, also are informal but provide more coverage.

HEADINGS

Because the heading of a curtain or drapery accommodates the pole or rod, its style reveals the type of hanging hardware it requires. Also, by considering the spacing between its gathers, pleats,

Café and tiered curtains, above and below left, are great for providing adjustable light and privacy control. **The sheer floor-length curtain panels,** opposite, reduce glare and offer some privacy when closed.

tabs, loops, or ties, you'll be able to tell how the panel will drape and fall.

Pocket Headings

The simplest and most common heading style is the rod-pocket heading. Here, a double row of stitching forms the casing for a curtain rod or pole. The top of the rod pocket may rest on the rod or, in the case of a ruffled heading, can extend 2 to 4 inches above it. Rod-pocket headings work well for curtains that don't often need to be pulled aside. If your panels will remain apart, exposing the rod, try bridging the gap between panels with a coordinating rod sleeve.

Gathered Headings

Behind a gathered heading, you may find a draw-cord strip that was used to shirr the fabric evenly. Rings or hooks connect this type of heading to the rod. Shallow, gathered headings look subtle, whereas deep gathers appear more dramatic. Full gathers can be bunched some more and sewn, taking the place of another top treatment.

Pleated Headings

Pleated headings give panels a tailored, formal appearance and add shaping to the fabric, which drapes in folds down its length. Pleats have many varieties. A pinch pleat, for example, is a large pleat subdivided into three smaller pleats. Divided in two, a simple pleat becomes a butterfly pleat. A fan pleat is a large, simple pleat extending above the top of the panel with two or four smaller pleats forming fanlike projections to either side. Narrow pencil pleats are spaced closely together. A goblet pleat consists of a 2- to 4-inch-wide tube pinched together at its base, and a button may highlight the pinch-point. A line of stitching flattens and secures the bases of cartridge pleats.

Floor-length draperies grace this master bedroom. To control light and privacy, install panels like these on a traverse rod or a pole with rings that allow you to open and close curtains easily.

Flat Headings

Tabbed, tied, plain, and pierced headings are considered flat headings. With these headings, the rod or pole is as important as the fabric because the rod is always visible. **Tab and Tie Tops.** These consist of loops spaced about 4 inches apart across the panel. Made of fabric, ribbon, or cord to match or contrast with the panel, both ends of each loop are usually sewn into the heading. One style has a free end with a buttonhole that slips over a button sewn to the heading. Tied loops are formed with ribbons or fabric strips sewn into the heading.

Pulled-back panels, above and left, frame these seating areas. The fabrics help set the tone. **A simple rod-pocket panel**, opposite, hung and tied back with twine, is the perfect dressing for this cabin window.

Plain or Pierced Headings. These panels hang from rings or holes made in the heading. Curtain rings or café clips, threaded on a rod, often secure panels having plain headings. A pierced heading is a series of evenly spaced, reinforced holes—buttonholes or grommets—that range along the top of the panel. Like pleated headings, pierced headings benefit from the use of buckram or interfacing. The pierced heading threads easily onto a rod as long as the holes in the panel are larger than the rod's diameter. You also can thread ties through a pierced heading to attach it to the rod.

Unusual but beautiful fabrics, left and below left, can become stunning curtains. Beaded fringe on the lower one adds special detail. **The shaped heading** of the panel below uses snaps to fasten it around a metal pole.

Design Tip

Follow length guidelines for foolproof results, but remember that they're not rules. Go ahead and play with curtain and drapery lengths. Instead of shortening long panels at the hem, for instance, take up excess material by blousing them over tiebacks for a pleasing effect.

Fabric Types

The pattern and texture of your window treatment will be in the limelight, and more than headings, panel type, or length, it's the fabric that everyone will notice first. Surprisingly, fabric is also the element that affords you the most leeway. While it's easy to pick a print that suits your design, the fabric itself may not be the correct choice. The information in the table below will familiarize you with the traditional uses of a variety of materials. The care instructions included in the table are good guidelines, but follow the cleaning instructions given by the manufacturer for any fabric you choose. In addition, always test a sample before cleaning the entire curtain or drapery.

Fabric	Use	Care
Brocade: Weighty fabric in silk, wool, cotton, or a combination featuring a raised (jacquard) design	Draperies and top treatments	Cotton: Machine wash cold / tumble dry low / expect shrinkage Silk: Dry clean only Wool: Dry clean only
Cambric: Plain, tightly woven cotton or linen having a sheen on one side	Curtains	Linen: Dry cleaning preferred Hand wash / line dry / may shrink Cotton: Machine wash cold / tumble dry low / expect shrinkage / may lose sheen
Canvas: Coarse, woven cotton. Can be heavy- or lightweight	Curtains, draperies, and shades	Machine wash cold / tumble dry low / expect shrinkage
Chintz: Cotton, all-over print fabric, often floral. Coated with a resin that gives it a sheen	Curtains, draperies, and top treatments	Dry clean only to maintain sheen
Damask: A material made with cotton, silk, wool, or a combination of these fibers with a satin raised (jacquard) design	Draperies and top treatments	See Brocade
Gingham: Plain-woven cotton fabric with block or checked prints	Curtains, draperies, and trimmings	Machine wash cold / tumble dry low / expect shrinkage
Lace: Cotton or a cotton and polyester material featuring open-worked designs	Curtains, top treatments, and shades	Some dry clean only Machine wash cold / gentle cycle / line dry / may shrink
Linen: Strong fabric made from flax. Creases easily	Curtains, draperies, and shades	Dry cleaning preferred Hand wash / line dry / expect shrinkage
Moiré: Acetate or silk fabric having a wavy, watermark pattern	Draperies	Dry clean only
Muslin: A coarse, plain-woven cotton in white or cream. Often sheer	Curtains	Machine wash cold / tumble dry low / expect shrinkage
Organdy: Light cotton washed in acid for a crisp finish	Curtains, top treatments, and trimmings	Dry clean only
Satin: A cotton, linen, or silk fabric with a glossy surface and dull back, sometimes with a moiré finish	Draperies and top treatments	Dry clean only
Silk: A soft, shiny fabric made from the fine fibers produced by silkworms	Draperies and top treatments	Dry cleaning preferred Hand wash / line dry / expect shrinkage
Taffeta: Acetate or silk fabric that appears shiny and maintains shape	Draperies, top treatments, and trimmings	Dry clean only
Toile de Jouy: Cotton or linen printed with pastoral scenes	Curtains, draperies, and top treatments	Dry clean only
Velvet: Cotton, silk, polyester, or viscose rayon fabric with a smooth, iridescent-looking pile	Draperies	Dry clean only

Choose panel style, length, and fabric to complement the room and window.

"Clothes make the man," or woman, and curtains and draperies can make the window—even the room. Window fashions, in fact, are a lot like couture. Today's renditions tend to be simpler, lighter, and less fussy than ones in recent years.

shades, blinds & shutters

Today's **attractive** shades, blinds, and shutters look fabulous **alone** or **paired** with other treatments.

Whether installed by themselves, combined with curtain or drapery panels, or paired with a treatment spanning the top of the window, shades, blinds, and shutters give you the power to easily control the amount of light and privacy you want in that particular room. While a particular type of shade—the plain white vinyl roller shade—is still practical and very serviceable in certain situations, it does not offer the style and versatility of all the different types of shades, blinds, and shutters on the market today. Because they come in a range of styles, share materials, and frequently are misnamed by their manufacturers, it's often hard to distinguish between shades and blinds and sometimes even between blinds and shutters.

A shade, constructed from a single piece of fabric or vinyl, regulates light and privacy by the amount it is raised or lowered via a cord system or a spring-tension roller. Blinds, either the horizontal or vertical type, adjust light and privacy levels as they are lowered or closed and as the angle of their movable slats is adjusted. While these slats once were made strictly of wood, metal, or plastic, today they may be vinyl or covered in fabric. Shutters installed with hinges swing and fold open and closed. Some have adjustable louvers that regulate the light in almost the same way blinds do. Others are merely hinged frames that can be fitted with the material of your choice. All of these types of window treatments are available as ready-mades or can be custom-made to fit your particular window or door.

SHADES

S hades fall into six groups—roller shades, Roman shades, festoon shades, pleated shades, cellular shades, and woven-wood, or natural, shades. A shade's ability to block light depends on its material, and pale or lightweight shades may be lined. Whichever shade you choose, make sure that it not only looks good but suits your needs for privacy and light control.

Roller Shades

Roller shades are spring-operated. They come in vinyl, textured or plain fabric, and an array of colors, making these simplest of shades an attractive option. A fancy hem design—scalloped, fringed, ruffled, or notched and fitted with a rod—can change a shade's personality to anything from elegant to whimsical.

Roman Shades

Streamlined Roman shades feature flat, horizontal pleats that may be 4 to 6 inches deep. You operate them with a cord and, like roller shades, they are available in a variety of colors and materials. A Roman shade can be made from a single layer of fabric, or it may be lined.

Festoon Shades

Festoon shades are especially decorative, and their opulent gathers appear soft and feminine. Styles include balloon shades, cloud shades, and Austrian shades. Some festoon shades are operable or adjustable, but many are stationary.

Pleated Shades

Made of permanently folded paper or fabric, pleated shades stack compactly enough to be nearly invisible under curtains. Some of these shades have a double cord system that lets you lower the shades from the top and

Fabrics and cord systems define the style of Roman shades, above and below left. **Roman shades,** right, offer light and privacy control for this breakfast bay.

raise them from the bottom. You can rest them up, down, or somewhere in between. Because pleated shades have 1- to 2-inch-wide pleats, they usually look best in solid colors: some incorporate texture or a tone-on-tone pattern for variety. Retailers also offer pleated shades with room-darkening or insulating properties.

Cellular Shades

Cellular, or honeycomb, shades feature layers of fabric that are pleated accordion-style and joined, back to back, at the pleat valleys. Newer versions of honeycomb shades have no exposed cords and operate like roller shades. Although cellular shades resemble pleated shades, their air-cushioned fabric layers provide better UV protection and superlative insulation.

Woven-Wood Shades

Sometimes called natural shades and often referred to as blinds, this category of window coverings includes shades made from bamboo, matchsticks, hemp, jute, woven reeds, grasses, and other natural or natural-looking materials. Natural shades are operated with rollers or cords, and the tightness of their weave determines their light-blocking capability.

BLINDS

Blinds, which come in a range of materials, have either horizontal or vertical slats. Their linear quality complements contemporary settings, but they also enhance traditional rooms when they are paired with curtains or draperies.

Venetian Blinds

Venetian blinds feature convex horizontal slats that vary in width from $\frac{1}{2}$ to 3 inches. You can raise and lower the

---

Woven-wood shades fit right in with this room setting. The lines and geometric shapes displayed by the light passing through the shades add even more interest.

Design Tip

If you're pairing your blinds with a curtain treatment, consider purchasing ready-made rather than custom blinds. While custom blinds offer more decorative options, the cost difference is enormous. Stock blinds come in many colors and sizes, and you may receive substantial discounts for buying in quantity.

slats with a cord or keep the blind in the lowered position and adjust the angle of the slats to direct light.

Commonly made of aluminum, vinyl, or wood, standard-width Venetian blinds come in a variety of colors, while custom blinds may have pearlized, metallic, suedelike, or other specialty finishes. Custom-made blinds also offer decorative ladder tapes in $^1\!/_2$- to 1-inch widths that cover the cords joining the slats.

Venetian blinds made of wood feature natural, stained, or painted slats. Because they are thicker than metal and plastic blinds, wood blinds don't stack as compactly. You can purchase wood blinds with squared or rounded slats, decorative ladder tapes, and even coordinating cornices that conceal the top of the blind. Faux-wood blinds constructed from PVC offer the look of wood blinds for less expense. Sometimes blinds must be custom-ordered, but they also come in standard sizes.

Special pleated shades, left, can be lowered from the top and raised from the bottom. Most, as those above, only move up. **A shutter,** right, is adjusted with tilt bar.

Measuring Windows

Correct measurements will help you determine whether ready-made options will work for you. Without them, you cannot accurately price the elements you need. Use a metal measuring tape for accuracy and record the measurements on paper. See "Inside or Outside Mount," page 34, for more advice.

Inside Mount for Shades, Blinds, and Tension Rods

Inside the window frame, measure the width across the top, center, and bottom. Use the narrowest measurement, and round down to the nearest ⅛ inch. Measure the height of the window from the top of the opening to the sill.

Outside Mount for Shades, Blinds, Cornices, or Curtain or Drapery Rods or Poles

Figure out the amount of space on each side of the window and above and below the window that you want to cover with your treatment. Then decide on bracket placement—on the window frame or the wall.

- Professionals recommend that outside-mounted shades or blinds extend 2 inches beyond the window sash on each side.
- To determine the appropriate rod length, measure from bracket to bracket. For a decorative pole with finials, add 5 to 8 inches on each side; the actual amount depends on the finial style. Be sure that you have enough room on either side of window before you buy the pole and finials.
- For a fuller curtain look, the width of the panels you use should be at least twice the measurement from bracket to bracket. Some opulent looks call for fabric measuring three times the bracket-to-bracket measurement.
- To determine the appropriate length of curtain and drapery panels, measure from the bracket placement down to the top of the sill, to below the sill, or to the floor, depending on the length you desire. If the panel heading extends above the rod or pole, add that measurement to the length as well.

Vertical Blinds

While you can fit any window with vertical rather than horizontal blinds, vertical blinds suit very large windows and sliding doors particularly well. Vertical blinds' free-hanging slats, or vanes, are cord-controlled and move back and forth on a track, stacking neatly to one side. Slats come in many colors, and you can angle or close them to control light. Special textured slats mimic stucco designs, leather, linen, tweed, and crushed fabric. You may purchase optional coordinating valances, really just heading strips, to conceal hardware.

Natural shades with valances dress the windows and door, above. Those at the windows are set inside the window frame, leaving the decorative trimwork exposed.

Fabric slats, which contain a stiffener, can hang free or slide into channeled vinyl casings that increase their durability, light-blocking ability, and price. These casings cover only the back of each slat, hooking over the edges to be barely visible from the front. Transparent casings display the slat back, while solid-color casings present a uniform appearance to passersby.

SHUTTERS

The weight and permanence of shutters almost qualify them as architectural embellishments. While shutters function like shades or blinds, they control light more effectively. Shutters feature flat or louvered panels or fabric panels set into a frame, and they look

Wooden shutters are a bold statement for any window. These stained shutters, near right, are installed on top of the window frame; those painted white, opposite, are set inside the frame.

Inside or Outside Mount

Sometimes you have an option of installing a shade or blind on the inside or outside surface of the window frame. Often the decision is based on whether you are buying stock items, which are available in a limited number of sizes, or custom-made treatments. When deciding where to install your blind or shade, take accurate measurements of the window and blind or shade, and use the information below as guidelines.

Outside Mount

- May be necessary if buying a stock item that will not fit the inside width measurement across the window frame
- May be necessary if the window frame is not deep enough to contain at least the shade or blind mounting brackets, if not the entire depth of the unit
- Can compensate for unattractive or nonexistent window trim
- Can make a too narrow window look wider

Inside Mount

- Cannot be used if the blind or shade will not fit within the inside measurements of the window opening
- Is recommended if the blind or shade will be covered by draw curtains or draperies, which may be impeded by the shade or blind
- Allows handsome trimwork around the window to remain visible
- Can make a wide window appear narrower

handsome alone or when paired with a soft treatment. Because they become part of the window, shutters look best when painted or finished the same as the rest of the window frame. You can mount shutters inside or outside the window frame, but wide windows may require extra framing to support the shutters.

Louvered Shutters

These shutters may feature a tilt bar that is used to angle the louvers to control and direct light. Vertical louvered shutters have 1- to 1¼-inch-wide louvers that may pivot from side to side. Plantation shutters fill the window opening and feature 2- to 4-inch-wide horizontal louvers that may tilt up and down. Café shutters cover just half of the window—usually the lower portion. Double-hung tiered sets can cover a window, giving you more ways to regulate the light and privacy.

Panel Shutters

In place of louvers, panel shutters feature solid, inoperable panels that you need to open to admit light or air. Panel shutters commonly consist of flat wood or a fabric or paper insert that blocks or filters sunlight.

Shades, blinds, or shutters can suit all types and styles of rooms.

Concerned about the cost of custom shades, blinds, or shutters? Relax. You can find great-looking ones in many standard sizes, including ones to fit today's popular "architectural" windows. More versatile options include patterned and textured finishes and a range of colors. Installation in most cases is an easy do-it-yourself project.

3

valances &
cornices

The **perfect** valance or cornice
can transform an **ordinary** window
into an **extraordinary** one.

A pelmet, the catchall term for valances and cornices, is a versatile decorating element that can establish the style or ambiance of your room. Though it's not essential, except in period rooms, a pelmet can be an attractive and useful feature in a room. For example, if your room scheme is contemporary, casual, or minimal, a simple chic top treatment—such as a gracefully gathered valance—will soften the lines of shutters or blinds. In richly decorated or traditional rooms, a cornice of crown molding can lend architectural importance to undistinguished windows, and opulent pelmets will balance elegant furnishings. Pelmets can also be used to cover worn window frames, conceal nondecorative hardware, and cap too tall windows, making them appear in better proportion to the room.

To ensure that your pelmet blends with the rest of the window treatment's design and doesn't overwhelm or dominate it, keep its proportion in mind. A pelmet should not be so short as to appear skimpy, and you'll naturally need longer ones for taller windows. Ideally, a valance won't be longer than one-quarter of the window's length, and the tails of a shaped valance should extend to one-third its length.

While searching for inspiration, look to the details within the room. For example, the colors in a stained-glass window could be in the fabric for a balloon valance. Or perhaps the simplicity of the elements in the room could be a perfect contrast for a box cornice decorated with tapestry and exquisite trim molding.

VALANCES

A valance is a soft top treatment made of fabric. It may dress a window by itself, coordinate with existing panels or café curtains, top a drapery treatment, or soften a hard top treatment, such as a cornice. Valances share some features with curtain and drapery panels. For example, valances attach to window hardware, as do curtains and draperies, and often have the same headings as curtains. An overview of valance types follows.

Balloon Valances

Like the balloon shade, a balloon valance features soft, romantic-looking poufs created by gathered material. But unlike the shade, this valance is stationary. One type of balloon valance, a puff valance, is basically one long pocket. You can pull apart its two layers to form a pouf, or stuff the opening with batting or tissue paper for more fullness. A cloud valance has more fullness at its scalloped bottom edge, and the Austrian valance features shirring evenly along most of its length.

Pleated Valances

The popular, traditional pleated valance is available in many varieties. Aside from its pleated heading, this tailored valance often has additional folds or gathers along its length. The box-pleat valance features uniform, hard-edged, inverted pleats. A pleated-and-gathered valance has a heading that features alternating pinch pleats and gathers; it falls more softly than a valance having box pleats, and appears more formal. Triple- and butterfly-pleat valances have pleated headings that release into soft folds. Bell-pleat valances consist of wide, soft cone-shaped pleats.

A plaid pelmet, upper left, combines an upholstered cornice and a gathered shaped valance. **The simple valances**, left, are tied to decorative rods. **A series of rectangular panels** outlined with contrasting trim form the unique valance and side panels, opposite.

Distinctive Valances

Valances that are both unique and beautifully decorative can be made from unconventional materials. If it's a material that you prefer not to cut, perhaps it can be draped and fastened around a pole or rod, or folded and stapled to a mounting board and then installed. When the material can be finished with a rod-pocket heading, it can be threaded onto a rod or pole and then installed across the window. Here are several suggestions.

- Hang graduated lengths of heavy, wide grosgrain ribbons side by side with their lower ends producing a shaped lower edge for the valance.
- Fold and drape a fringed shawl, points down, over a rod.
- Tie strings of beads or shells onto a rod and set it across the window.
- Use entire or partial pieces of lace or antique linens that have embroidery, monograms, decorative cutwork, or handmade trimmings. Some popular

choices might include all or part of a lace tablecloth, depending on the amount needed for the window. You might also consider pillowcases, kitchen towels, or hand towels for narrow windows or the upper portion of an embroidered or eyelet-trimmed flat bedsheet for wider windows. Several linen or cotton napkins or doilies, overlapping each other and with their corners pointing down, also make charming valances.

Tabbed Valances

A tabbed valance attaches to window hardware with loops, ties, or rings and, because it does not fully conceal the rod, needs attractive hardware. Gathered tabbed valances have a fuller appearance but must be at least one-and-a-half times the window's width. A tabbed valance with a shaped hem looks best when it's pulled flat. It should equal the width of the window.

Gathered Valances

A gathered valance is simply a rod-pocket valance that measures two to three times the width of the window. It may feature a ruffled heading or a shaped hem. Shirring the valance onto a rod creates its fullness. An arched rod can add a distinctive look to the top of a ruffled valance.

Toga Valances

A toga valance resembles a short curtain panel with rod pockets at both ends. The toga effect comes from

---

Tasseled pennants, above, arranged in a mirror image, continue the eclectic theme of this room. **The structured box cornice,** opposite, is a handsome architectural feature.

alternating at least three panels—one of which may contrast with the others—on the rod. If, for example, you have two blue panels and one white panel, thread them onto the rod in this order: one end of the first blue panel, one end of the white panel, the free end of the first blue panel, one end of the second blue panel, the free end of the white panel, and the free end of the second blue panel. When installed, the white will overlap the blue.

CORNICES

A cornice is a hard, permanent valance that is usually made of wood embellished with architectural molding. Although it is designed to remain in place when curtains and draperies change, there is a trend toward creating cornices of softer materials to match specific curtains or draperies. If your cornice will add architectural detail, match it to nearby trim or keep it a neutral hue that will work with any window treatment.

Box Cornices

The box cornice consists of a face board (the front), two end boards (the sides), and a dust board (the top). The

basic box may be embellished with molding, then painted and mounted or draped with fabric swags. Sometimes a box cornice is upholstered and trimmed with tufting, pleats, buttons, or studs. A cornice may cap a fabric valance that softens its lower edge and gives it a finished, layered appearance.

Shaped Cornices

Typically, a shaped cornice consists of intricately cut panels of buckram-stiffened fabric attached to a cornice shelf. Painted or fabric-covered cardboard can also be used. A shaped cornice might feature scallops, notched designs, S-curves, or pendent shapes along its lower edge and be further embellished with moldings, piping, tassels, or bands of trim.

Lambrequins

A lambrequin cornice fits around the window and extends to the floor or at least two-thirds of the way down the sides of the window. Like a box cornice, a lambrequin usually consists of wooden sides, front panels, and a top that may be painted, stained, or upholstered.

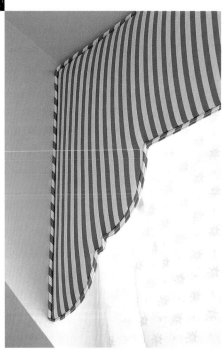

A cornice with interesting fretwork, opposite, sits like a crown above majestic windows. **An attractive lace panel,** above left, is only a part of this window dressing that includes gingham wallpaper and hand-painted flowers. **A shaped cornice,** above, is edge-finished with piping.

Make a Simple Cornice

You can buy inexpensive kits for making cornices that also include instructions. Or you can make a quick-and-easy cornice using the instructions below. You will need

- Measuring tape
- Straightedge
- Foam core board
- Razor knife or box cutter
- Polyester batting
- Hot glue gun and glue sticks
- Scissors
- Fabric
- Staple gun
- Optional decorative trim

Decide the height of the cornice from its top to bottom edges. Measure across the top of the window and add double the depth of the return (the sides of the cornice). For example, if each side of the cornice will be 6 inches deep, add 12 inches to your window length measurement. Cut the foam core board to this total length by the desired height. Measure in from each end of the board the depth of each return, and using a straightedge, score the front of the board with the blade, being careful not to cut all the way through it. Bend the board back

along the score marks to create the returns. Cut batting to fit the front and both returns of the cornice, and glue it in place. Cut the fabric 2 or more inches larger than the cornice on all sides. Lay the fabric flat with its wrong side facing up, and place the batting side of the cornice onto the fabric. Pull the fabric evenly around the cornice, and glue or staple its edges to the back of the board. Wrap the cornice around the window frame, and staple it in place through the valance and into the window frame. Decorate the cornice with trim or other embellishments.

Design Tip

Any new cornice or cornice shelf includes mounting hardware and directions for its installation. But you'll probably need to purchase mounting brackets to install older or homemade cornices. If you're not comfortable with the idea of working on a ladder, especially while handling the cornice and various tools, call a pro. A professional installer will charge a flat rate for coming to your house plus an additional fee for each treatment. Prices vary, but your location, the size of the treatment (measured by the foot), and the difficulty of the job will determine its price.

The beautifully shaped cornice and the puddled drapery panel, opposite, mimic the curves of the Victorian settee, and the sequined medallions add more glamour to the overall setting. A box cornice embellished with a hand-painted mural, above, complements the crewel embroidery on the drapery panels.

A variety of styling techniques can be used for valances and cornices.

Valances and cornices have made a comeback in recent years. One reason is that they offer a clever way to disguise or enhance the size and shape of a window or tie together mismatched windows. For example, add height to a short opening with a cornice or valance that is installed on the wall above the window.

swags & jabots

Versatile swag-and-jabot combinations **provide** over-the-top **styling** in all types of rooms.

Depending on the fabric and style, swags and jabots can take on almost any personality from sophisticated to casual or something else in between. A triple-swag treatment of lined silk flanked by piped jabots, for instance, looks regal and very different from an unlined plain linen scarf swag draped over a decorative wood or metal rod.

If you've wondered about the difference between a swag and a valance, you're not alone—even professionals who make swags and valances use the terms interchangeably. While a valance can be any of a range of soft treatments for dressing the top of a window, a swag has a very distinct form. It may help to remember that swags are shaped like crescents, and one or more swags can span the top of the window.

Jabots are the side pieces, long or short, that flank the swag. They are often referred to as cascades, or tails. Historically, a swag-and-jabot top treatment accompanied drapery panels, curtain panels, and blinds. But today's more casual approach to window coverings invites you to use the treatment by itself or pair it with only a blind. Swag-and-jabot treatments also look beautiful framing French and sliding doors.

Whether you use them in modern or traditional ways, the arrangement of swags flanked by cascading jabots maintains its place as a favorite of good design. Although shaped valances and curtain panels that have angled sides may simulate jabots, they lack a crescent-shaped element and are therefore not considered to be a true swag-and-jabot treatment.

SWAGS & JABOTS

Traditional swag-and-jabot treatments that use heavy, lined drapery fabrics are affixed to a board mounted over the window. But stylish hardware, such as decorative rods and specially designed swag holders, lets you mount swags and jabots in different ways for a variety of styles. Some arrangements using single, double, triple, and fan swags are merely updates of traditional styles. Others, such as swagged or wrapped window scarves, are today's cutting-edge window fashions.

Swag Styles

Conventional swag-and-jabot treatments are made up of separate pieces and feature at least one swag with a jabot at each end. A modern version may be a single piece of material—a window scarf—draped over a rod or threaded through swag holders to form both the swag and jabots.

Beautiful ribbon-print fabric set over a white lining, above, draws attention to the view outside. **A classic layering** of fringed swags and jabots over drapery panels, above right, stands out in this traditional room setting. **Self-lined swag and jabots** outlined with trim soften a Venetian blind in the library, opposite.

Design Tip

The number of swags to drape across a window will depend on the width of the window and the look you want to achieve. When planning how many swags you'll need for the treatment, consider the following:

- The most popular arrangement is an uneven number of swags with the middle one spanning the center of the window.
- The width of a swag should not exceed 40 inches; its depth (drop) can range from 12 to 20 inches.
- Swags should overlap each other slightly.

Traditional swag-and-jabot treatments rely on balance and symmetry, which means that you'll see the same arrangement on each side of the window. These swags and jabots are usually pleated, share the same fabric, and are generally lined. Swags and jabots, however, though traditional in shape, often are made with coordinating or contrasting fabrics that, when of similar weight and texture, can still look balanced.

Single Swag. A single swag is simply one swag flanked by individual jabots. A fan swag features a single swag pleated at its top center so that soft folds radiate from it.

Double Swags. The double swag version features two adjacent swags. For an elegant variation on the double swag, you might try a crown swag: a fluted or pipe jabot at the center raised higher than the rest of the treatment separates the swags, which slope down to meet jabots at each end of the window. (See "Jabot Styles," page 59, for more information.)

Cornice-topped swags and jabots, left, fit right in with this window seat. **Stripes and plaids,** above and above right, are popular choices and can suit almost any style room.

Design Tip

While planning your swag-and-jabot treatment, draw the window to scale. Then, using tissue paper as an overlay, sketch possible treatments over the base drawing of the window. Vary the number, size, and depth of the swags; add jabots between the swags as well as at the ends of the treatment; and experiment with different lengths for the jabots.

Intricate folding and draping, above, complete with cord, produces a distinctive top treatment. **Tasseled trim** finishes the swags and jabots, right.

Design Tip

Plaids and stripes are a traditional choice for swags and jabots. But how they are folded and draped has a significant effect on the resulting overall pattern. For example, the lines can be positioned to be vertical and horizontal, or they can be draped as a diagonal. In addition, installing the darker-value stripes as the outer part of the pleat will create a totally different look from the one produced by setting the lighter value there. Try folding the fabric in different ways and pleat depths before you finally decide on the look that you prefer.

Three or More Swags. The center element of a triple swag might hang over the other two swags or is simply hung between them. Sometimes, the center swag is larger than the others are and drapes lower than those beside it. Regardless of the number of swags, each side will mirror the other in this symmetrical arrangement.

Jabot Styles

Traditional jabots, like conventional draperies, look formal and well tailored. The cascade jabot, which is cut on a diagonal and pleated at the top, is the most common style. A fluted jabot is an open tube with a straight lower edge. A pipe jabot is a tube with a pointed edge.

It's best to line most jabots, because pleats and folds may reveal their undersides. The tops of separate jabots may be displayed or hidden by a swag.

WINDOW SCARVES

A window scarf is one of the newer "tools" for creating beautiful and dramatic treatments for the top of a window. The scarf is basically a long length of fabric, but the manner in which it is hung and draped defines its resulting swag or wrapped-pole shape.

To create these relaxed, casual, and often romantic treatments, you'll need three key ingredients: a relatively generous length of fabric; the correct hardware; and a willingness to pull, primp, and reposition the fabric until you achieve the right look. A helper can make this job much easier. Make sure that your scarf is long enough to form generous jabots because without enough fabric, the arrangement will appear skimpy. For best results, use a lightweight fabric that has no right or wrong side. Fabrics such as voile, lace, and lawn work particularly well. They are also easy to work with and form graceful folds, drapes, and wraps.

A magnificent treatment, opposite, frames a row of simple windows. **A plaid scarf with a plain lining,** right, is casually draped over decorative brackets.

Hanging a Scarf Swag

- Arrange the fabric by laying it out on a large, clean surface and softly pleating it lengthwise, accordion-style.
- Estimate at which two points the fabric will begin to descend the sides of the window, and pin or tie the pleats in place at those points.
- Place your fabric over the pole, or thread it carefully through the brackets, positioning the jabots in place.
- Pull at the lower pleats in the center of the swag to create an even drape.
- Release the pins or ties from the tops of the jabots.
- Stand back and study the arrangement; then go back and make any adjustments.

Wrapping a Window Scarf

The best way to wrap a window scarf around a pole is as follows:

- Lay out the material on a large, clean surface. Gather the fabric at the top of each jabot, and use elastic to hold it together.
- Swing one jabot into place over the pole and, starting from there, wind the swag portion as many times as you need around the pole until you reach the elastic at the second jabot, which should have landed at the opposite end of the pole.
- Readjust wraps along the pole. Generally, wrapped swags just touch or slightly overlap each other.
- For a dramatic effect, stuff the wrapped swags with tissue paper or thin foam, depending on the translucence and weight of your fabric.
- Release elastics at tops of jabots.

Scarf Swags

A scarf swag is formed by draping a window scarf over brackets or a pole to create a look of a swag and jabots. Scarf swags look best when their jabots fall about two-thirds of the way to the sill. The draping need not be symmetrically arranged. An asymmetrical treatment—one jabot longer than the other—can be dramatic.

Because the scarf fabric will not cover the hardware completely, it's important to choose a pretty pole with finials, or decorative swag brackets for securing the scarf crescent at each end. Some brackets feature ornate

A sheer, self-lined scarf, left, is draped over brass swag holders. Notice the separate pipe jabot. **Fringed scarves,** above, are held at the center by a holdback and at

plasterwork; others are simply rings through which you can pull the scarf. There are also special brackets that come with instructions for forming rosettes or other decorative fabric folds around them.

Wrapped Scarves

A wrapped scarf produces swags and jabots when wrapped loosely around a pole; it can require even more fabric than a scarf swag. The weight of this extra fabric and the difficulty of wrapping it while standing on a ladder make this treatment more ambitious.

---

other points are threaded through decorative brackets.
Each fringed scarf, right, is draped asymmetrically but when viewed as a pair form a symmetrical arrangement.

Swags and jabots of any styling can take center stage in a room.

A swag-and-jabot treatment suits almost any style interior or window. If a room is formal, a heavy, lined fabric in a traditional print is appropriate. Choose simple cottons, checks, plaids, or small prints for a country room. Sheers and asymmetrical swags pair best with contemporary or eclectic interiors.

decorative hardware

A marriage of **function** and **form** has produced a wide **variety** of **decorative** hardware.

P retty poles with fancy finials, inventive swag or scarf holders, and ingenious holdbacks are just a few of today's window accessories. Now, instead of relying only on the color and pattern of your curtain fabric to set the tone for your window and room, you can let the hardware take a supporting or even a leading role. You won't have far to search for what you need, either. Decorative hardware is the heart and soul of today's window fashions, and the most up-to-date, sought-after looks are within easy reach of everyone. Divine inspiration or a resident carpenter need not be on hand to create all the intriguing window treatments you see in books and magazines. Many of them can be replicated after a visit to your favorite home, curtain, or fabric store.

While decorative hardware takes center stage in many of the contemporary window fashions, traditional treatments also benefit from today's innovative hardware. Drapery poles and their decorative ends, finials, draw the most attention, and for the most part, these poles work just like their functional forerunners. But made-to-be-seen rings, clips, and pins pick up where old-fashioned drapery hooks leave off.

Today's array of swag holders has revolutionized swag-and-jabot treatments, setting off entirely new categories of top treatments such as scarf swags and wrapped window scarves. Holdbacks, which often coordinate with a pole's finials, replace or are used in conjunction with tieback treatments. They can also be installed at the top of a window or door and serve as holders for scarf swags.

DECORATIVE POLES

You've made up your mind to use a decorative pole with finials. You scour the stores, cut out possible candidates from magazines and catalogs, and surf the Web for a pole that's just right for your room. When it comes time to narrowing down your favorites, however, you find yourself looking at 50 pole and finial possibilities. How do you choose the most appropriate ones for your needs? Well, because it will look best if you tie it into some element already present in your decorating scheme, start by taking cues from the rest of the furnishings.

Wooden Poles

A wooden pole might match or complement the finish of the woodwork or wood furniture in the room. Can't find a match from all of the varieties of wooden poles available? Then, stain an inexpensive pine pole in a finish to match what you need. If your room features painted furniture or colorful furnishings, paint the pole as well as any rings

A stick serves as a pole for plain curtain panels with tie tabs, above. The combination fits perfectly with the other rustic elements of this bedroom, from a picket-fence headboard to a worn bench at the foot of the bed.

Drapery poles are supported by the brackets fastened to the window frame or wall. The brackets that are provided with the poles generally coordinate and blend in with the pole finish. Brackets can be simple but also decorative. If you opt for a spectacular, attention-grabbing bracket, consider choosing less showy finials for the ends of the pole.

The pole with decorative finials, above left, supports draperies hung from rings. **A twig,** above, serves as a bracket for a stick pole. **A family of birds** and their nest, left, sits above a panel hung with red clothespins.

that will slide along it. Be aware that you can buy or replicate on a wooden pole practically any finish that you might find on wood, including stained, painted, gilded, pickled, marbled, and verdigris finishes.

Metal Poles

If you're leaning toward a metal pole, zero in on the metallic elements in the room to help you determine which type will best suit the room. You may not think many are present, but a careful look around will demonstrate otherwise. Study the picture frames, lamps, switch plates, and fireplace screens and tools. And don't forget to look at decorative panels, collectibles, ceiling fan hardware, heat registers, and radiators. If the room has a predominance of gold or brass accents, as is often the case in traditional rooms, choose a brass pole. Perhaps it's a contemporary setting, or one that features silver, pewter, or wrought iron, where a brushed chrome pole would look best. Rustic rooms accented with folk art and Americana are natural homes to wrought-iron poles, but this metal can also be an eye-catching contrast in many contemporary rooms.

Finials

Unless you want to repeat an element or motif in your room, simply choose a finial you like. You may fancy a finial's shape or texture so much that you'll want to repeat it as a motif elsewhere in the room. The variety of finials seems endless, but common designs include fleur-de-lis, shepherd's crook, ball, spear, urn, acorn, flame, twig, acanthus leaf, and scroll motifs. Typical finial materials are wood and metal, and they usually match the material of the pole with which they are paired. Sometimes, though, the finial provides a contrast to the pole. Ceramic and glass finials, for example, stand out like jewels against their typically metal rods. Elaborate finials that would be too

---

Delicate branches painted gold, above right, hold lightweight panels. **Twisted wood and colorful rings and finials,** opposite, are perfect for these curtains. **A sunny holdback,** right, peeks out from behind yards of fabric.

Design Tip

Because they're designed to stand out, decorative poles and their finials require more room for installation than conventional drapery rods. Finials add inches to the ends of a window treatment, so make sure you have enough wall room to display your hardware to its full advantage. And because decorative rods are often heavy, be certain your window frames and walls can support the additional weight.

Installing Rods and Poles

The way to install a rod or pole depends on the type it is, the brackets that will hold it, the weight of the window treatment, and the surface to which it is being fastened. Given below are some general guidelines, but for specific installation procedures, refer to the instructions that accompany the rod or pole.

- Use a stepladder to reach high places.
- Use the proper tools.
- Take accurate measurements.
- Work with a helper.
- If attaching a bracket to wood, first drill small pilot holes to avoid splitting the wood.
- Consider using wall anchors, particularly for the heavier window treatments.
- Use a level as needed to help you position the brackets for the pole or rod.
- Take care not to drill or hammer into any pipes or electrical wiring.

A plain holdback, left, is used as a swag holder. A simple curtain ring and a fleur-de-lis hook, above, combine to hold back a panel banded with a bold plaid. The metal rod with glass finials, opposite, reiterates the chrome and silver accents gracing the table below it.

heavy in metal are frequently made of a plastic resin or another lightweight composite and finished to resemble metal or another substance.

RINGS, CLIPS, PINS

Most curtain and drapery panels are attached to a pole through the use of rings or clips. With them, you can open or close the treatment at will. Certain lightweight panels are secured in place with decorative drapery pins. These treatments, however, are stationary.

Rings and Clips

Drapery rings slide along a pole and are the means for connecting the drapery or curtain panels to the pole. For best results, the ring finish, of which there are many, should coordinate with that of the pole. The method for attaching the panel will depend on the type of ring. One kind has a small clip for grabbing the fabric directly, and another has a small ring for receiving a hook already in place at the top of the panel. Others open like rings used for hanging shower curtains, fastening around a rod and into buttonholes or grommets in the top of the panel.

Pins

Pins are like scaled-down, knob-styled holdbacks, and they're used to fasten smaller amounts of lightweight fabric permanently in place. Available in a range of decorative styles and materials, pins can be used to instantly create such top treatments as swags and scalloped valances. You can also use them to hold up a lightweight curtain.

HOLDBACKS

Holdbacks can be hooks, pegs, or knobs in various materials and motifs, many of which are meant to coordinate with or match a decorative finial. With most treatments, each piece of a pair of holdbacks is mounted to a side of the window so it's ready to support a pulled-back curtain or drapery panel. A holdback may also serve

Concealed Rods

Some window fashions just look better when hung from concealed rods. Here's an overview of some types of rods.

Bay window rod. This single- or double-rod variety eliminates the need for each window of a bay window unit to have separate hardware.

Ceiling-mounted rod. This rod attaches to the ceiling or the underside of a window frame. It can be useful for hanging window treatments in tight spaces like corners and dormers.

Combination rod. A pair of two or a set of three stationary rods that share the same brackets, these rods accommodate multiple layers of rod-pocket treatments.

Continental rod. This is a wide stationary rod for a window treatment having a rod-pocket opening of equal width to the rod. It can also be used to make a decorative rod sleeve.

Corner rod. Available in single- or double-rod versions, a corner rod eliminates the problem of lining up separate hardware that meets exactly on windows set into a corner.

Double-track rod. The same concept as a traverse rod (below), a double-track rod has two tracks for layering window treatments. A triple-track version is also available.

Swivel rod. Also known as a French door rod, this hinged rod is ideal for treatments that can swing out of the way on occasion.

Tension rod. This adjustable rod has rubber tips and a built-in tensioning device so that it can sit within the window frame.

Traverse or concealed-track rod. This rod provides a track onto which drapery is hooked and, through the use of a cord system, can be drawn open and closed. It can also be bent to fit a particular contour.

Wire or cable rod. Great for curved or angled areas, this consists of a metal cable threaded through brackets on the wall.

as a "hook" for a working tieback. The level at which to install holdbacks depends on the look you want. Do you prefer the panels pulled back high, at the middle of the window, or somewhere in between? When installing holdbacks, be sure they'll be hidden behind the panels when they're not in use. Holdbacks can also serve as swag or scarf holders.

Ornate swag holders and tasseled ties, above, contain this billowy arrangement. **These swag holders,** opposite, differ in style but not in color or purpose.

SWAG & SCARF HOLDERS

Decorative swag and scarf holders add more pizzazz to an already beautiful top treatment. Swag and scarf holders can be plain holdbacks or complex brackets that come complete with instructions for incorporating rosettes into the swag or scarf as you hang the material across the window. And although a decorative pole is not typically thought of as a swag holder, swags can be beautifully draped over one or wrapped across it. (See "Window Scarves," page 59, for more information.)

Another type of swag and scarf holder is a decorative bracket, sometimes referred to as a corbel or sconce when used for this purpose. Often made to imitate beautifully ornate architectural elements, brackets can be very formal in nature, but in an otherwise plain room, they become the defining detail. Usually made from plaster or resin composites, these brackets are installed at the top of the window or door to either the wall or casing and are structured with an opening through which a swag or a drapery rod can be threaded. The brackets are available prefinished in various looks or as plain white ones that can be tailored to fit your specific decorating scheme.

Decorative hardware can be traditional or inventive.

Use your imagination to create your own artful hardware. Make a pole from a tree branch that's not too heavy but sturdy enough to support your fabric. Paint a new finish on a store-bought bracket to match your décor. Lightly sand the bracket and wipe it with a tack cloth before applying the new paint and stain.

Details make the difference.
That's why it's so exciting to
find such an array of styles in
poles, finials, holdbacks, and
tiebacks in today's market.
Use these items to underscore
your decorating theme,
whether it is rustic country,
Old World elegant, clean-lined
contemporary, or refined
American traditional.

finishing
touches

Flourishes such as trims, tassels, or tiebacks **finish** a window treatment and give it a **professional** look.

There are many types of finishing touches that can be added to a window treatment to give it a rich, professional look that captures the eye and sets it apart from the rest. Even just one carefully chosen embellishment can transform an otherwise perfect window treatment into a unique, hard-to-overlook feature in a room.

If you are purchasing custom-made window treatments, incorporating these details is simply a matter of taking the time to select trimmings to match the fabrics and hardware. If you're buying ready-made treatments or constucting them yourself, you can embellish them with store-bought or handmade trims and accents. It's not that difficult to do. Besides time and a bit of patience, you'll need the basic ability to stitch, fuse, or glue the trims in place. That's it. Craft and some fabric stores will have the supplies. Your challenge will be in trying to narrow down your choices from the outstanding selection of trimming materials and colors. The best advice: keep it simple and choose a design that is in keeping with the style of the fabric and the room. Reserve ornate details for traditional fabrics and formal interiors.

You may find it useful to sketch ideas before deciding finally what size and shape works the best with your design. In many instances, the window treatment itself will lead you in the right direction. For example, you may want to accentuate the pretty shape of a scalloped edge with trim. To focus attention on the meeting point of a set of swags, add a rosette.

Design Tip

If conventional trims and braids don't excite you, look for untraditional or unusual elements for decorating your window treatments. Attach single beads, small shells, or crystal drops at regular intervals along the edge. Either glue them in place or, if they have holes, sew them on. A series of stars, leaves, or some other appropriate shape made of stiffened fabric and then glued or stitched on is another idea. Consider old or new buttons, jewelry, or metal chains. If your embroidery skills are good, use them to embellish the window treatment.

Tassels

Tassels, whether alone or as part of a tieback, are often the crowning touch of a window treatment. Available in a wide range of sizes, styles, colors, and materials, they basically consist of long strands of thread (often silk) that are tied and folded in half and then wrapped tightly just beyond the fold. Below the tie is the skirt of the tassel. Often a casing encloses the top of the tassel. Fancy tassels might have brass, chrome, pewter, or gilt tops; ceramic and carved wood tassel tops are also available. The strands of thread in the top and skirt can be partitioned and tied or decorated in a tremendous variety of ways to increase the beauty and complexity of the tassel. Tassel varieties include the key tassel, a large tassel with rows of smaller tassels all around it, and the frog tassel, which features a pair of tassels falling below a series of decorative loops and is further embellished with a rosette.

TRIMS

A trim of any kind—braid, fringe, ruffles, piping—can further enhance the personality of almost any window dressing, whether it is a curtain or drapery panel, a top treatment, or a shade. It can match or contrast with the color, pattern, or texture of the fabric; it can be placed along its edge or at an appropriate area on the face of the treatment. All of these factors combine to build the look you want for the treatment. For example, ornate braiding or opulent fringe on a heavy drapery panel can back up a period treatment beautifully. A gathered, matching-fabric ruffle along an edge will soften the look of even a

Tasseled fringe, above, restates the colors of the drapery panel. **Tassels,** opposite, are just one of the types of embellishments used for this unusual valance.

Design Tip

You don't have to limit yourself to tiebacks made from matching or contrasting fabric. Achieve creative custom looks by making tiebacks from unexpected items. Some materials to consider are old cotton bandannas or silk scarves, strings of beads, lengths of leather, or old belts and chains.

lightweight curtain, giving it a fussy, feminine feeling, while a pleated ruffle will bring a formal, traditional note to a curtain. Rickrack trim applied to the face of a treatment or inserted into the seam along its edge is playful and casual—perfect for a child's room, a playroom, a modern kitchen, or a rustic den. Simple bands of contrasting fabric trim following the edge can reiterate and perhaps reinforce the edge so that it can stand up to more tugging over the years.

Choosing Trims

When selecting a trim, choose one having the same care requirements as the fabric in the panel and of a weight that will not overwhelm it. Bring a sample of the fabric with you to match it with the trim. If your plan is to embellish ready-made curtains, buy an extra panel and make your trim from it. If you're making your own panels and fabric trim, buy adequate yardage.

Applying Trims

Some trims—flat braids, ribbons, appliqués—can be applied to the face of the window treatment; others—piping, cord with a selvage—are meant to be inserted into a seam. To fasten trim to the face of a window treatment, use a fusible web product, hot glue and a glue gun, or a special fabric adhesive. The better method,

Beads, opposite, add sparkle and glamour to a plain curtain. **Piping and a pleated ruffle,** above left, form a distinctive edge finish. **Three fabric ties,** above, with pinked edges are simple in form but elegant in look.

Types of Trimmings

Despite the enormous variety of trimmings available, certain types, as listed below, appear over and over in window treatments. Perhaps you'll find them to be just what you need.

Ruffles. A strip of gathered fabric; a double ruffle features two layers of frill. For a pleated ruffle, the fabric is pressed into neat folds. Both edges of a ruffle can be finished; if the ruffle is for insertion into a seam, only one edge is finished.

Picot Braid. A flat braid patterned with small loops or scallops along one or both edges.

Cord. Yarns or strings twisted together to form a rope. Thick cord is typically used for tiebacks.

Flanged Cord. Cord having a selvage for inserting the trim into a seam.

Fan-Edge Braid. A flat trim with a straight upper edge and a lower edge with an open fanlike pattern formed by looped cords.

Piping. Folded bias-fabric strip, often covering cord, that is inserted into a seam so only a portion of the folded edge is visible. Also known as welting.

Fringe. A trim having a braided upper part and a lower portion of lengths of cord that are patterned in various ways. Many types of fringe are available; the name usually describes the effect formed by the fringe. Here are a few examples.

- **Brush fringe** has a row of thin cords, cut to form a straight, brushlike edge.
- **Bullion fringe** is a thick fringe made of uncut twisted cord.
- **Campaign fringe** is made up of one or more rows of bell-shaped tassels.
- **Tasseled fringe** is a type of brush fringe, but the strands are grouped and tied together at regular intervals along the length of the trim.
- **Minitasseled fringe** is made of a row of brush fringe overlaid with small tassels.
- **Onion fringe** is a tasseled fringe with a tie at the bottom of each tassel to produce bulblike shapes.
- **Looped fringe** positions the cords in a definite open-loop pattern.

however, is to sew it in place using hand or machine stitches before adding a lining fabric, if there is one. You have more control, the staying power is usually stronger, and if need be, it will be easier to remove the trim later.

ROSETTES

A rosette is a decorative window accessory typically placed between swags or where a swag meets a jabot or a valance reaches a panel. One might also be used as part of a tieback treatment. Made from fabric, usually to match that of the curtain or drapery, a rosette is ruffled or folded to form a roselike pouf that's then attached to the window treatment. The rosette can take a wide variety of forms. Common rosette styles are the *choux* (cabbage), fabric rose, and Maltese cross. If you're going the custom route, a fabricator might present you with design sketches of other shapes. If you want rosettes to complement a ready-made treatment or curtains you are making, purchase an extra panel or additional yardage from which you can fashion your own. Because edges require finishing and many fabrics are not reversible, creating rosettes usually requires sewing skills. Many home sewing project books can give you step-by-step instructions for fashioning all kinds of rosettes, and there are easy patterns you can buy. Or try the Maltese cross, referring to "Making a Simple Rosette," on page 86.

Scarf Rosettes

Typically, the rosette is a separate item that is attached once the rest of the window treatment is in place. Today, however, the rosettes that we see most often are those formed using special hardware that is designed specifically to accommodate scarf treatments. Unlike traditional rosettes, these are formed from the scarf fabric itself while it is being draped across the window. When considering this type of scarf, remember to add extra fabric, about 10

Custom-made fabric roses, left, coordinate in fabric and are defining features for this swag treatment.

to 15 inches per rosette, to the total yardage necessary for the window scarf. Specific instructions for creating the rosettes are included with the specialty hardware.

Without the special hardware as an aid, you can create rosettes for a scarf by knotting the material at the appropriate points. Start out with a small knot, and then loosely knot the material over it until it looks generous. Once you've created the rosette, you can primp it and tack it in place. Before buying fabric, knot it to determine how much will be required for each rosette. Lightweight gauzy fabrics that have no right or wrong side work best with this treatment.

TIEBACKS

Besides being decorative, a tieback holds in place curtains or draperies that have been pulled back, usually to the side of a window. In this way they are similar to holdbacks. (See "Holdbacks," page 70.) There are three main categories of tieback—fabric, braided, and tasseled—and within each category is a wide range of styles, one more attractive than the next.

Tiebacks are typically attached to hooks installed discreetly on the window frame. Rings, loops, or ties on the ends of the tieback are the usual means for fastening it in place. A tasseled tieback, however, because it is a loop of cord, simply latches on to the hooks. For a more decorative approach, a tieback can be hooked over stylish knobs or peg holdbacks.

Positioning Tiebacks

The beauty of this style of window treatment is in the lines and curves formed in the draping of the curtain panels. Most treatments use two tiebacks, one for each half of the window covering. The preferred location for

Buillon fringe and tasseled tieback, opposite, restate the colors in the fabric. **Tassels,** one plain, above right, and another ornate, right, dress these panels beautifully.

Making a Simple Rosette

One of the simplest rosettes to make is a Maltese cross. For each cross, you will need 24 inches of a wide, sturdy reversible ribbon (such as wired ribbon) that complements the window fabric; a 4-inch-square swatch of window fabric; a 3-inch-square piece of cardboard; a few cotton balls; a stapler and staples; a hot glue gun and glue; and scissors. Work on a hard, flat surface.

- Cut the ribbon in half, and arrange the two strips in a cross pattern. Staple the strips together at the center. Then fold all four ends of the ribbon to the center, and staple them in place. For a fuller Maltese cross, add more 12-inch lengths of the same ribbon or other colored ribbons to the cross, and position them diagonally to form an X. Fold these ribbon ends to the center, and then staple them in place.
- Cut a 2-inch-diameter circle from the cardboard, and staple it once to the center of the cross. Glue two or three cotton balls onto the cardboard circle, and let them dry. Then, with the right side of the window fabric swatch up, cover the cotton-padded cardboard with the fabric, tucking and gluing the edges of the fabric onto the reverse side of the cardboard. Let the rosette dry, and then pin or sew it in place.

---

hooking tiebacks is slightly above or below the center of the window. A low placement makes a window appear taller than it really is; a high tieback creates a tight, short curve of fabric. Another effective treatment is to use multiple tiebacks drawn to the same side of the window but hooked at different levels. Before installing any hooks, decide where you want the tiebacks. Experiment by pulling back the curtain or drapery at various spots until you find what looks best for the window and room.

Fabric Tiebacks

Most fabric tiebacks are flat strips, stiffened with buckram or fusible interfacing and lined. Plain or fancy in shape, fabric tiebacks can match exactly, coordinate with, or provide a contrast to the curtain panels they hold. Fabric tiebacks are suitable candidates for all the same trimmings as window panels. You can sew piping into the edges, add fabric bands, or border panels with ruffles. For a formal effect, attach tassels or fringe.

For a very simple bow tieback, wrap a long length of wide ribbon around the panel, and tie its ends into a bow, positioning it at a strategic point of the panel. Then, "hook" the ribbon onto the holdback or hook.

Simple in design yet stylishly attractive is a ruched tieback. It consists of an inner core of buckram or thick cord covered by a sleeve of fabric that is twice the length

of the cord. The extra fabric creates a soft, gathered effect along the length of the tieback.

Braided Tiebacks

A braided tieback comprises three or more strands of decorative cord or fabric-covered cord that are plaited together. A braid made from silky cord of jewel tones interspersed with gold strands will look rich, upscale, and formal, while cords covered in a calico print will be a perfect choice for a casual country-style window treatment. For a contemporary room setting, consider braiding lengths of wire or leather cord; for a romantic theme, use strings of beads.

Tasseled Tiebacks

Usually formal in nature, tasseled tiebacks are lengths of cord featuring either a single tassel in the center of the tieback or a pair of tassels, one on each each end. They are available in a range of colors and weights of cord. The tassels can be simple or ornate, and match or contrast with the cord. (See "Tassels," page 78.)

Striped fabric and grommets, opposite, combine to form an effective trim for this curtain. The choice of grommet used in holding back the panel will alter the drape.

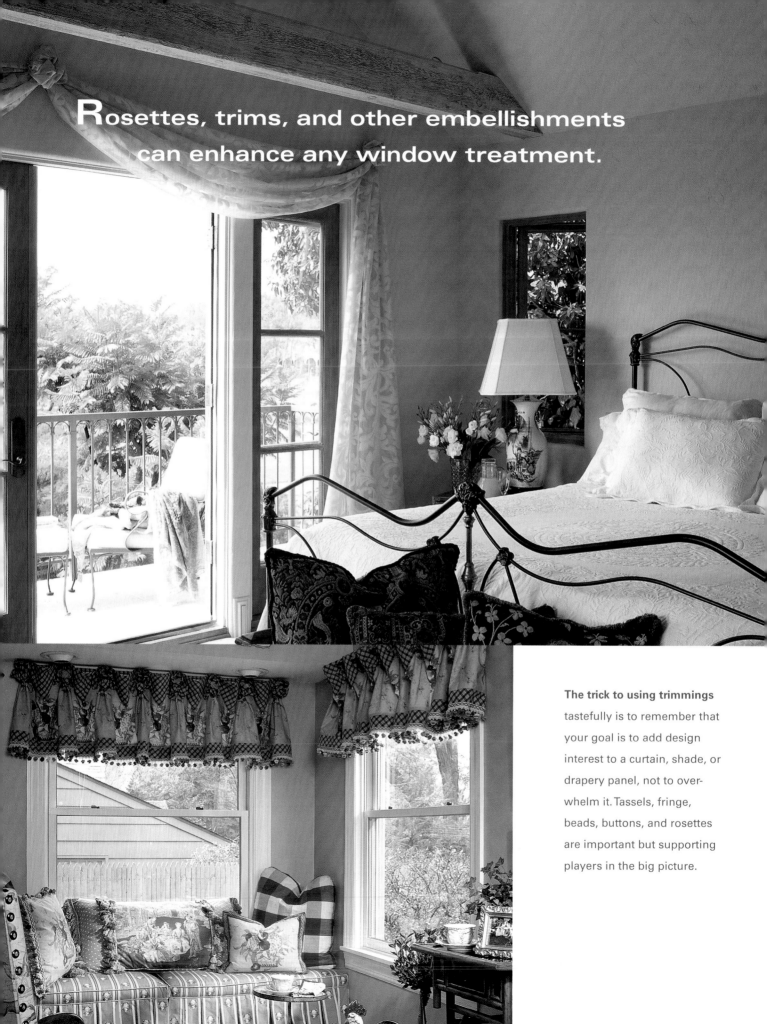

Rosettes, trims, and other embellishments can enhance any window treatment.

The trick to using trimmings tastefully is to remember that your goal is to add design interest to a curtain, shade, or drapery panel, not to overwhelm it. Tassels, fringe, beads, buttons, and rosettes are important but supporting players in the big picture.

7

challenges & solutions

Whether it's due to size, shape, or location, some windows can be a challenge to treat.

ertain windows typically pose problems. These include bay, bow, casement, and dormer windows; too large, small, tall, or short windows; and specialty or unusually shaped windows, such as cathedral, round, elliptical, arched, or triangular units. Occasionally even ordinary windows, particularly when they are at corners or are different in size and shape from the other windows in the room, can be a challenge to dress properly. Glazed doors, because of their movement, have other needs. Sometimes the answer is the installation of special hardware. (See "Concealed Rods," page 72, for more information.) Other times you can rely on the creative use of fabric or decorative elements to solve the problem.

A window treatment that is well designed will remove any awkwardness of the window and shift your focus from the problem to the decorative quality of the treatment itself. Alternatively, if the shape of the window is more important, then the window treatment could be an accent rather than the focus. The first step in successfully dressing a difficult window is to consider all types of coverings—curtains, shades, valances, swags and jabots, and so on—imagining them on the window and visualizing what they accomplish. Try combining the types, by adding a valance over a shade or a set of side panels, for example. Make a pencil sketch of the window as a base and then, using tissue-paper overlays, sketch various arrangements, adding embellishments as needed to complete a look. As you shop for the elements and trims, attach samples to your drawing, making note of the prices and sources.

BAY & BOW WINDOWS

Bay and bow windows are multiple-window units that project out from the exterior wall of a house to form a recessed area inside the house. The primary difference between the two is that the recess of the bay window is angled, whereas the bow window's is curved.

There are several options for dressing a bay window. A casual treatment might consist of dressing each window in the unit with a valance on top and then a shade, blind, or set of café curtains on the bottom. Another solution is

Each bay window setting, opposite and below, is dressed differently to suit style, light, and privacy concerns.

Design Tip

Occasionally too little room exists between the window frame (if there is one) and the ceiling. In this situation you might be able to use ceiling-mounted hardware. Alternatively, a cornice across the top and a rod mounted inside the cornice will give you the dual benefit of visually lowering the top of the window and concealing the hardware.

to hang curtain panels from a single bay window rod installed directly above all the windows. The bay window rod is essential because individual rods above the windows would be crowded for space, and the treatment will not flow. Using a double bay window rod, a traditional formal treament could consist of a pair of curtain panels for each window opening hanging from the inside rod and two drapery panels—one at each end of the unit—from the outer rod. Another choice is to hang drapery panels and a top treatment on a straight rod, fastened outside and across the top of the recess of the window unit.

A bow window generally requires the use of a curved rod installed directly above all the windows of the unit. It's a custom item well worth the investment because from it you can hang anything from a full drapery treatment to a simple top treatment. Professionally bent traverse rods, also called concealed track rods, are even more versatile. Another option for a bow window is a wire or cable rod that will take on the shape of the curve. They are best suited for lighter-weight treatments.

Both bay windows, left and opposite, have a treatment inside the alcove; **the bay,** opposite, has another outside.

Visual Tricks

Some windows can be difficult to treat just because they're not the right size or proportion. Several of these dilemmas can be solved with fool-the-eye tricks. Other times it will be a matter of using a treatment that does not conform to the precise measurements of the window.

To make a wide window appear narrower

- Use a fabric the same color as the wall.
- Hang side panels within the frame of the window.
- Use a treatment whose lines will break up the horizontal line of the window.

To make a narrow window appear wider
- Extend the treatment beyond each end of the window.
- Use tieback curtains, which tend to add width visually.

To make a tall window appear shorter
- Use a longer, fuller top treatment.
- Cap it with a valance having points or lines that will pull the eye downward.

To make a small window appear larger
- Install a treatment that extends just beyond the dimensions of the window. If the treatment is movable, as is a shade or blind, don't go too far beyond the actual size of the window, because the difference will be very apparent when the treatment is open.

CASEMENT & DORMER WINDOWS

A casement window, which opens out, presents no special problems in terms of window covering. Keep in mind, however, that you will want easy access to the crank handle that operates the unit. A good choice for any casement window is to hang panels from swivel rods, which allow you to swing the panels out of the way when you need to open the window.

A dormer window, because it's recessed in an alcove and has a wall on each side of it, leaves little room for treatments such as draperies that stack when they're open. One solution is to hang panels from swivel rods. Another is to install your hardware outside the alcove and choose a window treatment—a valance and two side panels, for example—to frame the whole area.

CORNER WINDOWS

W indows that converge at the corner of a room look best when treated as a unit. When dressing them, use any elements you would use for a pair of windows adjacent to each other on a flat wall. If you want to "join" the two and make the corner the focus, hang a drapery panel on each outer edge and a set to fill the space in the corner between the windows. Corner rods available in double- or single-rod versions eliminate the awkwardness of installing separate rods on each window, and they ensure that your treatment will fill in the corner of the wall without leaving a gap. Try mirror-imaging two halves of a treatment. For example, cover each window with a tieback curtain or drapery panel, and pull each panel to the outside edge of the window. Another successful look is achieved by dressing the windows with swags and jabots, setting a pair of jabots at the corner.

A **ceiling-mounted rod,** opposite, and **a cornice,** above right, are features of these corner-window treatments. **A simple shade,** right, adorns a small window.

SPECIALTY WINDOWS

Various shaped windows, such as arched, round, half-round, elliptical, and angular, sometimes placed above one or more large windows, are favorites with new-house builders. Aesthetically, it is usually best to leave as much as possible of these beautiful windows unadorned because their pleasing shapes and muntins are meant to be on display. Perhaps a valance or a creatively draped scarf is all that's needed. On the practical side, however, this does not allow for the control of light, especially sunlight and its glare and heat, nor does it provide privacy. This could be particularly problematic if the window is large, as is a cathedral window or the arch-topped Palladian window.

If you must cover an "architectural" window, there are options. You can buy custom cellular shades for many

Specialty windows, left, below, and opposite, are best when unadorned or dressed simply with treatments that can be moved aside to fully reveal the window's features.

Design Tip

Some windows are set so close to corners that no area exists for certain treatments such as draperies that stack when they are open. One possible solution is to use lightweight panels, which are less bulky when they are stacked. Otherwise, choose coverings that are confined to the limits of the window—blinds, shades, café curtains, valances, or even swags and jabots.

configurations. Shutters are another made-to-order option, although you can sometimes purchase ones that will fit standard-size windows. Kits allow you to create a rod-pocket curtain for a variety of window shapes, but any one of these curtain treatments is fairly stationary once it is in place. For an angled window, consider shirred curtains on ordinary adjustable rods affixed to the top and bottom of the window or on tension rods set within the window frame. An arched rod is another option to investigate for a window with a curved top. Available in a large variety of sizes, an arched rod allows you to treat an arched window as you would a square or rectangular unit. You can install the rod as you would an ordinary one, mounting it inside or outside the window opening. Once the treatment is up, however, it is stationary.

To enjoy the architectural beauty of a large specialty window such as a cathedral or arch-top Palladian-style window but still have some light control, consider a covering for the lower portion only. Use a treatment, such as draperies on rings and a decorative rod, that can be drawn open or closed at will.

GLAZED DOORS

The most important consideration for any treatment on a glazed door is that all the elements will clear the opening and not interfere with the operation of the doors. The quintessential treatment for sliding glass patio doors and French doors that open out is draperies on a decorative or traverse rod. Long panels puddled at the floor, however, aren't suitable because they may catch onto the bottom of a sliding door.

If the doors open into the room, you also have to pay attention to the top of the treatment so that it won't interfere with the door swing. When the wall space above the door is adequate, you could top it with a valance or a scarf wrapped around a pole. Or consider sheer sash curtains that attach directly to the doors. Another alternative is to hang panels from swivel, or French door, rods.

One long decorative rod, below, set high above French doors, supports draperies on rings. **Woven-wood shades,** opposite, provide a unified look for dissimilar windows.

Design Tip

If the windows in the room are dissimilar but your design calls for treating all of them the same, work out variations of a treatment based on the different sizes. Keep the fabrics and other elements coordinated to create a harmonious overall effect. In one situation, a large window might have drapery panels and a valance as well as some kind of shade or blind, while the smaller window might wear only a matching valance.

Possible Solutions for Challenging Windows

Some windows are more difficult than others to dress. Frequently the solution is in the form of specialty hardware. Other times it involves a unique placement of ordinary hardware and the treatment. Listed below are some suggested ways for treating these windows.

Type	Solutions
Bay Window	• Use a specially designed bay window rod. • Place a treatment outside the alcove. • Treat windows singly, perhaps each with a shade and a simple top treatment.
Bow Window	• Use a curved rod, a professionally bent traverse rod, or a wire or cable rod.
Casement Window	• Try swivel rods (sometimes called French door rods) to swing the treatment out of the way when necessary.
Corner Window	• Use a specially designed corner window rod. • Use a wire or cable rod. • Try mirror-imaging two halves of the treatment.
Dormer Window	• Try swivel rods to swing the treatment out of the way when necessary. • Hang the treatment outside the alcove.
Glazed Door	• Use panels that cover only the windows of the door. • Install a traverse rod above the opening and make sure the treatment and its stack back clear door openings. • Try swivel rods to swing the treatment out of the way when necessary.
Specialty Windows	• Use bent-rod kits designed for round, elliptical, octagonal, arched, or eyebrow windows. • Use custom cellular shades or shutters.

Blend your ingenuity and design skills when dressing a challenging window.

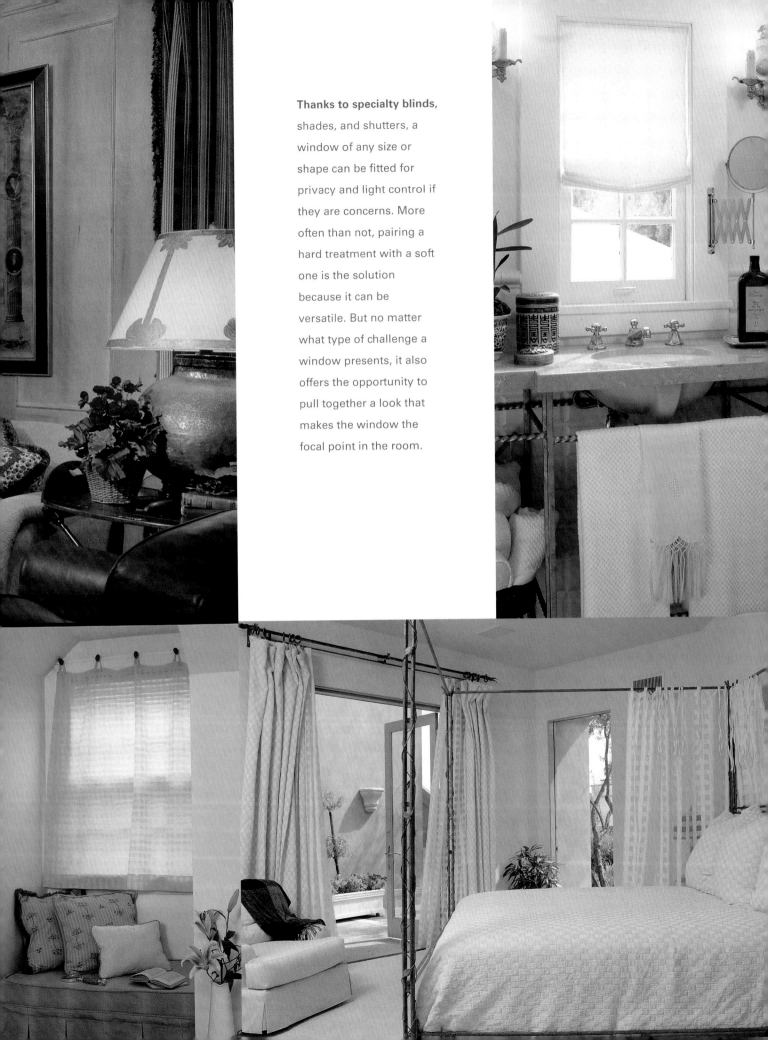

Thanks to specialty blinds, shades, and shutters, a window of any size or shape can be fitted for privacy and light control if they are concerns. More often than not, pairing a hard treatment with a soft one is the solution because it can be versatile. But no matter what type of challenge a window presents, it also offers the opportunity to pull together a look that makes the window the focal point in the room.

8

minimal
looks

Sometimes **less** is more when it comes to choosing the **right** window **treatment** for its surroundings.

Rooms with a minimal or uncluttered look can be striking in their simplicity, emphasizing space and architecture rather than decorative objects, prints, or patterns. To a decorating minimalist, one who prefers clean lines and fewer personal effects, layers of fabric, buttons, bows, and showy hardware go against the grain. If you prefer an unfussy interior with open and airy windows or you live in a contemporary clean-lined house, you need a minimal window treatment—one that reinforces the lines and perhaps textures already present in the architecture and interior surfaces.

Dressing a window to coordinate with a minimal design scheme does not mean limiting the solution to a plain blind or a simple top treatment, although these are options, especially for informal rooms. Some minimal environments are complex and formal, however, and call for window treatments to echo that. Also typical of this style are large windows or a wall of glass, where the treatment must be an unobtrusive frame for a good-looking window, an accompaniment to the elements inside the room, and a controlling device for light and air. In some cases, a sheer or translucent covering is all you need. Other times the best treatment can be none at all, particularly if there's a great view outside and privacy isn't a concern.

In this chapter you'll see how simple or streamlined window fashions provide the perfect solution to numerous interior design situations. In addition, you'll find inspiration for creating unique looks with unexpected objects.

CONVENTIONAL TREATMENTS

Line definition plays an essential role in a minimal environment. Instead of focusing on busy, colorful upholstery and window treatments, your eye follows the geometry of the surfaces and furniture in the room. The architectural features are more likely to stand out in an uncluttered room, too. For this reason, hard elements that can add lines or restate ones that are already in play are natural choices. Contrary to what you may think, soft elements such as fabric are not taboo in a minimal setting. The type of fabric you choose and how you use it, however, can make or break the design scheme.

Hard Elements

Used alone, window treatments such as blinds, shades, shutters, and cornices work well in a minimal setting.

Louvered blinds or fitted shutters offer optimal light regulation and privacy in a minimal environment, and the louvers of either are easily adjustable. You can choose vertical or horizontal blinds according to what suits the room. Natural shade types such as matchstick, bamboo, and other woven woods, reeds, grasses, and synthetic look-alikes offer interesting light play and texture. If you're also using curtains or draperies, you might choose a translucent fabric so that the line play of the shade, blind, or shutter is not lost behind the fabric.

As the day progresses, the muntins of a window with multiple panes provide the geometric structure for a play of shadows that travel on the floor and the wall opposite the window. An angled skylight can also be the force

Roman shades, opposite and above, work well in minimal settings. When they're open, the window, room, and view share the glory. When closed they provide privacy.

Too Much Light?

Windows dressed in volumes of sheer fabric create a spectacular effect, but it may not be appropriate. Does it complement the the style of the house, the architecture of the windows, and the rest of the furnishings in the room? Will the light streaming in be too much for the time of day when you will use the room the most? Rooms having east-facing windows get lots of morning light, while those facing south and west get a great deal of sunlight that you might want to control, particularly in the afternoon. North-facing rooms, however, can use every bit of daylight available.

Also consider glare, particularly if you have shiny floors or furniture or if the room is your media center. Besides being annoying, blinding glare could be a hazard for those who are visually impaired.

When choosing fabric for the treatment, select one that can stand up to the damaging effects of the sun. Silk in particular is prone to sun damage; cotton, linen, and many of the synthetic fabrics are sturdier. But no matter what type of fabric you use, sunlight can cause its color to fade. Lighter colors and fabrics treated to resist fading will stand up better.

behind another light-and-shadow show. Curvy lines present in a minimal room can be echoed and emphasized by the look of light shining through a window that is framed by a cornice or lambrequin, the edges of which are shaped to restate these curves in the room or to add a sensuous element to a rectilinear space.

Soft Elements

Minimalist designs can also rely on the power of textures to create interest. When choosing a fabric for a window treatment, look for one with a surface that invites you to touch it. Raised damask or brocade tone-on-tone fabrics with patterns that tie in with something else in the room are examples, as well as some linens. Heavy or coarse fabrics and materials with distinctive patterning such as tweeds or twills are also possibilities. Avoid floral prints, busy patterns, frilly laces, and any fabrics that will defeat your contemporary or spare design goals—reserve such fabrics for a traditional or country room.

Other appealing choices for this style of interior are sheer see-through fabrics. Sheers are versatile. They can be tailored or relaxed, patterned or plain. Long curtain or drapery panels made from a sheer fabric can add a simple sculptural shape to an otherwise boxy window. Sheer materials are also great for the way they soften the light streaming through them, sometimes also providing

a shadowy display of the structure and lines of the window or door right behind them.

In terms of color, curtains and draperies are often best when kept neutral or subtle in color, sometimes with a tone-on-tone look. Pattern and lively prints, unless they are geometric, should be avoided because they can be distracting. Remember, your goal is to make the window treatment unobtrusive and let the space itself, the window's architecture, or the view take the spotlight.

Hardware

When choosing decorative hardware for a spare design, look for choices that are simple, elegant, and harmonious with furnishings or accents already present. Avoid ornate styles, especially elaborate finials. Brushed-metal finishes look most appropriate, but wood painted to blend in with a window's frame and trim works well, too. If you are using holdbacks, keep to simple styles that will not detract from the rest of the overall design. Resist any temptation to add accents that will defeat your intention to make either the window itself or the window beyond it the focus of attention.

The sheer curtains, opposite, are a simple, soft decoration for these second-story bedroom windows and the panorama of nature beyond them. In such a secluded spot, privacy concerns are minimal at best.

OTHER "MINIMAL" TREATMENTS

When you can't produce a minimal treatment using conventional components, try using elements that are not thought of as typical window dressings. Some suggestions are given here. They are not presented as how-to projects but simply to inspire you to create unusual but minimal window treatments of your own. Instructions and supplies for making some of them are available in craft stores.

Grilles and Grids

Metalwork can be stunning and, with light behind it, casts lovely images onto the floor or an opposite wall. You can sometimes find vintage grillwork at antique stores or where architectural salvage is sold. Shoji screens, made of wood framing and textured papers, imbue a room with understated elegance and pattern. Sections of old weathered picket fencing are another possibility for adding texture. New fencing and latticework, finished to suit the room, can also work.

Stained and Leaded Glass

Scour antique shops and art-glass stores for stained- or leaded-glass panels that you can suspend in front of or set into your windows. Depending on the weight of the glass and the way you install it, this may be a choice more suitable for stationary windows. You might also want a professional to install the panel.

Glasswork, Beads, and Shells

Where strong light is not a problem, shelves of colored glasswork or strings of pretty beads provide some coverage while creating interesting color and light reflections inside the room. Strings of shells can do the same. Choose your elements with a sense of proportion to the window, reserving fine, delicate objects for small openings and big ones for larger windows. As always, trying to achieve proper scale and proportion is often a trial-and-error process, so be patient and experiment until you get the desired effect.

Plants

When properly chosen for their care and light needs, plants can flourish as a window decoration that adds fresh natural color to an interior. Try various shapes and heights of plants. Look for ones with interesting fronds or leaves that can create patterns in front of a window or provide some privacy. To accommodate hanging plants, suspend a shelf from the ceiling or from wall brackets, varying the height of the shelf according to the area the plants will cover. Or display the plants in hanging baskets. Install decorative hooks, using anchors for adequate support. Plants, especially large ones, can get very heavy after watering.

A stained- and leaded-glass window, right, is the focal point here. An antique metalwork piece, opposite above, makes a stunning window decoration. A red-and-white valance, opposite right, hides a closed miniblind.

Design Tip

You can easily stencil a work of art onto a windowpane, perhaps only as a border around the edge. Choose or create a design that gives you as little or as much privacy and light control as you need. Use a ready-made stencil or a piece of openwork fabric such as lace, or mask a design onto the glass using tape and a razor knife. Then apply glass paint or frosted glass spray, referring to the instructions and guidelines that come with the product.

Protecting Your Privacy

Often with the sparse unadorned features of a minimal window treatment, your privacy becomes a concern, particularly at night and for bedrooms and baths. Here are some things to do to make sure you are not inviting the curiosity of passersby.

• Stand outside the house and look at your window to see whether more covering is needed. You might want to do this during the day and again at night with the lights on in the room before you make a decision to leave a window bare or partially treated.

• Install an opaque, movable treatment to cover the lower part of a street-level window, the entire surface of a below-street-level window, or all or part of a high-rise-apartment window, depending on what you need to ensure your privacy.

• Consider putting frosted or one-way glass into all of the windows or just into those areas needed to provide privacy.

• Investigate automatic controls for opening and closing the window treatment at the appropriate times.

Aminimal treatment can be the best look for certain settings.

Window treatments that are barely there or starkly simple can be appealing alternatives to layered or "constructed" window fashions, especially if the architecture of the window itself is interesting. Beautifully shaped specialty windows or stained- and leaded-glass panels work well in a minimal setting. Lightweight sheer or lace curtains will allow filtered light inside without completely sacrificing privacy. Adjustable shades that roll up and are almost out of sight when not needed are another option for a spare design. Or try a simple valance or sheer scarf swag for an understated but pretty look.

resource guide

Associations

American Architectural Manufacturers Association *is an organization of window, door, and skylight manufacturers. The Web site offers a listing of window products and a section on national window safety.*
1540 East Dundee Rd., Suite 310
Palatine, IL 60067
Phone: 708-202-1350
www.aamanet.org

American Sewing Guild *is a nonprofit organization for people who sew. Members receive discounts for sewing-related materials.*
9660 Hillcroft, Suite 516
Houston, TX 77096
Phone: 713-729-3000
Fax: 713-721-9230
www.asg.org

Home Sewing Association *directs the sewer to projects, press releases, discussions, and sewing-related links.*
1350 Broadway, Suite 1601
New York, NY 10018
Phone: 212-714-1633
www.sewing.org

Window Covering Association of America *is a nonprofit trade organization for the window-covering industry. Its Web site offers tips, patterns, a Q & A message board, and a dealer directory.*

WCAA National Office
2339 Meadow Park Ct.
St. Louis, MO 63043
Phone: 888-298-9222
www.wcaa.org

Window & Door Manufacturers Association *promotes high-performance standards for windows, skylights, and doors.*
1400 E. Touhy Ave., Suite 470
Des Plaines, IL 60018
Phone: 800-223-2301
Fax: 847-299-1286
www.wdma.com

Manufacturers & Retailers

Soft Treatments

Country Curtains *specializes in curtains and accessories, with ideas and tips on the Web site.*
Country Curtains at The Red Lion Inn
Stockbridge, MA 01262
Phone: 800-456-0321
www.countrycurtains.com

Croscill Home Fashions *manufactures curtains and decorative hardware.*
261 Fifth Ave., 25th Floor
New York, NY 10016
Phone: 919-683-8011
www.croscill.com

Romanzia *creates custom-made fabric shades and valances. The customer provides the fabric.*
655 County Rd. A
P.O. Box 72
Chetek, WI 54728
Phone: 715-924-2960
Fax: 715-924-4244
www.romanzia.com

Smith & Noble *makes custom soft and hard window treatments.*
1801 California Ave.
Corona, CA 92881
Phone: 800-560-0027
www.smithandnoble.com

Spiegel *catalog's home accents collection offers everything related to window treatments: curtains, blinds, valances, and accessories, such as tiebacks, sconces, and decorative rods and finials.*
Spiegel Customer Satisfaction
P.O. Box 6105
Rapid City, SD 57709
Phone: 800-474-5555
www.spiegel.com

Waverly *manufactures fabrics and ready-made curtains. The Web site includes tips on how to decorate effectively and a product finder.*
Phone: 800-423-5881
www.waverly.com

Hard Treatments

BTX Window Automation, Inc. *manufactures motorized systems for window coverings.*
10880 Alder Circle
Dallas, TX 75238
Phone: 800-422-8839
Fax: 214-343-2252
www.btxinc.com

Hunter Douglas, Inc., *manufactures shades and blinds. The Web site will direct you to designers, dealers, and installers.*
2 Park Way
Upper Saddle River, NJ 07458
Phone: 800-937-7895
www.hunterdouglas.com

Levolor Home Fashions *manufactures blinds and shades, including cordless types.*
4110 Premier Dr.
High Point, NC 27265
Phone: 336-812-8181
Fax: 336-881-5862
www.levolor.com

The Pillow Parlor *sells ready-made decorative cornices and canopies for windows.*
56 North Federal Hwy. (U.S. 1)
Dania, FL 33004
Phone: 800-954-1515
www.pillowparlor.com

resource guide

Smith & Noble *(See Curtains & Soft Treatments.)*

Southwestern Blind Company *sells a wide variety of ready-made blinds.*
P.O. Box 10013
Austin, TX 78766
Phone: 888-792-5463
Fax: 512-331-9000
www.swblind.com

Spiegel *(See Soft Treatments.)*

Hardware

Atlas Homewares *sells decorative hardware. Ideas for unique tiebacks are found on the Web site.*
326 Mira Loma Ave.
Glendale, CA 91204
Phone: 800-799-6755
www.atlashomewares.com

Graber Window Fashions *manufactures curtain hardware. All questions can be answer by e-mail.*
www.graber.ws/index.html

Kirsch Window Fashions *manufactures blinds, rods, shades, holdbacks, and other window accessories in a variety of styles. The Web site has a glossary of various window treatment terms.*
524 W. Stephenson St.
Freeport, IL 61032
Phone: 800-817-6344
www.kirsch.com

Ona Drapery Company *manufactures rods, brackets, tiebacks, finials, and other accessories.*
5320 Arapahoe Ave.
Boulder, CO 80303
Phone: 800-231-4025
Fax: 303-786-7159
www.onadrapery.com

Fabric

Ainsworth Noah & Associates *sells fabric.*
351 Peachtree Hills Ave., Suite 518
Atlanta, GA 30305
Phone: 404-231-8787
www.ainsworth-noah.com

Benartex Incorporated *supplies cotton fabric designs from a variety of original collections.*
1460 Broadway, 8th Floor
New York, NY 10036
Phone: 212-840-3250
Fax: 212-921-8204
www.benartex.com

Calico Corners *sells a selection of fabrics and offers custom services in its stores nationwide.*
203 Gale Ln.
Kennett Square, PA 19348
Phone: 800-213-6366
www.calicocorners.com

F. Schumacher & Co. *manufactures fabric and coordinated wallcovering.*

939 Third Ave.
New York, NY 10022
Phone: 212-415-3900
www.fschumacher.com

Joann Fabrics and Crafts *sells fabrics, notions, patterns, and craft products in its stores nationwide.*
5555 Darrow Rd.
Hudson, OH 44236
Phone: 888-739-4120
www.joann.com

J.R. Burrows & Co. *supplies hand-printed art fabrics and lace, with reproductions from many design periods.*
6 Church St.
Boston, MA 02116
Phone: 617-451-1982
www.burrows.com

Motif Designs *manufactures fabric and coordinated wallcovering.*
20 Jones St.
New Rochelle, NY 10802
Phone: 800-431-2424

Old World Weavers *carries fabrics made of wool, cotton, silk, and more.*
D&D Building
979 Third Ave.
New York, NY 10022
Phone: 212-752-9000
Fax: 212-758-4342
www.old-world-weavers.com

Plaid Enterprises, Inc., *manufactures craft and home decorating products including fabric and glass paints, stamps, stencils, paints, and stitchery supplies.*
P.O. Box 2835
Norcross, GA 30092
Phone: 800-842-4197
www.plaidonline.com

Rashmishree *makes tassels, ribbons, and trims.*
P.O. Box 723
Pine Brook, NJ 07058
Phone: 973-808-1566
www.rashmishree.com

Sahco Hesslein *is an international textile manufacturer that creates original fabrics.*
3720 34th St.
Long Island City, NY 11101
Phone: 718-392-5000
www.sahco-hesslein.com

Scalamandré *manufactures and imports fabrics and trimmings.*
300 Trade Zone Dr.
Ronkonkoma, NY 11779
Phone: 800-932-4361
www.scalamandre.com

Waverly *(See Soft Treatments.)*

glossary

Apron: Molding installed at the bottom of a window, below the inside sill, or stool.

Austrian Shade: An opulent style of shade that hangs in cascading scallops from top to bottom. Often made of a sheer or lacy fabric, it is raised by a cord.

Balloon Shade: A fabric shade that falls in full blousy folds at the bottom; it is raised by a cord.

Bay Window: A multiple-window unit projecting out from the exterior wall of a house, forming an angled recess inside the house.

Bow Window: Similar to a bay window, but the recess is curved.

Box Pleats: Two folds turned toward each other, creating a flat-fronted pleat.

Brackets: Hardware to support a curtain or drapery rod or pole or, as with a scarf swag, a decorative holder for the treatment.

Brocade: A weighty, typically formal fabric in silk, cotton, wool, or a combination of these fibers. Woven on a Jacquard loom, it is distinguished by a raised, typically floral, design.

Buckram: A coarse, stiff fabric used as an interlining to give body and shape to curtain and drapery headings, cornices, and tiebacks.

Café Curtains: A window treatment that covers only the bottom portion of a window. Panels are most often hung at the halfway point of the window.

Calico: Lightweight, inexpensive cotton or cotton-blend fabric in brightly colored prints.

Casement Window: A hinged vertical window that opens out; often operated with a crank mechanism.

Cathedral Window: A triangular or trapezoidal window paired with and placed above a large fixed window. The top portion of a cathedral window is often left uncovered.

Chintz: A cotton fabric, typically having a floral or other overall print, coated with a resin to give it sheen.

Cloud Shade: A balloon shade having a gathered or pleated heading.

Combination Rods: Two or three rods sharing one set of brackets. They facilitate the layering of various treatments, such as draperies over sheers.

Cornice: A projecting decorative boxlike unit installed above a window, designed to hide a curtain rod.

Damask: A jacquard fabric of cotton, silk, wool, or a combination, woven with a raised design. Widely used for draperies and top treatments.

Dormer Window: A window set into the front face of a dormer. A dormer window brings light into the space provided by the dormer.

Double-Hung Window: The most common type, consisting of two sashes, one atop the other, which are moved up and down to open and close the window.

Draping: A technique of folding, looping, and securing fabric in graceful curves and lines.

Draw Draperies: Draperies that hang from a traverse rod and can be drawn to open or close over the window by means of a pulley.

Face Fabric: The main outer fabric of a window treatment, as opposed to its lining.

Festoon Shades: A class of adjustable or stationary shades that are made of gathered fabric. Styles include balloon, cloud, and Austrian.

Finials: The decorative ends of a drapery rod or pole.

French Doors: Two adjoining doors with hinges at

opposite ends and typically with 12 divided panes of glass in each door.

Fringe: A decorative trim attached to curtain panels, draperies, top treatments, and other window coverings as an embellishment.

Gingham: A light- to medium-weight, plain-weave fabric yarn dyed and woven to create checks or plaids.

Goblet Pleat Heading: A heading with tube-shaped pleats that are pinched together at their bases.

Heading: The horizontal area at the top of a curtain or a drapery. Its style determines how a curtain or drapery looks and hangs.

Holdback: Hardware (made of metal, wood, or glass) that is attached to the wall near the edge of a window and is used to hold in place a pulled-back curtain or drapery panel. It can also be used as a swag holder.

Interlining: Lightweight opaque fabric placed between the face and lining fabrics of a drapery to add body or to block light.

Jabot: The vertical tail that complements a swag in a swag-and-jabot treatment.

Jacquard: The name of the inventor and of the loom that revolutionized weaving by using punched cards to produce jacquard fabrics, which have intricate, raised designs. Brocade and damask are jacquard fabrics.

Lambrequin: A painted board or stiffened fabric that surrounds the top and sides of a window or a door.

Lining: A fabric added to the window treatment for body and a visually unified exterior appearance. It also helps to control light, air, and dust that filter through the window.

Moiré: A silk or acetate fabric having a finish that resembles watermarking.

Mounting Board: A wooden board installed either inside or outside the window frame to which some types of window treatments are attached.

Muntin: Wood trim that sets off smaller panes of glass in a window.

Muslin: A plain-weave cotton fabric ranging in weight from coarse to fine.

Piping: An edging trim made of folded bias-cut fabric, which is sewn into a seam. It often encases cord. Also known as welting.

Pleated Shades: Shades made of permanently folded paper or fabric.

Pole: Metal or wooden hardware that supports curtain or drapery fabric; also called a rod.

Repeat: The duplication of a design motif or pattern at consistent or random intervals in a fabric.

Return: The distance from the front face of a curtain or drapery rod to the wall or surface to which the brackets for the rod are attached.

Rod: See Pole.

Rod-Pocket Curtains (or Draperies): Panels that hang from a rod threaded through a stitched pocket across the top of the panel. The most common window treatment.

Roller Shade: A shade made of vinyl or fabric attached to a spring-loaded roller.

Roman Shade: A fabric shade that forms layers of straight, flat horizontal folds when open. It is lifted by pulling a cord threaded through rings attached to fabric tape on the back of the shade.

Ruching: Extremely tight gathers used as a decorative top finish to a panel.

glossary

Stack Back: The space along the sides of a window or door taken up by a curtain or drapery panel when it's pulled open.

Swag: The center drape or scallop of fabric in a swag-and-jabot treatment; it can have a deep or shallow drop.

Tab-Top Curtains (or Draperies): Panels that hang from a rod via looped fabric tabs.

Taffeta: A shiny silk or acetate fabric that maintains its shape. It is used for formal curtains and draperies.

Tail: A common term for jabot, the vertical lengths of fabric that complement a swag.

Tieback: A cord or fabric strip used to hold open curtains or draperies.

Toile de Jouy: An eighteenth-century print of pastoral scenes on cotton or linen, printed in one color, usually on a white background. It was first produced in Jouy, France.

Traverse Rod: A rod that opens and closes the window treatment by pulling a cord.

Valance: A short length of fabric that hangs along the top of a window, with or without a curtain, drapery, or other treatment underneath.

Venetian Blind: A blind made of metal or wood slats, attached to cloth tape, and worked by a cord on a pulley.

Welting: See Piping.

index

index

index

credits

page 1: Robert Harding Picture Library page 2: Giammarino and Dworkin page 5: Robert Harding Picture Library page 6: Mark Lohman page 7: *top to bottom* Jessie Walker; Brad Simmons; Robert Harding Picture Library; Jessie Walker page 8: Tria Giovan page 11: Giammarino and Dworkin page 12: Robert Harding Picture Library page 14: *top to bottom* Mark Samu; Tria Giovan page 15: Robert Harding Picture Library page 16: Nancy Hill page 18: *top to bottom* Mark Lohman; Mark Samu page 19: Brad Simmons page 20: *all* Robert Harding Picture Library page 21: Scalamandré page 22: *top* Jessie Walker; *bottom left* Robert Harding Picture Library; *bottom right* Brad Simmons page 23: *top to bottom* Mark Lohman; Tim Street-Porter/Beate Works page 24: Mark Lohman page 26: *all* Robert Harding Picture Library page 27–31: *all* Mark Lohman page 32: Tim Street-Porter/Beate Works page 33: Mark Lohman page 34: *left* Jessie Walker; *right* Mark Lohman page 35: Mark Lohman page 36: *top* Mark Lohman; *bottom*

Giammarino and Dworkin page 37: Phillip Ennis page 39: Mark Lohman page 40: *top to bottom* Jessie Walker; Mark Samu page 41: Mark Samu page 42: Jessie Walker page 43: Phillip Ennis page 44: Mark Lohman page 45: *top to bottom* Jessie Walker; Mark Lohman page 46: Jessie Walker page 47: Mark Samu page 48: *top and bottom left* Mark Lohman; *bottom right* Mark Samu page 49: *top left* Jessie Walker; *top right* Nancy Hill; *bottom* Mark Samu page 50: Mark Samu page 52: *all* Mark Lohman page 53: Jessie Walker page 54: Mark Lohman page 55: *all* Mark Samu page 56: Mark Lohman page 57: Mark Lohman page 58: Mark Lohman page 59: Mark Samu page 60: *all* Jessie Walker page 61: Mark Lohman page 63: *top left* Nancy Hill; *top right and bottom* Mark Lohman page 65: Mark Samu page 66: Giammarino and Dworkin page 67: *top and middle* Mark Samu; *bottom* Jessie Walker page 68: *top* Nancy Hill; *bottom* Mark Lohman page 69: Jessie Walker page 70: *left* Mark Lohman; *right* Jessie

Walker page 71: Mark Samu page 72: Tim Street-Porter/Beate Works page 73: Mark Lohman page 74: *left* Jessie Walker; *right* Mark Samu page 75: *top and bottom left* Mark Samu; *top right* Mark Lohman; *bottom right* Robert Harding Picture Library page 76: Time Street-Porter/Beate Works page 78: Jessie Walker page 79: Tim Street-Porter/Beate Works page 80: Giammarino and Dworkin page 81: *top* Mark Lohman; *bottom* Jessie Walker page 82: *top right* Scalamandré; *center* Mark Samu page 84: Mark Lohman page 85: Giammarino and Dworkin page 87: Tria Giovan page 88: *top* Grey Crawford/Beate Works; *bottom* Jessie Walker page 89: *top left* Jessie Walker; *top right* Mark Lohman; *bottom* Brad Simmons page 90: Mark Lohman page 92: Mark Lohman page 93: Mark Samu page 94–95: *all* Mark Lohman page 96: Mark Samu page 97: *top to bottom* Mark Samu; Mark Lohman page 98: *top* Tria Giovan; *bottom* Mark Samu page 99: Mark Lohman page 100: Phillip Ennis page 101: Mark Lohman page 102–103: *all* Mark

Lohman page 104: Jessie Walker page 106: Mark Samu page 107: Mark Lohman page 108: Mark Samu page 109: Giammarino and Dworkin page 110: Jessie Walker page 111: *top* Mark Lohman; *bottom* Brad Simmons page 112: *top* Mark Samu; *bottom* Mark Lohman page 113: *top* Robert Harding Picture Library; *bottom* Tria Giovan page 120: Mark Samu page 122: Mark Lohman page 125: Tim Street-Porter/Beate Works

Have a home improvement, decorating, or gardening project? Look for these and other fine Creative Homeowner books at your local home center or bookstore.

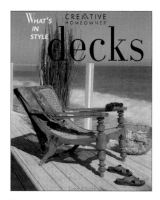

The latest in deck design and deck products. More than 200 color photos and illustrations.
128 pp.; 8½"×10⅞"
BOOK #: 277183

Fill your home with the spirit of country: fabrics, finishes, and furniture. More than 200 photos.
176 pp.; 9"×10"
BOOK #: 279685

Transform a dated kitchen into the spectacular heart of the home. Over 150 color photos.
176 pp.; 9"×10"
BOOK #: 279935

How to work with space, color, pattern, and texture. Over 300 photos.
256 pp.; 9"×10"
BOOK #: 279667

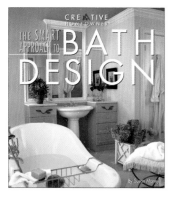

All you need to know about designing a bathroom. Over 150 color photos.
176 pp.; 9"×10"
BOOK #: 287225

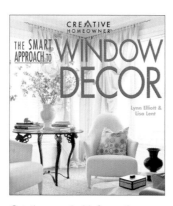

Get the practical information you need to choose window treatments. Over 100 illustrations & 125 photos. 176 pp.; 9"×10"
BOOK #: 279431

Turn an ordinary room into a masterpiece with decorative faux finishes. Over 40 techniques & 300 photos. 272 pp.; 9"×10"
BOOK #: 279550

Interior designer Lyn Peterson's easy-to-live-with decorating ideas. Over 350 photos.
304 pp.; 9"×10"
BOOK #: 279382

Impressive guide to garden design and plant selection. More than 600 color photos.
320 pp.; 9"×10"
BOOK #: 274615

Lavishly illustrated with portraits of over 100 flowering plants; more than 500 photos.
208 pp.; 9"×10"
BOOK #: 274032

Everything you need to know about setting ceramic tile. Over 450 photos and illustrations.
160 pp.; 8½"×10⅞"
Book #: 277524

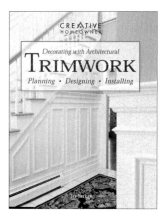

How to create a richly textured home. More than 450 color photos and illustrations.
208 pp.; 8½" ×10⅞"
BOOK #: 277495

For more information, and to order direct, call 800-631-7795; in New Jersey 201-934-7100.
Please visit our Web site at www.creativehomeowner.com

Fourth Edition

NorthStar 1

Listening & Speaking

Authors: Polly Merdinger
Laurie Barton

Series Editors: Frances Boyd
Carol Numrich

Dedication

This book is dedicated to Stratton Ray, whose love of teaching
was an inspiration, and whose friendship was a gift.
—*Polly Merdinger*

To Natasha and Madeleine, to whom I hope will see the world.
—*Laurie Barton*

NorthStar: Listening & Speaking Level 1, Fourth Edition

Copyright © 2020, 2015, 2009, 2004 by Pearson Education, Inc.
All rights reserved.

No part of this publication may be reproduced, stored in a retrieval system, or transmitted in any form or by any means, electronic, mechanical, photocopying, recording, or otherwise, without the prior permission of the publisher.

Pearson Education, 221 River St, Hoboken, NJ 07030

Staff credits: The people who made up the *NorthStar: Listening & Speaking Level 1, Fourth Edition* team, representing content creation, design, marketing, manufacturing, multimedia, project management, publishing, rights management, and testing, are Pietro Alongi, Stephanie Callahan, Gina DiLillo, Tracey Cataldo, Dave Dickey, Warren Fishbach, Sarah Hand, Lucy Hart, Gosia Jaros-White, Stefan Machura, Linda Moser, Dana Pinter, Karen Quinn, Katarzyna Starzynska - Kosciuszko, Paula Van Ells, Claire Van Poperin, Joseph Vella, Peter West, Autumn Westphal, Natalia Zaremba, and Marcin Zimny.

Project consultant: Debbie Sistino
Text composition: ElectraGraphics, Inc.
Development editing: Debbie King
Cover design: Studio Montage

Library of Congress Cataloging-in-Publication Data

A Catalog record for the print edition is available from the Library of Congress.

Printed in the United States of America

ISBN-13: 978-0-13-523265-1 (Student Book with Digital Resources)
ISBN-10: 0-13-523265-1 (Student Book with Digital Resources)

ISBN-13: 978-0-13-522697-1 (Student Book with MyEnglishLab Online Workbook and Resources)
ISBN-10: 0-13-522697-X (Student Book with MyEnglishLab Online Workbook and Resources)

5 2021

CONTENTS

WELCOME TO NORTHSTAR

A Letter from the Series Editors

We welcome you to the 4th edition of *NorthStar Listening & Speaking Level 1*.

Engaging content, integrated skills, and critical thinking continue to be the touchstones of the series. For more than 20 years *NorthStar* has engaged and motivated students through contemporary, authentic topics. Our online component builds on the last edition by offering new and updated activities.

Since its first edition, *NorthStar* has been rigorous in its approach to critical thinking by systematically engaging students in tasks and activities that prepare them to move into high-level academic courses. The cognitive domains of Bloom's taxonomy provide the foundation for the critical thinking activities. Students develop the skills of analysis and evaluation and the ability to synthesize and summarize information from multiple sources. The capstone of each unit, the final writing or speaking task, supports students in the application of all academic, critical thinking, and language skills that are the focus of unit.

The new edition introduces additional academic skills for 21st century success: note-taking and presentation skills. There is also a focus on learning outcomes based on the Global Scale of English (GSE), an emphasis on the application of skills, and a new visual design. These refinements are our response to research in the field of language learning in addition to feedback from educators who have taught from our previous editions.

NorthStar has pioneered and perfected the blending of academic content and academic skills in an English Language series. Read on for a comprehensive overview of this new edition. As you and your students explore *NorthStar*, we wish you a great journey.

Carol Numrich and Frances Boyd, the editors

New for the FOURTH EDITION

New and Updated Themes

The new edition features one new theme per level (i.e., one new unit per book), with updated content and skills throughout the series. Current and thought-provoking topics presented in a variety of genres promote intellectual stimulation. The real-world-inspired content engages students, links them to language use outside the classroom, and encourages personal expression and critical thinking.

Learning Outcomes and Assessments

All unit skills, vocabulary, and grammar points are connected to GSE objectives to ensure effective progression of learning throughout the series. Learning outcomes are present at the opening and closing of each unit to clearly mark what is covered in the unit and encourage both pre- and post-unit self-reflection. A variety of assessment tools, including online diagnostic, formative, and summative assessments and a flexible gradebook aligned with clearly identified unit learning outcomes, allow teachers to individualize instruction and track student progress.

Note-Taking as a Skill in Every Unit

Grounded in the foundations of the Cornell Method of note-taking, the new note-taking practice is structured to allow students to reflect on and organize their notes, focusing on the most important points. Students are instructed, throughout the unit, on the most effective way to apply their notes to a classroom task, as well as encouraged to analyze and reflect on their growing note-taking skills.

Explicit Skill Instruction and Fully-Integrated Practice

Concise presentations and targeted practice in print and online prepare students for academic success. Language skills are highlighted in each unit, providing students with multiple, systematic exposures to language forms and structures in a variety of contexts. Academic and language skills in each unit are applied clearly and deliberately in the culminating writing or presentation task.

Scaffolded Critical Thinking

Activities within the unit are structured to follow the stages of Bloom's taxonomy from *remember* to *create*. The use of APPLY throughout the unit highlights culminating activities that allow students to use the skills being practiced in a free and authentic manner. Sections that are focused on developing critical thinking are marked with 🔍 to highlight their critical focus.

Explicit Focus on the Academic Word List

AWL words are highlighted at the end of the unit and in a master list at the end of the book.

The Pearson Practice English App

The **Pearson Practice English App** allows students on the go to complete vocabulary and grammar activities, listen to audio, and watch video.

ExamView

ExamView Test Generator allows teachers to customize assessments by reordering or editing existing questions, selecting test items from a bank, or writing new questions.

MyEnglishLab

New and revised online supplementary practice maps to the updates in the student book for this edition.

THE NORTHSTAR UNIT

1 FOCUS ON THE TOPIC

Each unit begins with an eye-catching unit opener spread that draws students into the topic. The learning outcomes are written in simple, student-friendly language to allow for self-assessment. Focus on the Topic questions connect to the unit theme and get students to think critically by making inferences and predicting the content of the unit.

UNIT 1

Unique Homes

1 FOCUS ON THE TOPIC

1. What kind of house do you see in the photo? How would you describe this house?
2. What is unique or unusual about this house?
3. Is this a good house to live in? Why or why not?

Unique Homes **3**

LEARNING OUTCOMES

> Infer both sides of a story
> Take notes with + and /
> Identify and understand advantages and disadvantages

> Use the present and past of *be*
> Stress *not*
> Ask for more information

Go to **MyEnglishLab** to check what you know.

2 UNIT 1

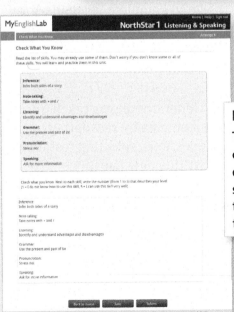

MyEnglishLab

The "Check What You Know" pre-unit diagnostic checklist provides a short self-assessment based on each unit's GSE-aligned learning outcomes to support the students in building an awareness of their own skill levels and to enable teachers to target instruction to their students' specific needs.

2 FOCUS ON LISTENING

A vocabulary exercise introduces words that appear in the listenings, encourages students to guess the meanings of the words from context, and connects to the theme presented in the final speaking task.

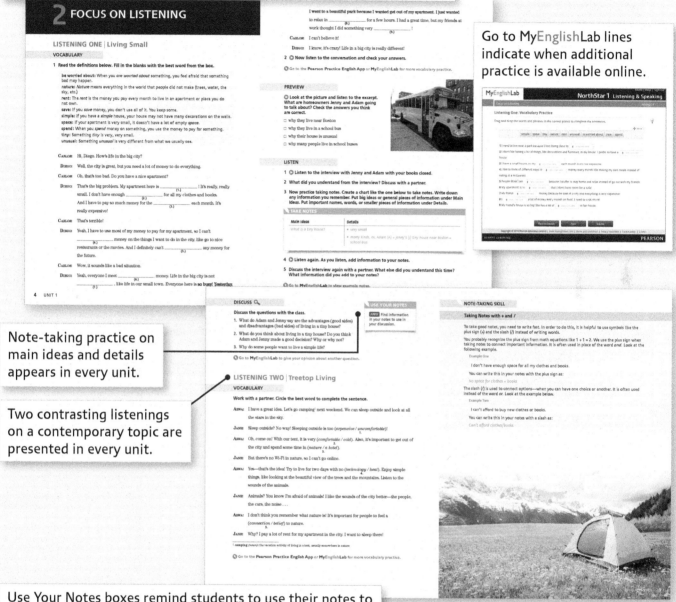

Note-taking practice on main ideas and details appears in every unit.

Two contrasting listenings on a contemporary topic are presented in every unit.

Use Your Notes boxes remind students to use their notes to complete exercises that support language, academic skills, production and critical thinking.

Every unit focuses on noting main ideas and details and features an additional note-taking skill applicable to the listenings. Activities are designed to support students in successfully completing the final speaking tasks.

EXPLICIT SKILL INSTRUCTION AND PRACTICE

Step-by-step instructions and practice guide students to move beyond the literal meaning of the listenings. 🔍 highlights activities that help build critical thinking skills.

MAKE INFERENCES 🔍

Inferring Both Sides of a Story

An inference is a guess about something that is not said directly. When people talk about themselves or tell a personal story, there are often two sides to the story: a good side and a bad side. People usually focus on the good side of things. But if we listen closely, we can also understand the bad side, even if they don't say it.

▶ **Listen carefully to the example and choose _a_ or _b_.**

Example

When Adam says, "And it's crazy, but that same day, we bought this bus!" he is focusing on the good side: He and Jenny made a great and unusual decision very quickly. What's the bad side that Adam didn't talk about?

a. Adam and Jenny made a bad decision when they bought the bus.
b. Adam and Jenny didn't think a lot about a very important decision.

Explanation

The correct answer is _b_. Adam and Jenny were not crazy when they bought the bus, and it wasn't a bad decision. However, living in a school bus is a very unusual thing to do. Most people think for a long time before they make an unusual decision. But Adam and Jenny decided to live in a school bus, and they bought the bus in one day. This means they didn't think a lot before they made this important decision.

▶ **Listen to the excerpts from the interview. Circle _a_ or _b_ to choose the bad side of the story.**

Excerpt One

Good side: Adam and Jenny were happy because they usually can't make decisions quickly.

Bad side: **a.** They were still worried about making a quick decision.

ve space.
keep your things.

ed.
ed.

Unique Homes **7**

MyEnglishLab

NorthStar 1 Listening & Speaking

Focus on Listening

Attempt **1**

Listening Practice: Identifying and Understanding Advantages and Disadvantages

Listen to the excerpts from a conversation. Select all the positive or negative words that you hear then choose whether the conversation talks about advantages or disadvantages.

▶ ○━━━ 00:00 ◀) ━━━○ ⚙

1 Select all the positive or negative words you hear.
- ☐ cool
- ☐ hotel
- ☐ lovely
- ☐ peaceful
- ☐ bad
- ☐ beautiful

Based on your answers above, this excerpt talks about:
- ☐ advantages
- ☐ disadvantages

▶ ○━━━ 00:00 ◀) ━━━○ ⚙

2 Select all the positive or negative words you hear.
- ☐ treehouse
- ☐ uncomfortable
- ☐ tiny
- ☐ city
- ☐ fun
- ☐ boring

Based on your answers above, this excerpt talks about:
- ☐ advantages
- ☐ disadvantages

MyEnglishLab
Key listening skills are reinforced and practiced in new contexts. Autograded skills-based activities provide instant scores, allowing teachers and students to identify where improvement is needed.

Back to course   Save   Submit

ALWAYS LEARNING

PEARSON

3 FOCUS ON SPEAKING

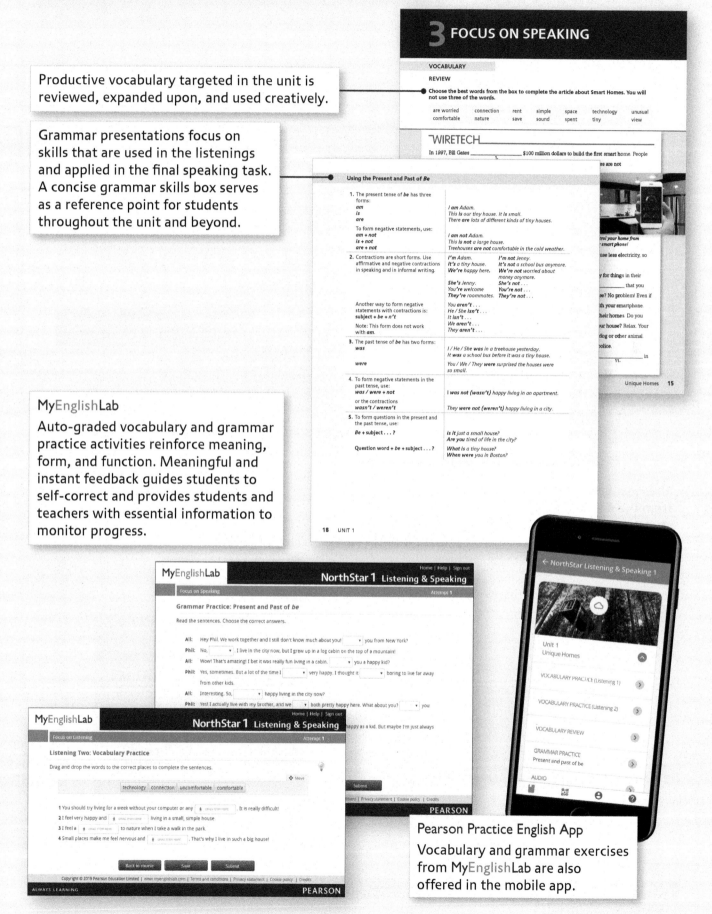

Productive vocabulary targeted in the unit is reviewed, expanded upon, and used creatively.

Grammar presentations focus on skills that are used in the listenings and applied in the final speaking task. A concise grammar skills box serves as a reference point for students throughout the unit and beyond.

MyEnglishLab

Auto-graded vocabulary and grammar practice activities reinforce meaning, form, and function. Meaningful and instant feedback guides students to self-correct and provides students and teachers with essential information to monitor progress.

Pearson Practice English App

Vocabulary and grammar exercises from MyEnglishLab are also offered in the mobile app.

A TASK-BASED APPROACH TO PROCESS WRITING

Pronunciation and Speaking Skill tasks are focused on learning outcomes which are later used in the final speaking task, helping students develop their professional and academic public speaking skills.

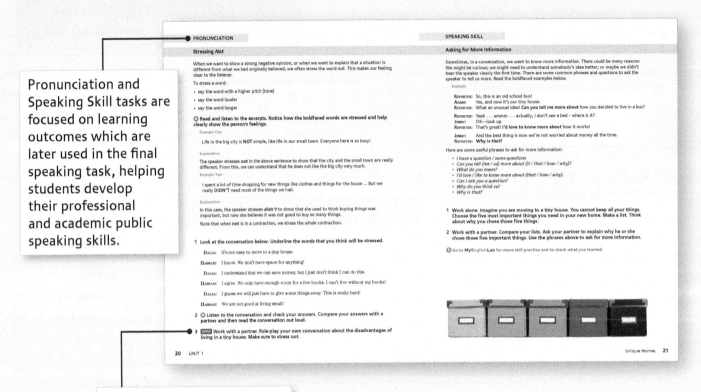

Stressing *Not*

When we want to show a strong negative opinion, or when we want to explain that a situation is different from what we had originally believed, we often stress the word *not*. This makes our feeling clear to the listener.

To stress a word:

- say the word with a higher pitch (tone)
- say the word louder
- say the word longer

⊙ Read and listen to the excerpts. Notice how the boldfaced words are stressed and help clearly show the person's feelings.

Example One

Life in the big city is **NOT** simple, like life in our small town. Everyone here is so busy!

Explanation

The speaker stresses *not* in the above sentence to show that the city and the small town are really different. From this, we can understand that he does not like the big city very much.

Example Two

I spent a lot of time shopping for new things like clothes and things for the house ... But we really **DIDN'T** need most of the things we had.

Explanation

In this case, the speaker stresses *didn't* to show that she used to think buying things was important, but now she believes it was not good to buy so many things.

Note that when *not* is in a contraction, we stress the whole contraction.

1 Look at the conversation below. Underline the words that you think will be stressed.

DALIA: It's not easy to move to a tiny house.

HASSAN: I know. We don't have space for anything!

DALIA: I understand that we can save money, but I just don't think I can do this.

HASSAN: I agree. We only have enough room for a few books. I can't live without my books!

DALIA: I guess we will just have to give some things away. This is really hard!

HASSAN: We are not good at living small!

2 ⊙ Listen to the conversation and check your answers. Compare your answers with a partner and then read the conversation out loud.

3 **APPLY** Work with a partner. Role-play your own conversation about the disadvantages of living in a tiny house. Make sure to stress *not*.

Asking for More Information

Sometimes, in a conversation, we want to know more information. There could be many reasons: We might be curious; we might need to understand somebody's idea better; or maybe we didn't hear the speaker clearly the first time. There are some common phrases and questions to ask the speaker to tell us more. Read the boldfaced examples below.

Example

REPORTER: So, this is an old school bus!
ADAM: Yes, and now it's our tiny house.
REPORTER: What an unusual idea! **Can you tell me more about** how you decided to live in a bus?

REPORTER: Yeah . . . ummm . . . actually, I don't see a bed - where is it?
JENNY: OK—look up.
REPORTER: That's great! **I'd love to know more about** how it works!

JENNY: And the best thing is now we're not worried about money all the time.
REPORTER: **Why is that?**

Here are some useful phrases to ask for more information:

- *I have a question / some questions*
- *Can you tell (me / us) more about (it / that / how / why)?*
- *What do you mean?*
- *I'd love / like to know more about (that / how / why).*
- *Can I ask you a question?*
- *Why do you think so?*
- *Why is that?*

1 Work alone. Imagine you are moving to a tiny house. You cannot keep all your things. Choose the five most important things you need in your new home. Make a list. Think about why you chose these five things.

2 Work with a partner. Compare your lists. Ask your partner to explain why he or she chose those five important things. Use the phrases above to ask for more information.

⊙ Go to **MyEnglishLab** for more skill practice and to check what you learned.

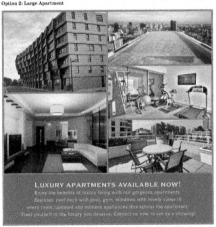

APPLY calls out activities that get students to use new skills in a productive task.

The Final Speaking task incorporates themes and skills from the unit in a final productive task that engages students in a variety of public speaking genres, from interactive role-plays to academic presentations.

A role-play is a short performance. Students take roles in a situation. You are going to role-play a discussion between two friends who are looking for a place to live near their university. You are talking about what kind of house you will move into.

STEP 1

Form two groups: Group A and Group B. Follow the instructions for your group.

Group A

- You want to move to a tiny house. Your roommate wants to live in a large apartment. You need to change your roommate's mind.
- Look at the pictures of the tiny house in Option 1. As a group, take notes on the advantages of living in this house.
- Look at the pictures of the large apartment in Option 2 on the next page. As a group, take notes on the disadvantages of living in this apartment.

Option 1: Tiny House

Group B

- You want to move to a large apartment. Your roommate wants to live in a tiny house. You need to change your roommate's mind.
- Look at the pictures of the large apartment. As a group, take notes on the advantages of living in this apartment.
- Look at the pictures of the tiny house on page 22. As a group, take notes on the disadvantages of living in a tiny house.

Option 2: Large Apartment

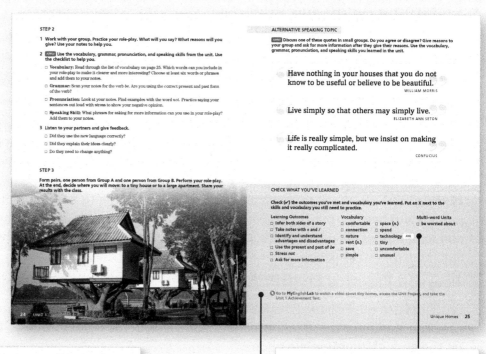

At the end of the unit, students are directed to MyEnglishLab to watch a video connected to the theme, access the Unit Project, and take the Unit Achievement Test.

Academic Word List words are highlighted with **AWL** at the end of the unit.

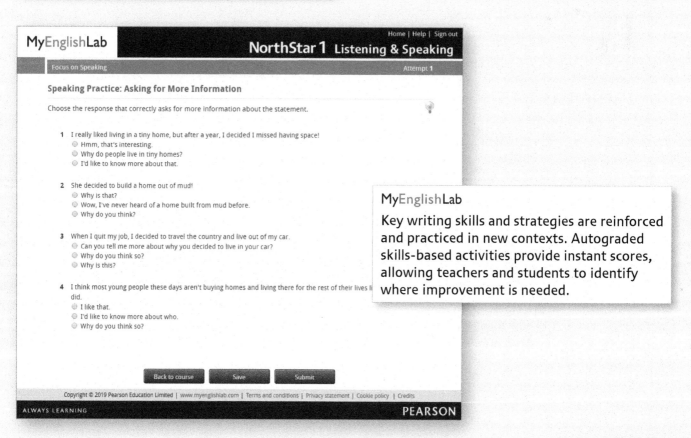

MyEnglishLab

Key writing skills and strategies are reinforced and practiced in new contexts. Autograded skills-based activities provide instant scores, allowing teachers and students to identify where improvement is needed.

COMPONENTS

Students can access the following resources on the Pearson English Portal.

- **Classroom Audio and Videos**

  Classroom audio (the readings for the Reading & Writing strand and the listenings and exercises with audio for the Listening & Speaking strand) and the end-of-unit videos are available on the portal.

- **Etext**

  Offering maximum flexibility in order to meet the individual needs of each student, the digital version of the student book can be used across multiple platforms and devices.

- **MyEnglishLab**

  MyEnglishLab offers students access to additional practice online in the form of both auto-graded and teacher-graded activities. Auto-graded activities support and build on the academic and language skills presented and practiced in the student book. Teacher-graded activities include speaking and writing.

- **Pearson Practice English App**

  Students use the Pearson Practice English App to access additional grammar and vocabulary practice, audio for the listenings and readings from the student books, and the end-of-unit videos on the go with their mobile phone.

INNOVATIVE TEACHING TOOLS

With instant access to a wide range of online content and diagnostic tools, teachers can customize learning environments to meet the needs of every student. Digital resources, all available on the Pearson English Portal, include **MyEnglishLab** and ExamView.

Using MyEnglishLab, *NorthStar* teachers can

Deliver rich online content to engage and motivate students, including

- student audio to support listening and speaking skills, in addition to audio versions of all readings.
- engaging, authentic video clips tied to the unit themes.
- opportunities for written and recorded reactions to be submitted by students.

Use diagnostic reports to

- view student scores by unit, skill, and activity.
- monitor student progress on any activity or test as often as needed.
- analyze class data to determine steps for remediation and support.

Access Teacher Resources, including

- unit teaching notes and answer keys.
- downloadable diagnostic, achievement and placement tests, as well as unit checkpoints.
- printable resources including lesson planners, videoscripts, and video activities.
- classroom audio.

Using ExamView, teachers can customize Achievement Tests by

- reordering test questions.
- editing questions.
- selecting questions from a bank.
- writing their own questions.

SCOPE AND SEQUENCE

	1 Unique Homes Pages: 2–25 Listening 1: Living Small Listening 2: Treetop Living	**2 Making Unusual Art** Pages: 26–51 Listening 1: Mia Pearlman Listening 2: The Quilts of Gee's Bend
Inference	Inferring both sides of a story	Inferring why someone is surprised
Note-Taking	Taking notes with + and /	Using initials to reference people in your notes
Listening	Identifying and understanding advantages and disadvantages	Identifying main ideas and details
Grammar	Present and past of *be*	Simple present
Pronunciation	Stressing *not*	Using correct intonation in questions
Speaking	Asking for more information	Expressing opinions
Final Speaking Task	Role-play: discussion between two friends looking for a place to live near their university (tiny house or large apartment)	Role-Play: museum curators choose unusual art for a modern art museum
Video	Tiny Homes	Art

Assessments	Pre-Unit Diagnostic:
	   Check What You Know
	Checkpoint 1
	Checkpoint 2
	Unit Achievement Test
		Pre-Unit Diagnostic:
		   Check What You Know
		Checkpoint 1
		Checkpoint 2
		Unit Achievement Test

Unit Project	Research and give a report on a tiny house	Research and present pictures of traditional paper art

SCOPE AND SEQUENCE

	5 Understanding Fears and Phobias Pages: 102–125 Listening 1: Human Minds: A Radio Show Listening 2: Crossing a Bridge	6 Risks and Challenges Pages: 126–151 Listening 1: The Amazing Swimmer, Diana Nyad Listening 2: An Outward Journeys Experience
Inference	Inferring the meaning of exaggerations	Inferring the meaning of rhetorical questions
Note-Taking	Taking notes with bullets and dashes	Taking notes on cause and effect
Listening	Recognizing contradictions	Recognizing and understanding negative questions
Grammar	Simple past	Present progressive
Pronunciation	Pronouncing -ed endings	Pronouncing the vowels /iy/ and /ɪ/
Speaking	Giving orders, advice, and encouragement	Describing photos and visuals
Final Speaking Task	Role-play: a conversation about water phobia	Role-play: interview between a news reporter and a risk-taker
Video	Weird phobias	A heroic pilot

Assessments	Pre-Unit Diagnostic:
	    Check What You Know
	Checkpoint 1
	Checkpoint 2
	Unit Achievement Test
		Pre-Unit Diagnostic:
		    Check What You Know
		Checkpoint 1
		Checkpoint 2
		Unit Achievement Test

Unit Project	Research and prepare an oral report on a phobia	Research and present pictures of a risk-taker

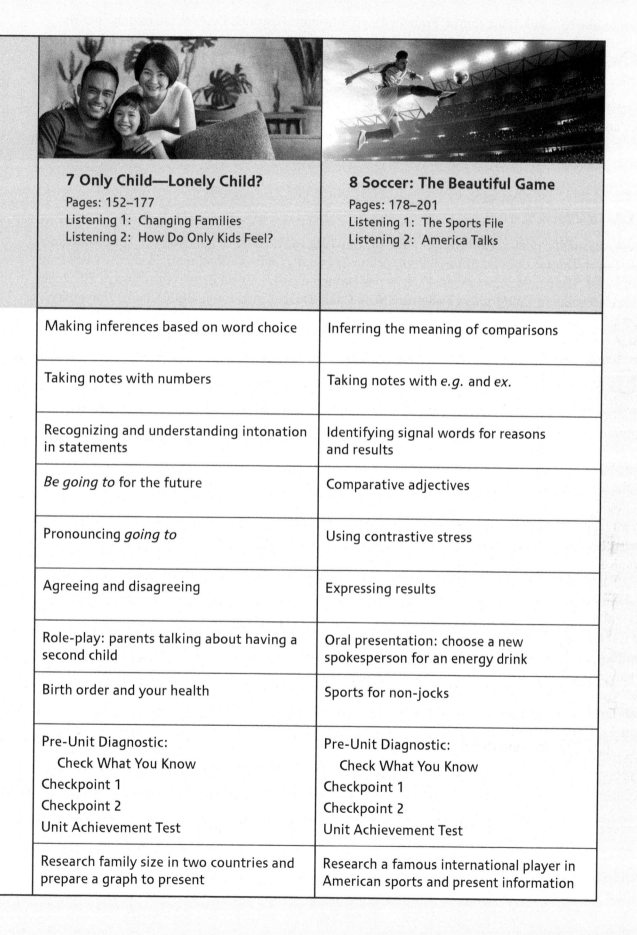

7 Only Child—Lonely Child? Pages: 152–177 Listening 1: Changing Families Listening 2: How Do Only Kids Feel?	**8 Soccer: The Beautiful Game** Pages: 178–201 Listening 1: The Sports File Listening 2: America Talks
Making inferences based on word choice	Inferring the meaning of comparisons
Taking notes with numbers	Taking notes with *e.g.* and *ex.*
Recognizing and understanding intonation in statements	Identifying signal words for reasons and results
Be going to for the future	Comparative adjectives
Pronouncing *going to*	Using contrastive stress
Agreeing and disagreeing	Expressing results
Role-play: parents talking about having a second child	Oral presentation: choose a new spokesperson for an energy drink
Birth order and your health	Sports for non-jocks

Pre-Unit Diagnostic:
    Check What You Know
Checkpoint 1
Checkpoint 2
Unit Achievement Test
	Pre-Unit Diagnostic:
	    Check What You Know
	Checkpoint 1
	Checkpoint 2
	Unit Achievement Test

Research family size in two countries and prepare a graph to present	Research a famous international player in American sports and present information

ACKNOWLEDGMENTS

I would like to thank Dana Pinter, Frances Boyd, Autumn Westphal, Peter West, and the entire NorthStar team for their exceptional support over the past year. And thank you to my husband, Rick Yaverbaum, for his love, support, and understanding.

—Polly Merdinger

I would like to thank my husband Craig Binns. This book could not have been written without his love and support.

—Laurie Barton

REVIEWERS

Chris Antonellis, Boston University – CELOP; Gail August, Hostos; Aegina Barnes, York College; Kim Bayer, Hunter College; Mine Bellikli, Atilim University; Allison Blechman, Embassy CES; Paul Blomquist, Kaplan; Helena Botros, FLS; James Branchick, FLS; Chris Bruffee, Embassy CES; Joyce Cain University of California at Fullerton; Nese Cakli, Duzce University; Molly Cheny, University of Washington; María Cordani Tourinho Dantas, Colégio Rainha De Paz; Jason Davis, ASC English; Lindsay Donigan, Fullerton College; Mila Dragushanskaya, ASA College; Bina Dugan, BCCC; Sibel Ece Izmir, Atilim University; Érica Ferrer, Universidad del Norte; María Irma Gallegos Peláez, Universidad del Valle de México; Vera Figueira, UC Irvine; Rachel Fernandez, UC Irvine; Jeff Gano, ASA College; Emily Ellis, UC Irvine; María Genovev a Chávez Bazán, Universidad del Valle de México; Juan Garcia, FLS; Heidi Gramlich, The New England School of English; Phillip Grayson, Kaplan; Rebecca Gross, The New England School of English; Rick Guadiana, FLS; Sebnem Guzel, Tobb University; Esra Hatipoglu, Ufuk University; Brian Henry, FLS; Josephine Horna, BCCC; Judy Hu, UC Irvine; Arthur Hui, Fullerton College; Zoe Isaacson, Hunter College; Kathy Johnson, Fullerton College; Marcelo Juica, Urban College of Boston; Tom Justice, North Shore Community College; Lisa Karakas, Berkeley College; Eva Kopernacki, Embassy CES; Drew Larimore, Kaplan; Heidi Lieb, BCCC; Patricia Martins, Ibeu; Cecilia Mora Espejo, Universidad del Valle de México; Oscar Navarro University of California at Fullerton; Eva Nemtson, ASA College; Kate Nyhan, The New England School of English; Julie Oni, FLS; Willard Osman, The New England School of English; Olga Pagieva, ASA College; Manish Patel, FLS; Paige Poole, Universidad del Norte; Claudia Rebello, Ibeu; Amy Renehan, University of Washington; Lourdes Rey, Universidad del Norte; Michelle Reynolds, FLS International Boston Commons; Mary Ritter, NYU; Ellen Rosen University of California at Fullerton; Dana Saito-Stehiberger, UC Irvine; Dariusz Saczuk, ASA College; Miryam Salimov, ASA College; Minerva Santos, Hostos; Sezer Sarioz, Saint Benoit PLS; Gail Schwartz, UC Irvine; Ebru Sinar, Tobb University; Beth Soll, NYU (Columbia); Christopher Stobart, Universidad del Norte; Guliz Uludag, Ufuk University; Debra Un, NYU; Hilal Unlusu, Saint Benoit PLS; María del Carmen Viruega Trejo, Universidad del Valle de México; Reda Vural, Atilim University; Douglas Waters, Universidad del Norte; Emily Wong, UC Irvine; Leyla Yucklik, Duzce University; Jorge Zepeda Porras, Universidad del Valle de México

LEARNING OUTCOMES

> Infer both sides of a story
> Take notes with + and /
> Identify and understand advantages and disadvantages

> Use the present and past of *be*
> Stress *not*
> Ask for more information

🔵 Go to **MyEnglishLab** to check what you know.

Unique Homes

1 FOCUS ON THE TOPIC

1. What kind of house do you see in the photo? How would you describe this house?
2. What is unique or unusual about this house?
3. Is this a good house to live in? Why or why not?

LISTENING ONE | Living Small

VOCABULARY

1 Read the definitions below. Fill in the blanks with the best word from the box.

be worried about: When you *are worried about* something, you feel afraid that something bad may happen.

nature: *Nature* means everything in the world that people did not make (trees, water, the sky, etc.)

rent: The *rent* is the money you pay every month to live in an apartment or place you do not own.

save: If you *save* money, you don't use all of it. You keep some.

simple: If you have a *simple* house, your house may not have many decorations on the walls.

space: If your apartment is very small, it doesn't have a lot of empty *space*.

spend: When you *spend* money on something, you use the money to pay for something.

tiny: Something *tiny* is very, very small.

unusual: Something *unusual* is very different from what we usually see.

CARLOS: Hi, Diego. How's life in the big city?

DIEGO: Well, the city is great, but you need a lot of money to do everything.

CARLOS: Oh, that's too bad. Do you have a nice apartment?

DIEGO: That's the big problem. My apartment here is __very small__ ! It's really, really
(1.)
small. I don't have enough __space__ for all my clothes and books.
(2.)
And I have to pay so much money for the __rent__ each month. It's
(3.)
really expensive!

CARLOS: That's terrible!

DIEGO: Yeah, I have to use most of my money to pay for my apartment, so I can't
__save__ money on the things I want to do in the city, like go to nice
(4.)
restaurants or the movies. And I definitely can't __save__ any money for
(5.)
the future.

CARLOS: Wow, it sounds like a bad situation.

DIEGO: Yeah, everyone I meet __be worried about__ money. Life in the big city is not
(6.)
__simple__ , like life in our small town. Everyone here is so busy! Yesterday,
(7.)

I went to a beautiful park because I wanted get out of my apartment. I just wanted to relax in _Space_ (8.) for a few hours. I had a great time, but my friends at work thought I did something very _Nature_ (9.)!

CARLOS: I can't believe it!

DIEGO: I know, it's crazy! Life in a big city is really different!

2 ▶ Now listen to the conversation and check your answers.

↗ Go to the **Pearson Practice English App** or **MyEnglishLab** for more vocabulary practice.

PREVIEW

▶ **Look at the picture and listen to the excerpt. What are homeowners Jenny and Adam going to talk about? Check the answers you think are correct.**

☐ why they live near Boston

☐ why they live in a school bus

☐ why their house is unusual

☐ why many people live in school buses

LISTEN

1 ▶ **Listen to the interview with Jenny and Adam with your books closed.**

2 **What did you understand from the interview? Discuss with a partner.**

3 **Now practice taking notes. Create a chart like the one below to take notes. Write down any information you remember. Put big ideas or general pieces of information under Main Ideas. Put important names, words, or smaller pieces of information under Details.**

TAKE NOTES

Main Ideas	Details
What is a tiny house?	• very small
	• many kinds, ex. Adam (A) + Jenny's (J) tiny house near Boston = school bus

4 ▶ **Listen again. As you listen, add information to your notes.**

5 **Discuss the interview again with a partner. What else did you understand this time? What information did you add to your notes?**

↗ Go to **MyEnglishLab** to view example notes.

MAIN IDEAS

Choose the correct answer. Use your notes to help you.

1. Jenny and Adam weren't happy with their apartment in Boston because it was _____ .

   (a.) small and expensive

   b. in a big city

2. They bought a school bus because they thought _____ .

   a. it was really interesting

   (b.) it could be a good tiny house

3. In a tiny house, you only have space for _____ .

   (a.) the things you need

   b. things that are small

4. Jenny and Adam's life is simple because they have _____ .

   a. fewer friends visit their house

   (b.) fewer things in their house

5. Jenny and Adam are _____ their simple life.

   (a) happy with

   b. sad about

DETAILS

1 ▶ **Listen again and add to your notes. Write _T_ (true) or _F_ (false) next to each statement. Correct the false information. Use your notes to help you.**

   __T__ 1. Jenny and Adam saw a video about tiny houses.

   __F__ 2. They bought the school bus the week after they saw it.

   __F__ 3. Jenny and Adam's bed is under the floor.

   __F__ 4. Jenny and Adam keep their shoes in a closet.

   __T__ 5. Now Jenny and Adam have more free time.

   __F__ 6. The school bus cost more than four months of rent in the city.

   __F__ 7. Jenny and Adam are still worried about money.

2 **With a partner, take turns summarizing your notes. Then discuss how your notes and your answers in Preview helped you understand the listening.**

🔊 Go to **MyEnglishLab** for more listening practice.

MAKE INFERENCES 🔍

Inferring Both Sides of a Story

An inference is a guess about something that is not said directly. When people talk about themselves or tell a personal story, there are often two sides to the story: a good side and a bad side. People usually focus on the good side of things. But if we listen closely, we can also understand the bad side, even if they don't say it.

▶ **Listen carefully to the example and choose *a* or *b*.**

Example

When Adam says, "And it's crazy, but that same day, we bought this bus!" he is focusing on the good side: He and Jenny made a great and unusual decision very quickly. What's the bad side that Adam didn't talk about?

a. Adam and Jenny made a bad decision when they bought the bus.
b. Adam and Jenny didn't think a lot about a very important decision.

Explanation

The correct answer is *b*. Adam and Jenny were not crazy when they bought the bus, and it wasn't a bad decision. However, living in a school bus is a very unusual thing to do. Most people think for a long time before they make an unusual decision. But Adam and Jenny decided to live in a school bus, and they bought the bus in one day. This means they didn't think a lot before they made this important decision.

▶ **Listen to the excerpts from the interview. Circle *a* or *b* to choose the bad side of the story.**

Excerpt One

Good side: Adam and Jenny were happy because they usually can't make decisions quickly.

Bad side: a. They were still worried about making a quick decision.

             b. They knew their decision was a big mistake.

Excerpt Two

Good side: In a tiny house, it's possible to find some unusual ways to save space.

Bad side: a. Tiny houses don't have many normal or typical places to keep your things.

             b. Tiny houses are too small for big things like a bed.

Excerpt Three

Good side: Your life will be simple, but you can have everything you need.

Bad side: a. A tiny house doesn't have enough space for things you need.

             b. You have to give away things that you like but don't need.

Discuss the questions with the class.

1. What do Adam and Jenny say are the advantages (good sides) and disadvantages (bad sides) of living in a tiny house?

2. What do you think about living in a tiny house? Do you think Adam and Jenny made a good decision? Why or why not?

3. Why do some people want to live a simple life?

🔾 Go to **MyEnglishLab** to give your opinion about another question.

USE YOUR NOTES

APPLY Find information in your notes to use in your discussion.

LISTENING TWO | Treetop Living

VOCABULARY

Work with a partner. Circle the best word to complete the sentence.

ARWA: I have a great idea. Let's go camping[1] next weekend. We can sleep outside and look at all the stars in the sky.

JANE: Sleep outside? No way! Sleeping outside is too (*expensive* / *uncomfortable*)!
1.

ARWA: Oh, come on! With our tent, it is very (*comfortable* / *cold*). Also, it's important to get out of
2.
the city and spend some time in (*nature* / *a hotel*).
3.

JANE: But there's no Wi-Fi in nature, so I can't go online.

ARWA: Yes—that's the idea! Try to live for two days with no (*technology* / *heat*). Enjoy simple
4.
things, like looking at the beautiful view of the trees and the mountains. Listen to the sounds of the animals.

JANE: Animals? You know I'm afraid of animals! I like the sounds of the city better—the people, the cars, the noise . . .

ARWA: I don't think you remember what nature is! It's important for people to feel a
(*connection* / *belief*) to nature.
5.

JANE: Why? I pay a lot of rent for my apartment in the city. I want to sleep there!

---

[1] **camping** (*noun*): the vacation activity of living in a tent, usually somewhere in nature

🔾 Go to the **Pearson Practice English App** or **MyEnglishLab** for more vocabulary practice.

Taking Notes with + and /

To take good notes, you need to write fast. In order to do this, it is helpful to use symbols like the plus sign (+) and the slash (/) instead of writing words.

You probably recognize the plus sign from math equations like $1 + 1 = 2$. We use the plus sign when taking notes to connect important information. It is often used in place of the word *and*. Look at the following example.

Example One

I don't have enough space for all my clothes and books.

You can write this in your notes with the plus sign as:

No space for clothes + books

The slash (/) is used to connect options—when you can have one choice or another. It is often used instead of the word *or*. Look at the example below.

Example Two

I can't afford to buy new clothes or books.

You can write this in your notes with a slash as:

Can't afford clothes/books

1  **Listen to the excerpts from Listening One and Two. Use the plus sign (+) and slash (/) to take notes.**

Excerpt One

Main Ideas	Details
What is a tiny house?	• very small house, like _____

Excerpt Two

Main Ideas	Details
Tiny life = simple life	ex.: _____

Excerpt Three

Main Ideas	Details
Treehouse ≠ perfect	• difficult to have _____
	• if weather too _____ → uncomfortable
	• $$ to have _____

2 **Compare your notes with a partner's. Did you both use the plus sign (+) and slash (/)? Did you write the same words?**

Go to **MyEnglishLab** for more note-taking practice.

Life in a tree house

COMPREHENSION

1 ▶ **Listen to the podcast episode titled "Treetop Living." Create a chart like the one below to take notes. Try to use the plus sign (+) and slash (/) in your notes.**

◤ **TAKE NOTES   Treetop Living**

Main Ideas	Details

2 Choose the correct answer. Use your notes to help you.

1. The podcast is about treehouses _____ .

   a. to live in   b. to play in

2. People in treehouses want to spend more time _____ .

   a. with children   b. in nature

3. When you live in a treehouse, you enjoy _____ .

   a. singing in the forest   b. the quiet sounds of the forest

4. Masahiro Sato says, "People today spend too much time _____ ."

   a. in nature   b. with technology

5. Sato says, "People who live in _____ are usually happy."

   a. treehouses   b. Japan

6. Living in a treehouse may be _____ for some people.

   a. too warm   b. uncomfortable

7. Another problem is that treehouses are very _____ .

   a. small   b. high up off the ground

8. Some people don't live in their treehouses all the time. They _____ .

   a. rent them to other people   b. give them away to other people

9. Some treehouses are not homes. Instead, they are _____ .

   a. schools   b. hotels

◤ **USE YOUR NOTES**

Compare your notes with a partner's. How can you improve your notes next time?

1 ▶ **Listen to the excerpt. Are Jenny and Adam talking about positive points or negative points about their tiny house? How do you know?**

Identifying and Understanding Advantages and Disadvantages

When you listen to an explanation of a new experience or an uncommon situation, you often hear advantages and disadvantages. An **advantage** is a good or positive side of a situation. It helps you understand why people like something. A **disadvantage** is a bad or negative side of a situation. It helps you understand why people dislike something. By understanding the advantages and disadvantages, you can also create your own opinion on the topic.

A speaker sometimes does not use the words *advantage* or *disadvantage* in a description of something. You need to listen for other clues. To identify advantages, listen for positive words and phrases. To identify disadvantages, listen for negative words and phrases.

▶ **Listen carefully to the example.**

Example One

Is the host talking about advantages or disadvantages? How do you know?

Explanation

In this excerpt, the host uses positive words like ***beautiful, quiet,*** and ***peaceful.*** These ideas are connected with the word ***and*** which is often used to connect positive points. This is how we know that these are advantages of living in a treehouse.

▶ **Now listen to Jenny and Adam talk about their apartment in Boston.**

Example Two

Are Jenny and Adam talking about advantages or disadvantages? How do you know?

Explanation

Jenny says the Boston apartment was **expensive** and **very small.** She also uses the word ***but,*** which is often used to introduce a negative point. This is how we know she is talking about disadvantages.

2 ▶ **Listen to the excerpts from Listening Two. Decide if the excerpt talks about advantages or disadvantages. Take notes on the words and phrases that helped you find the answer.**

Excerpt One

Word and phrases to help you find the answer:

_____

This excerpt talks about:

☐ advantages of treehouses   ☐ disadvantages of treehouses

Word and phrases to help you find the answer:

_____

This excerpt talks about:

☐ advantages of treehouses   ☐ disadvantages of treehouses

Go to **MyEnglishLab** for more skill practice.

CONNECT THE LISTENINGS 🔍

ORGANIZE

A Venn diagram has three circles that show how different ideas about a common topic are connected. In this case, we can see the advantages, disadvantages, and similar points of treehouses and tiny homes.

1 Work in two groups: Group A and Group B.

Group A: Complete the Venn diagram about the advantages of unique homes. On the left side of the diagram, write the advantages of tiny homes. On the right side, write the advantages of treehouses. In the middle of the diagram, write the advantages that fit both tiny homes and treehouses.

Advantages of Unique Homes

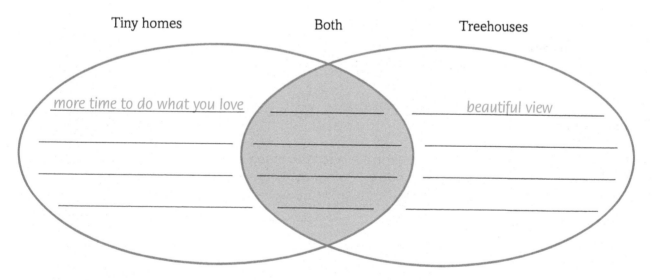

Tiny homes   Both   Treehouses

more time to do what you love   _____   beautiful view

cheaper than living in a city apartment   peaceful   save money
~~beautiful view~~   break from technology easy to find things
~~more time to do what you love~~   connect with nature   simple life
easy to clean   quiet

Group B: Complete the Venn diagram about the disadvantages of unique homes. On the left side of the diagram, write the disadvantages of tiny homes. On the right side, write disadvantages of treehouses. In the middle of the diagram, write the disadvantages that fit both tiny homes and treehouses.

Disadvantages of Unique Homes

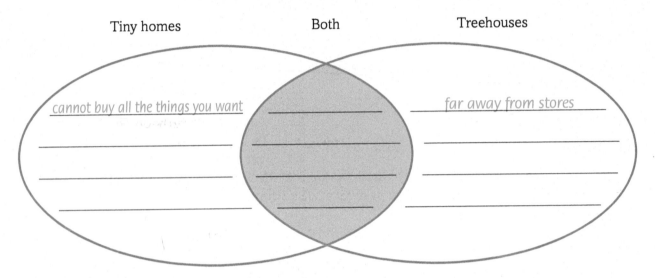

Tiny homes   Both   Treehouses

cannot buy all the things you want _____ far away from stores

can be uncomfortable   far away from stores
not a lot of room for many things   cannot have normal furniture
expensive to have heat/AC   can be uncomfortable
cannot keep all your stuff   cannot buy all the things you want
small

2 Share your Venn diagrams with the class. Discuss any questions.

SYNTHESIZE

Make a pair with one person from Group A and one person from Group B. Decide if you should live in a tiny home or a treehouse. Role-play a conversation about the advantages and disadvantages of each choice with the information from Organize.

A: I think the treehouse is perfect for us!

B: Ummm, I'm not sure . . . Where can I put all my clothes?

A: That's true. You won't be able to keep all your clothes. Just keep your favorite things!

B: I'm not sure that is a good idea. Also, . . .

Go to **MyEnglishLab** to check what you learned.

VOCABULARY

REVIEW

Choose the best words from the box to complete the article about Smart Homes. You will not use three of the words.

are worried	connection	rent	simple	space	technology	unusual
comfortable	nature	save	sound	spent	tiny	view

WIRETECH

In 1997, Bill Gates **spent** [1] $100 million dollars to build the first smart home. People thought it was amazing! But today, many people have smart homes. These homes are not **view** [2]. The **_____** [3] to change your home into a smart home is very **comfortable** [4]. You only need one **space** [5] computer chip. This very small chip can make a **connection** [6] between your smartphone and everything in your house that uses electricity. For example, many people use smart-home technology for the lights in their house. In a smart home, the lights go on when you enter a room, and they go off when you leave the room. There is no reason to have the lights on in a **spent** [7] that has no people! Smart-home technology helps you use less electricity, so you **save** [8] money.

Control your home from your smart phone!

an oven

Some people also use smart-home technology for things in their kitchen. **are worried** [9] you **view** that you forgot to turn off the oven before you left the house? No problem! Even if you are far away from home, you can turn it off with your smartphone.

Smart homes also help people to feel safe in their homes. Do you hear a strange **sound** [10] outside your house? Relax. Your smartphone can tell you if it is a person or just a dog or other animal. And if it's a person, the smartphone will call the police.

A smart home does many things for you, so you can just relax and feel **comfortable** [11] in your high-tech home!

EXPAND

Answer each question in a full sentence using one of the phrasal verbs in the box. Then read your answers aloud.

Verb phrases with *save*, *spend*, and *waste*

- *save*, *spend*, and *waste* **time**
- *save*, *spend*, *waste* **money**

- *save*, *waste* **space**
- *save*, *waste* **energy**

1. Sofia brought her bicycle to the university, but her dorm room is tiny, so she hung her bike on the wall. Why did she do that?

   She wanted to ___spend___ .

   She didn't want to __·and wast spend__ .

2. Why do some students buy used textbooks?

   They want to ___save money___ .

   They don't want to ___spend___ a lot of money on books.

3. Why do some students turn off the lights and air conditioner when they leave their room?

   They want to ___save energy___ .

   They don't want to _____ .

4. Why do some students read their textbooks while they are exercising on a treadmill?

   It's a good way to __save time__ .

5. What do some students do when they take a break from studying?

   They __wast space__ with their friends.

6. Why do some students plan their schedules to have their classes close together?

   So they don't __wast time__ waiting between classes.

CREATE

APPLY **Work in small groups. Discuss these questions using the vocabulary from Expand.**

1. What are some ways you can **save space** when you live in a small room?

2. How can university students **save money**?

3. What are some ways university students can **save time**?

4. How can people **save energy**?

5. How much time do you usually **spend** on your phone every day? Do you always use it for important things, or do you **waste a lot of time,** too?

6. What are some useful ways to **save time** when you go shopping for food or clothes? What are some useful ways to **save money**?

7. In your opinion, what do people often **waste money** on?

🌐 Go to the **Pearson Practice English App** or **MyEnglishLab** for more vocabulary practice.

GRAMMAR FOR SPEAKING

1 Read the excerpts. Follow the directions.

Excerpt One

REPORTER: So, what is a tiny house? Is it just a small house? Well, no. A tiny house is very, very small—about the same size as a trailer or a bus! There are lots of different kinds of tiny houses.

Excerpt Two

ADAM: I know, we were surprised, too! But we needed to change our lives, and we both thought a tiny house was a good idea, so . . . here we are!

Excerpt Three

ADAM: So our life is very simple, but it's great because we're not worried about money anymore.

1. Underline all the present forms of **be**. Circle all the past forms of **be**.

2. What **negative** form of **be** can you find? _____

1. The present tense of ***be*** has three forms:
am
is
are

*I **am** Adam.*
*This **is** our tiny house. It **is** small.*
*There **are** lots of different kinds of tiny houses.*

To form negative statements, use:
am + not
is + not
are + not

*I **am not** Adam.*
*This **is not** a large house.*
*Treehouses **are not** comfortable in the cold weather.*

2. Contractions are short forms. Use affirmative and negative contractions in speaking and in informal writing.

***I'm** Adam.*	***I'm not** Jenny.*
***It's** a tiny house.*	***It's not** a school bus anymore.*
***We're** happy here.*	***We're not** worried about money anymore.*
***She's** Jenny.*	***She's not** . . .*
***You're** welcome*	***You're not** . . .*
***They're** roommates.*	***They're not** . . .*

Another way to form negative statements with contractions is:
subject + *be* + *n't*

Note: This form does not work with ***am***.

*You **aren't** . . .*
*He / She **isn't** . . .*
*It **isn't** . . .*
*We **aren't** . . .*
*They **aren't** . . .*

3. The past tense of ***be*** has two forms:
was

*I / He / She **was** in a treehouse yesterday.*
*It **was** a school bus before it was a tiny house.*

were

*You / We / They **were** surprised the houses were so small.*

4. To form negative statements in the past tense, use:
was / were + not

*I **was not (wasn't)** happy living in an apartment.*

or the contractions
wasn't / weren't

*They **were not (weren't)** happy living in a city.*

5. To form questions in the present and the past tense, use:

***Be* + subject . . . ?**

Is it just a small house?
Are you tired of life in the city?

Question word + *be* + subject . . . ?

What is a tiny house?
When were you in Boston?

2 Complete the transcript of a podcast called *Tiny Living* with the correct form of *be*. Use contractions whenever possible. The first one has been done for you.

TINY LIVING:
Questions and Answers with an Expert

JUN: Welcome to "Living Small." This _____is_____ Ana. She lives in a tiny house with her roommate, and she
1.
_____ here to answer questions about her experience.
2.

ANA: Thanks for having me, Jun. I _____ happy to answer any questions you have!
3.

JUN: What kinds of tiny homes _____ available for people to live in?
4.

ANA: Well, there _____ more options than you think! Some homes _____ perfect for people
5.   6.
interested in nature and other homes _____ better for people interested in saving money.
7.

JUN: _____ it necessary to move away from a city?
8.

ANA: No, it _____! Living small works well in nature and in a big city.
9 neg.

JUN: I _____ really interested in a tiny home, but I have a lot of things, like books and clothes. What if I
10.
can't fit all my things in my new house?

ANA: It _____ true. It _____ easy to fit everything in a tiny house. You will have to give away
11.   12 neg.
some of your things before you move. When my roommate and I moved into our tiny house, I _____
13.
worried about this, too. But, after we packed our bags, we _____ surprised at how happy we felt. At first,
14.
we _____ happy to give things away, but in the end it _____ a really nice feeling to have fewer
15 neg.   16.
things. All of the things we didn't keep _____ important anymore. We felt free!
17 neg.

JUN: That sounds really nice, Ana! ! Before we end our show, can you answer one more question? What

_____ the most important piece of advice you have for a new tiny house owner?
18.

ANA: Great question! It _____ important to remember why you want to live small. Sometimes, in the
19.
beginning, you _____ going to be comfortable in a small space, and you might feel frustrated. You have
20 neg.
to keep your goal in mind and that will help you stay happy in your new home!

JUN: Thanks so much for sharing your thoughts, Ana!

ANA: My pleasure!

3 ▶ Listen and check your answers with a partner. Then read the conversation aloud. Remember to use contractions whenever possible.

4 APPLY Talk with a partner. Describe your house now and describe your house when you were a child. Was it big or small? Did you have a simple home? Why or why not? Remember to use the present and past forms of *be*. Use contractions whenever possible.

Go to the **Pearson Practice English App** or **MyEnglishLab** for more grammar practice. Check what you learned in **MyEnglishLab**.

Stressing *Not*

When we want to show a strong negative opinion, or when we want to explain that a situation is different from what we had originally believed, we often stress the word *not*. This makes our feeling clear to the listener.

To stress a word:

- say the word with a higher pitch (tone)
- say the word louder
- say the word longer

▶ **Read and listen to the excerpts. Notice how the boldfaced words are stressed and help clearly show the person's feelings.**

Example One

Life in the big city is **NOT** simple, like life in our small town. Everyone here is so busy!

Explanation

The speaker stresses **not** in the above sentence to show that the city and the small town are really different. From this, we can understand that he does not like the big city very much.

Example Two

I spent a lot of time shopping for new things like clothes and things for the house … But we really **DIDN'T** need most of the things we had.

Explanation

In this case, the speaker stresses ***didn't*** to show that she used to think buying things was important, but now she believes it was not good to buy so many things.

Note that when **not** is in a contraction, we stress the whole contraction.

1 **Look at the conversation below. Underline the words that you think will be stressed.**

DALIA: It's not easy to move to a tiny house.

HASSAN: I know. We don't have space for anything!

DALIA: I understand that we can save money, but I just don't think I can do this.

HASSAN: I agree. We only have enough room for a few books. I can't live without my books!

DALIA: I guess we will just have to give some things away. This is really hard!

HASSAN: We are not good at living small!

2 ▶ **Listen to the conversation and check your answers. Compare your answers with a partner and then read the conversation out loud.**

3 APPLY **Work with a partner. Role-play your own conversation about the disadvantages of living in a tiny house. Make sure to stress *not*.**

Asking for More Information

Sometimes, in a conversation, we want to know more information. There could be many reasons: We might be curious; we might need to understand somebody's idea better; or maybe we didn't hear the speaker clearly the first time. There are some common phrases and questions to ask the speaker to tell us more. Read the boldfaced examples below.

Example

REPORTER: So, this is an old school bus!
ADAM: Yes, and now it's our tiny house.
REPORTER: What an unusual idea! **Can you tell me more about** how you decided to live in a bus?

REPORTER: Yeah . . . ummm . . . actually, I don't see a bed - where is it?
JENNY: OK—look up.
REPORTER: That's great! **I'd love to know more about** how it works!

JENNY: And the best thing is now we're not worried about money all the time.
REPORTER: **Why is that?**

Here are some useful phrases to ask for more information:

- *I have a question / some questions*
- *Can you tell (me / us) more about (it / that / how / why)?*
- *What do you mean?*
- *I'd love / like to know more about (that / how / why).*
- *Can I ask you a question?*
- *Why do you think so?*
- *Why is that?*

1 Work alone. Imagine you are moving to a tiny house. You cannot keep all your things. Choose the five most important things you need in your new home. Make a list. Think about why you chose those five things.

2 Work with a partner. Compare your lists. Ask your partner to explain why he or she chose those five important things. Use the phrases above to ask for more information.

⚫ Go to **MyEnglishLab** for more skill practice and to check what you learned.

A role-play is a short performance. Students take roles in a situation. You are going to role-play a discussion between two friends who are looking for a place to live near their university. You are talking about what kind of house you will move into.

STEP 1

Form two groups: Group A and Group B. Follow the instructions for your group.

Group A

- You want to move to a tiny house. Your roommate wants to live in a large apartment. You need to change your roommate's mind.

- Look at the pictures of the tiny house in Option 1. As a group, take notes on the advantages of living in this house.

- Look at the pictures of the large apartment in Option 2 on the next page. As a group, take notes on the disadvantages of living in this apartment.

Option 1: Tiny House

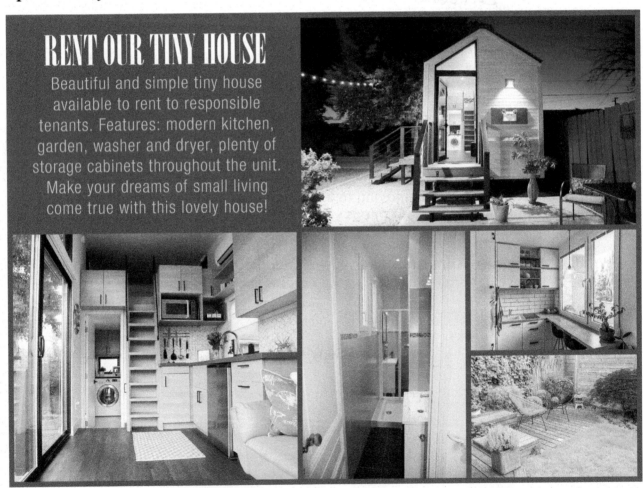

RENT OUR TINY HOUSE

Beautiful and simple tiny house available to rent to responsible tenants. Features: modern kitchen, garden, washer and dryer, plenty of storage cabinets throughout the unit. Make your dreams of small living come true with this lovely house!

Group B

- You want to move to a large apartment. Your roommate wants to live in a tiny house. You need to change your roommate's mind.

- Look at the pictures of the large apartment. As a group, take notes on the advantages of living in this apartment.

- Look at the pictures of the tiny house on page 22. As a group, take notes on the disadvantages of living in a tiny house.

Option 2: Large Apartment

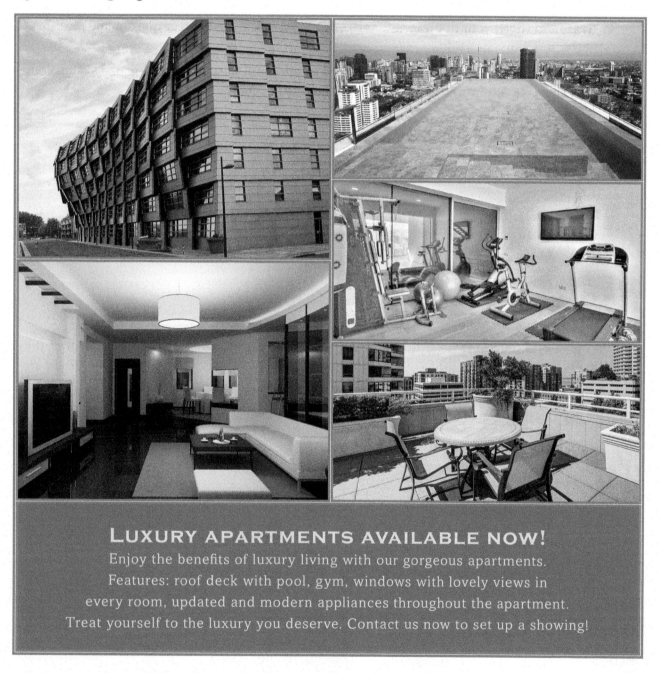

LUXURY APARTMENTS AVAILABLE NOW!

Enjoy the benefits of luxury living with our gorgeous apartments. Features: roof deck with pool, gym, windows with lovely views in every room, updated and modern appliances throughout the apartment. Treat yourself to the luxury you deserve. Contact us now to set up a showing!

STEP 2

1 **Work with your group. Practice your role-play. What will you say? What reasons will you give? Use your notes to help you.**

2 **APPLY Use the vocabulary, grammar, pronunciation, and speaking skills from the unit. Use the checklist to help you.**

☐ **Vocabulary:** Read through the list of vocabulary on page 25. Which words can you include in your role-play to make it clearer and more interesting? Choose at least six words or phrases and add them to your notes.

☐ **Grammar:** Scan your notes for the verb *be*. Are you using the correct present and past form of the verb?

☐ **Pronunciation:** Look at your notes. Find examples with the word *not*. Practice saying your sentences out loud with stress to show your negative opinion.

☐ **Speaking Skill:** What phrases for asking for more information can you use in your role-play? Add them to your notes.

3 **Listen to your partners and give feedback.**

☐ Did they use the new language correctly?

☐ Did they explain their ideas clearly?

☐ Do they need to change anything?

STEP 3

Form pairs, one person from Group A and one person from Group B. Perform your role-play. At the end, decide where you will move: to a tiny house or to a large apartment. Share your results with the class.

APPLY Discuss one of these quotes in small groups. Do you agree or disagree? Give reasons to your group and ask for more information after they give their reasons. Use the vocabulary, grammar, pronunciation, and speaking skills you learned in the unit.

> **Have nothing in your houses that you do not know to be useful or believe to be beautiful.**
>
> WILLIAM MORRIS

> **Live simply so that others may simply live.**
>
> ELIZABETH ANN SETON

> **Life is really simple, but we insist on making it really complicated.**
>
> CONFUCIUS

CHECK WHAT YOU'VE LEARNED

Check (✔) the outcomes you've met and vocabulary you've learned. Put an X next to the skills and vocabulary you still need to practice.

Learning Outcomes
- ☐ Infer both sides of a story
- ☐ Take notes with + and /
- ☐ Identify and understand advantages and disadvantages
- ☐ Use the present and past of *be*
- ☐ Stress *not*
- ☐ Ask for more information

Vocabulary
- ☐ comfortable
- ☐ connection
- ☐ nature
- ☐ rent (*n.*)
- ☐ save
- ☐ simple
- ☐ space (*n.*)
- ☐ spend
- ☐ technology AWL
- ☐ tiny
- ☐ uncomfortable
- ☐ unusual

Multi-word Units
- ☐ be worried about

➤ Go to **MyEnglishLab** to watch a video about tiny homes, access the Unit Project, and take the Unit 1 Achievement Test.

LEARNING OUTCOMES

> Infer why someone is surprised
> Use initials to reference people in your notes
> Identify main ideas and details

> Use the simple present
> Use correct intonation in questions
> Express opinions

▶ Go to **MyEnglishLab** to check what you know.

2

Making Unusual Art

1 FOCUS ON THE TOPIC

1. Look at the photo. What kind of art is this? What did the artist use to make it?

2. What does this art look like? How is this art unusual?

3. How many different kinds of art can you name (paintings, drawings, etc.)? What do artists use to make art?

VOCABULARY

1 ▶ Read and listen to the information about how Mia Pearlman makes sculptures. Mia uses paper to make very big sculptures. You can see them in many museums and galleries all over the world. Notice the boldfaced words. Try to guess their meanings.

Frequently Asked Questions About
Mia Pearlman's Paper Art

Q: HOW DOES MIA PEARLMAN MAKE HER SCULPTURES?

A: Mia is very different from other artists. She makes her art in a very unusual way. First, Mia goes to the museum or gallery, and she looks at the space. She needs to know: "How big is the space? Does it have any windows? Does it have any sunlight?" This is important because Mia makes each sculpture for one **specific** space.

Mia likes to use black ink on white paper.

After Mia sees the space, she goes home and she starts to **draw**. She uses black ink and long pieces of white paper. She draws many different lines on the paper. She doesn't have a specific plan for these lines.

Mia cuts the white paper.

Then Mia **cuts** the paper on the black lines. She usually cuts 30 to 80 pieces for each sculpture.

Mia lays out the paper in the gallery.

Mia goes back to the museum or gallery space. She puts all the pieces of paper on the floor. She thinks about how to make the sculpture. She doesn't have a plan. She decides her plan when she's in the space.

Mia's art makes you feel like you are in a cloud.

Finally, she puts all the pieces together to make the sculpture.

Mia Pearlman standing in front of her sculpture, *Inrush*

Q: PAPER ISN'T A VERY STRONG **MATERIAL**. WHY DOES MIA USE PAPER FOR HER SCULPTURES?

A: Mia loves paper! She says paper is like everything in nature. It always moves and changes, and it doesn't **last** forever.[1]

Q: WHY DO MANY OF MIA'S SCULPTURES LOOK LIKE CLOUDS?

A: Clouds are a beautiful **part** of nature, and people cannot **control** or change them. Mia's art helps people remember that nature is a very important **part of** the world.

[1]**forever:** for always; with no end

2 Take turns with a partner. Student A, read the sentence and choose the correct meaning of the word from the box. Student B, say, "Yes, I agree" or "No, I don't think so. I think . . ."

7 to make someone or something do what you want

6 to make pictures with a pencil or pen

3 to stay in good condition

4 something people use to make art, clothes, furniture, and other things

2 special or exact

5 to use scissors or a knife to make pieces

~~art that you usually make with stone, metal, or clay~~

1 a piece of the whole thing

Example

sculpture

> **A:** A **sculpture** is art that you usually make with stone, metal, or clay.
>
> **B:** Yes, I agree.

1. **A:** A **part of** something means . . .   **B:** (Yes . . . / No . . .)

2. **A:** **Specific** means . . .   **B:** (Yes . . . / No . . .)

3. **A:** To **draw** means . . .   **B:** (Yes . . . / No . . .)

4. **A:** **Material** is . . .   **B:** (Yes . . . / No . . .)

5. **A:** To **cut** something means . . .   **B:** (Yes . . . / No . . .)

6. **A:** To **last** means . . .   **B:** (Yes . . . / No . . .)

7. **A:** To **control** something means . . .   **B:** (Yes . . . / No . . .)

Go to the **Pearson Practice English App** or **MyEnglishLab** for more vocabulary practice.

PREVIEW

Look at the photo and discuss these questions with the class:

What does this sculpture look like to you? What does it show? What will people think about when they see it?

1 ▶ A magazine writer is interviewing a museum guide about the artist, Mia Pearlman. Listen to the interview with your books closed.

2 What did you understand from the interview? Discuss with a partner.

3 Now practice taking notes. Create a chart like the one below to take notes. Write down any information you remember. Put any big ideas or general pieces of information under Main Ideas. Put important names, words, or smaller pieces of information under Details.

TAKE NOTES **Mia Pearlman**

Main Ideas	Details
MP—interested in world	Kids make up stories with dolls. NOT Mia
	• MP made "Barbie world"
	• knew ppl = only small part of world

4 ▶ Listen again. As you listen, add information to your notes.

5 Discuss the interview again with a partner. What else did you understand this time? What information did you add to your notes?

↖ Go to **MyEnglishLab** to view example notes.

MAIN IDEAS

Circle the correct answers. Use your notes to help you.

1. Mia is interested in people and the ___world___ they live in.

   a. houses   (b.) world

2. Mia's art is about things that people cannot ___Control___

   (a.) control   b. understand

3. Mia's art helps people to feel their connection to ___Nature___ Несли.

   (a.) nature   +е   b. museums

4. Mia's sculptures teach people that everything in life _____.

   (a. has an end)   (b.) is beautiful

DETAILS

1 ▶ **Listen again and add to your notes. Write _T_ (true) or _F_ (false) next to each statement. Correct the false information. Use your notes to help you.**

_T_ 1. Mia thinks that people are the most important part of the world.

_F_ 2. Mia's sculptures use paper and sunlight.

_F_ 3. Some of Mia's sculptures are about life in a city.

_T_ 4. The sculpture _Inrush_ looks like it is moving.   _alurado_

_T_ 5. With _Inrush_, people can feel like they are inside a _cave_.   _weva sikei_

_T_ 6. Mia thinks that her sculptures are similar to a dance or a play in a theater.

2 **With a partner, take turns summarizing your notes. Then discuss how your notes and your answers in Preview helped you understand the listening.**

🎧 Go to **MyEnglishLab** for more listening practice.

MAKE INFERENCES 🔍

Inferring Why Someone Is Surprised

An inference is a guess about something that is not said directly.

Sometimes, a speaker says something that is surprising to the listener. The speaker may tell the listener unusual information, or use a word in a new or unusual way. In these situations, we have to make an inference to understand why the listener feels surprised.

Here are some phrases we use to express surprise:

Really?   _Interesting!_   _That's (a little/very) unusual._   _I don't understand._

▶ **Listen to an excerpt from the interview. Choose the best answer to question 1. In question 2, circle _a_ or _b_ to explain why the information is surprising.**

Examples

1. Why is the writer surprised?

   Mia (played with Barbie dolls / made "Barbie worlds") when she was very young.

Explanation

The correct answer is **Mia made "Barbie worlds" when she was very young.** Many little girls play with Barbie dolls, so that is not surprising.

Most girls make up stories about their dolls' lives. But when Mia played with dolls, she didn't make up stories about their lives. She wanted to make the world where the dolls lived.

2. This is surprising because the museum guide _____ .

   a. gives the writer unusual information

   b. uses a word in a new or unusual way

Explanation

The correct answer is **a.** Most children think only about their lives and about their family and friends. They don't think about the world. This is **unusual.**

▶ **Listen to the excerpts from the interview. Choose the best answer to complete the sentence in number 1. Then circle *a* or *b* in number 2 to explain why the writer was surprised.**

Excerpt One

1. Why is the writer surprised?

   She doesn't understand how a sculpture can (*end / go to a different museum*).

2. This is surprising because the museum guide:

   a. tells the writer unusual information.

   b. uses a word in a new or unusual way.

Excerpt Two

1. Why is the writer surprised?

   Mia doesn't want her sculptures to (*last for a long time / be in a museum*).

2. This is surprising because the museum guide:

   a. tells the writer unusual information.

   b. uses a word in a new or unusual way.

DISCUSS ⚲

> **USE YOUR NOTES**
>
> **APPLY** Find information in your notes to use in your discussion.

Discuss the questions with the class.

1. When Mia Pearlman was a child, she understood that "the world is very big, and people are just a very small part of it." Do young children often think about the world like Mia did? Why or why not?

2. Mia takes down her sculptures and never makes them again. Why do you think Mia does this? What does this tell you about Mia's way of making art?

➤ Go to **MyEnglishLab** to give your opinion about another question.

LISTENING TWO | The Quilts of Gee's Bend

VOCABULARY

**Work with a partner. Fill in the blanks with one of the words or phrases from the box.
Then take turns reading the sentences aloud.**

| expensive | inside | outside | put . . . together | throw . . . away |

The women in Gee's Bend make a lot of quilts. To make each quilt, we ___*put togethre*___ many

1.

pieces of cloth ___*expensive*___ . Since we make so many quilts, when the quilts get old, we

don't keep them. We just ___*throw away*___ them ___*throw away*___ , and we make a new one.

2.

I had one very old quilt, and I didn't want it anymore, so I took it ___*outside*___ , and I put it

3.

near the garbage behind my house. And then one day, a man came to Gee's Bend, and he saw my

old quilt. He said, "Look at that beautiful quilt!"

I thought he was crazy. I said, "Here, you can have it."

He asked me, "Do you have any more quilts like this?"

So we went ___*outside*___ my house, and I showed him all my quilts. He paid me $2,000 for

4.

three of my quilts! Two thousand dollars?! How could my old quilts be so _____? I

5.

thought they were old and dirty, but he said they were art.

Then he bought a lot of quilts from different women in Gee's Bend, and he put them in a museum!

Can you believe that? It's true.

Gee's Bend is the name
of a very small town in
Alabama. The women of
Gee's Bend are famous
for their quilts (blankets
made of many small
pieces of cloth).

🔊 Go to the **Pearson Practice English App** or **MyEnglishLab** for more vocabulary practice.

Using Initials to Reference People in Your Notes

When you listen to an interview, a discussion, or any kind of conversation between or about people, it can be helpful to use initials in your notes. An **initial** is the first letter of someone's name.

In Listening One, you took notes about Mia Pearlman. Rather than writing her full name many times in your notes, you can use one or both of her initials: *M* or *MP*. It's usually helpful to write out the person's full name the first time you write it in your notes; put the initials in parentheses ( ) after it, so you can remember who they refer to: *Mia Pearlman (MP)*.

Sometimes, you won't know the name of the person who is talking, but you want to write down his or her opinions or ideas. In those cases, you can use initials based on other information you may know. For example, you may know the person's job—such as writer *(W)* or museum guide *(MG)*. Another option when you don't know a person's name is to use initials to refer to the person's gender: *man (M)*, *male (M)*, *woman (W)*, or *female (F)*. If there are multiple male and female speakers, you can put numbers after them: *M1, M2, F1, F2*, etc.

Remember: Sometimes the idea is more important than the person who says it, so you don't always need to write down a speaker's name or initials. But if there are people who you refer to multiple times in your notes, using initials instead of their names can help you take notes more quickly.

1 ▶ **Create initials for the people in the excerpt. Then listen to the excerpt. Write the correct initials to complete the notes.**

The women in Gee's Bend: _WGB_

The woman telling the story: _W_

Main Ideas	Details
1 _Gee's Bend_ make lots of quilts	• throw away old quilts, make new ones 2 • _outside_ put old quilts near garbage

2 ▶ **Create initials for the people in the excerpt. Then listen to the excerpt. Use initials to take notes on important details.**

The man who bought the quilt: _W_

The woman telling the story: _____

Main Ideas	Details
Old quilts are worth a lot	

🅝 **Go to MyEnglishLab for more note-taking practice.**

1 ▶ **Listen to a podcast about the women of Gee's Bend. Create a chart like the one below to take notes. Try to use initials in your notes to refer to the people you hear about.**

◤ TAKE NOTES The Quilts of Gee's Bend	
Main Ideas	**Details**

2 **Complete the sentences. Use your notes to help you.**

1. The women in Gee's Bend make quilts _____ .

   a. because they are artists   b. to use on their beds *(circled)*

2. The women make the quilts with _____ .

   a. pieces of old clothes *(circled)*   b. expensive material

3. The quilts are art because _____ .

   a. they are beautiful and unusual *(circled)*   b. they have so many pieces

4. One woman made a quilt to remember _____ .

   a. her husband *(circled)*   b. her mother

5. The quilts have a special meaning because _____ .

   a. families make them together *(circled)*   b. they have many colors

6. When they make the quilts, the older women tell the younger women about _____ .

   a. their families *(circled)*   b. Africa

7. Now, many people can see these quilts because they are _____ .

   a. in a small town   b. in museums *(circled)*

◤ USE YOUR NOTES

Compare your notes with a partner's. How can you improve your notes next time?

1 Read this sentence from the podcast about the women of Gee's Bend. Do you think it is a main idea or a detail? Why?

To make a quilt, you cut the material into pieces.

Identifying Main Ideas and Details

When you listen to a story or report, it's important to separate main ideas and details.

Why are **main ideas** important?

Main ideas can:

- help you understand the purpose of the listening.
- help you find connected details.
- help you organize what you hear as you listen.

A **main idea** has **general** vocabulary like titles, names, and sometimes feelings and ideas. A main idea is often a statement or a sentence that explains the general topic of what you are listening to, just like an essay may have a general topic. There can also be subtopics in a listening that reflect additional main ideas, just like there may be subtopics in each paragraph of an essay.

Why are **details** important?

Details can:

- help you to understand the main idea.
- highlight the main idea—show why it is important.
- give you a clear example so you can remember the main idea.
- add interesting words and ideas to a story.

Details have **specific** vocabulary like actions (verbs) and descriptive words (adjectives). When you listen for details, you are identifying important words, examples, and supporting ideas and trying to understand how they connect to the main ideas.

▶ **Listen carefully to the vocabulary that the speaker uses in the example. Notice the difference between the main idea and the details.**

Example

Main Ideas	Details
G.B. Wom. → work just like artists	• choose how to put together pieces • always use new + different ways

Explanation

Artists is a general word. There are many kinds of artists, so the main idea is that the women in Gee's Bend are a kind of artist. The details give more information about how these specific artists (the women of Gee's Bend) work.

The details explain this with two examples:

1. They decide how to put all the pieces together.
2. They put them together in new and different ways.

2 ▶ **Listen to these excerpts and fill in the missing main ideas and details. Remember to listen for general words and specific words.**

Excerpt One

Main Ideas	Details
The quilts are unusual.	*Dc people no gjjomocrw*

Excerpt Two

Main Ideas	Details
They make quilts with old clothes.	

Excerpt Three

Main Ideas	Details
	Great-grandmother: "listen to story of my life"

🔖 Go to **MyEnglishLab** for more skill practice.

ORGANIZE

Complete the chart. Who might say these sentences?
Write *Yes* or *No* under *Mia Pearlman* and *A Woman from Gee's Bend.* Some answers have been done for you.

USE YOUR NOTES

APPLY Review your notes from Listening One and Two. Use the information in your notes to complete the chart.

	Mia Pearlman	A Woman from Gee's Bend
1. I am an artist.	Yes	No
2. I make sculptures.	Yes	No
3. I use unusual materials.	Yes	No
4. I use expensive materials.	No	No
5. I put together many pieces.	Yes	Yes
6. I always make a plan before I begin.	Yes	No
7. My work has many colors.	No	Yes
8. I work alone.	Yes	No
9. I make my art for one specific space.	Yes	No
10. My work is in museums.	Yes	Yes
11. My work has a special meaning.	Yes	Yes
12. My work lasts a long time.	No	Yes

SYNTHESIZE

A museum guide is speaking to two visitors to a museum. Role-play in groups of three. Complete the conversation with information from Organize. Each speaker should add at least four more sentences to the conversation.

VISITOR 1: Was this quilt made by an artist?

MUSEUM GUIDE: Well, the women of Gee's Bend don't think they are artists, but we think it is art!

VISITOR 2: What about this sculpture?

MUSEUM GUIDE: Yes, this was made by an artist named Mia Pearlman.

VISITOR 1: Do the Gee's Bend women use unusual materials?

MUSEUM GUIDE: Yes, and so does Mia Pearlman. They use . . .

VISITOR 2: Wow! That is unusual!

VISITOR 1: Yes, I think . . .

🔊 Go to **MyEnglishLab** to check what you learned.

REVIEW

Read about the Eggshell Sculptor. Fill in each blank with words from the box. You will not use all the words. Then take turns reading the paragraphs aloud with a partner.

control (v.)	expensive	~~material~~	put . . . together	specific
cut (v.)	inside	outside	sculpture	throw away
draws	last (v.)	parts of	space	unusual

THE EGGSHELL SCULPTOR

Some artists today make art with very unusual things, like old clothes, vegetables, old books,

butterflies, and stones. Gary LeMaster makes beautiful art with a different kind of unusual

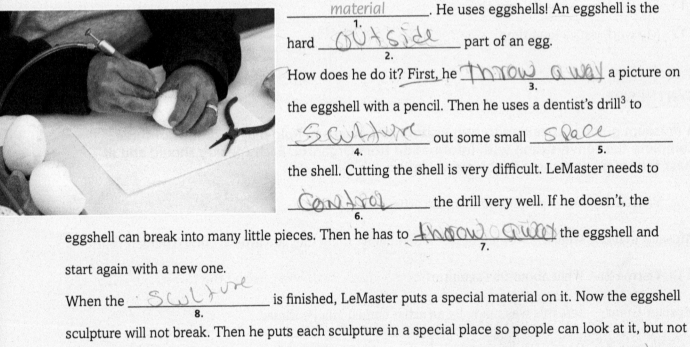

_____ *material* _____. He uses eggshells! An eggshell is the
            1.

hard ___ *outside* ___ part of an egg.
        2.

How does he do it? First, he ___ *throw away* ___ a picture on
                              3.

the eggshell with a pencil. Then he uses a dentist's drill[3] to

___ *sculpture* ___ out some small ___ *space* ___
        4.   5.

the shell. Cutting the shell is very difficult. LeMaster needs to

___ *control* ___ the drill very well. If he doesn't, the
        6.

eggshell can break into many little pieces. Then he has to ___ *throw away* ___ the eggshell and
                                                            7.

start again with a new one.

When the ___ *sculpture* ___ is finished, LeMaster puts a special material on it. Now the eggshell
              8.

sculpture will not break. Then he puts each sculpture in a special place so people can look at it, but not

break it. Sometimes he puts his sculptures under glass. This way, the sculptures ___ *outside* ___
                                                                                  9.

a long time.

_____

[3] **a dentist's drill:** a small machine that dentists use to make holes in teeth

LeMaster makes many different kinds of eggshell sculptures. Sometimes, people pay him to make a ____expensive____ sculpture that they
10.
want. For example, one man asked LeMaster to make a sculpture of a football with his football team's name on it. Some of LeMaster's sculptures are very ____expensive____. People pay $2,000 or more
11.
for some of his very unusual eggshell sculptures.

EXPAND

1 **Work with a partner. Read the expressions. Then write them on the scale from 0 to 5. (0 is for a very negative opinion, and 5 is for a very positive opinion.) Some of the numbers have two expressions with the same meaning.**

It's my favorite (kind of art).

I don't like it (at all).

I love it.

I hate it.

I can take it or leave it

I like it.

(It's OK, but) I'm not crazy about it.

I like it a lot.

I like it very much.

5: I love it. _____   _____

4: _____   _____

3: _____

2: _____   _____

1: _____

0: I hate it. _____

2 **Share your answers with the class.**

3 **Practice using the expressions with other students. Ask and answer the questions with two students:**

- Do you like Mia Pearlman's paper art?
- Do you like the quilts from Gee's Bend?
- Do you like Gary LeMaster's eggshell sculptures?

After each response, ask, "Why do you feel that way?"

CREATE

APPLY Work in small groups. Ask and answer the questions. Use the vocabulary in boldface and some of the words and phrases in parentheses.

1. Do you **like to draw**? If yes, what kinds of things do you **like to draw**? If you don't, why not?

2. Do you like to make art? If yes, what kind of art do you like to make? (painting, **sculpture,** etc.) What **materials** did you use? Are they unusual? If you don't like to make art, why not?

3. In general, do **you like** art? If yes, what kind of art do **you like**? Why do **you like it**? (**I love, I like** _____ **very much, I like . . .**, etc.) If you don't like art, why not?

4. Is there a kind of art that you **don't like**? If yes, what kind of art is it? Why don't you like it? (**I don't like, I can take it or leave it, I hate . . .** , etc.) If there is not a kind of art you don't like, why not?

5. Who is (or was) a great artist in your country? Do you **like** his or her art? Why or why not?

6. Do you have a **favorite** artist? If yes, is this artist's art unusual? What **materials** does this artist use? Does this artist have one **specific** work of art that is your **favorite**? If you don't have a favorite artist, talk about the **favorite** artist of someone you know.

🔊 Go to **MyEnglishLab** for more vocabulary practice.

GRAMMAR FOR SPEAKING

1 Read the excerpts from the interview. Notice the verbs in boldface.

a. WRITER: **I'm** very interested in Mia Pearlman's art.

b. GUIDE: When little girls **play** with dolls, like Barbie dolls, they usually **make up** stories about them.

c. GUIDE: **Do** you **see** that window?

d. GUIDE: And the sunlight from outside *really* **comes** through the window. . . . It **gives** the sculpture light.

   WRITER: So, the sculpture **is** like a part of nature inside the museum.

   GUIDE: Yes, and when you **stand** near the sculpture, you **feel** like you're a part of it, too.

e. GUIDE: I **know.** But Mia **thinks** sculptures are just like dances, or theater, or music concerts. You **enjoy** them, but they **don't last** forever. And that**'s** life too—everything **has** an end.

f. WRITER: I **have** some specific questions about how Mia **makes** these sculptures.

Look at the excerpts again.

1. Underline all the forms of the verbs *be* and *have*.

2. Look at all the other verbs and answer these questions.

   a. Which verbs end with *-s*?

   b. Why?

   c. After the subjects *I, you, we,* and *they,* what does the verb end with? Is there an *-s* or no *-s*?

Using the Simple Present

1. Use the simple present tense for everyday actions or facts.	*The Gee's Bend women* **make** *quilts.*
2. When the subject is *I, you, we,* or *they,* use the base verb (the form of the verb without any endings, such as *walk, run, work,* and *play*).	*The women* **work** *just like artists.* (= *They*)
3. When the subject is *he, she,* or *it* (the third-person singular), put an *-s* at the end of the main verb.	*Mia Pearlman* **makes** *sculptures.* (= *She*)
	Paper **moves** *and* **changes.** (= *It*)
This rule is also used when words like **this** or **that** are the subject.	*This (sculpture)* **reminds** *me of nature.*
SPELLING RULES: If a verb ends with *-s, -z, -sh,* or *-ch,* add *-es.*	*rush –* **rushes** *watch –* **watches**
If a verb ends with consonant + *y,* change the *y* to *i* and add *-es.*	*try –* **tries**
NOTE: After the subjects **everything, something, nothing, anything, everybody, somebody, nobody,** and **anybody,** use *-s* with the main verb.	*Everything in the world* **changes.**
NOTE: The verbs **be** and **have** are irregular. This means you do not add *-s* like you do with most verbs.	**be: am, is, are** *(See Unit 1.)* **have:** *I / You / We / They* **have** *some questions.* *He / She* **has** *some questions.*
3. To form negative statements with contractions (the short form), use: **Subject +** *doesn't / don't* **+ base verb.**	*Paper* **doesn't last** *forever.* *The women in Gee's Bend* **don't have** *a plan for their quilts.*
4. For *yes / no* questions, use: *Do / Does* **+ subject + base verb?**	*Do you* **see** *the window?*
5. For *Wh-* questions, use: *Wh-* **word +** *do / does* **+ subject + base verb?**	**Why does** *Mia Pearlman* **use** *paper?*

2 **Read the conversation silently. Fill in the correct form of the verb in parentheses in the simple present tense. Some verbs are negative or use the question form. Remember, if the subject is *he, she, it* (third-person singular), you must add *-s* or *-es*.**

GUIDE: Hello, everyone. This __is__ 1. (be) Mia Pearlman's new sculpture. Its name

__is__ *Inrush.*
2. (be)

VISITOR 1: Excuse me. What __it__

Inrush _____ ?
3. (mean)

GUIDE: Well, __es__ you

__sees__ the window up
4. (see)

there? The sunlight from outside always

__comes__ into the room and
5. (come)

_____ the sculpture a lot of light. So the paper _____
6. (give)   7. (look)

like it is shining. This sculpture _____ that nature _____
8. (show)   9. (be)

a part of art.

VISITOR 2: It _____ very beautiful, and it _____ so big! How much
10. (be)   11. (be)

time _____ Mia _____ on each sculpture?
12. (spend)

GUIDE: Well, it _____ on how big the sculpture is. Sometimes she
13. (depend)

_____ on one sculpture for a few months.
14. (work)

VISITOR 1: And how long _____ her sculptures _____ in the
15. (stay)

museum?

GUIDE: They usually _____ for a few weeks or months.
16. (stay)

VISITOR 1: And _____ they _____ to another museum after that?
17. (go)

GUIDE: No, Mia's sculptures _____ anywhere. When the show at the museum
18. (neg. / go)

_____ , Mia _____ down all the pieces of paper, and she
19. (end)   20. (take)

_____ that sculpture together again.
21. (neg. / put)

VISITOR 2: I _____ it!
22. (neg. / believe)

GUIDE: I _____ ! Many people _____ the same thing when they
23. (understand)   24. (say)

_____ this.
25. (hear)

VISITOR 2: But I _____ ! Her sculptures _____ beautiful! Why
                    26. (neg. / understand)   27. (be)

_____ she _____ that?
                              28. (do)

GUIDE: Mia _____ an unusual idea about art. She _____ her
                  29. (have)   30. (think)

paper sculptures _____ like dances or theater or music performances.
                          31. (be)

Those things _____ forever. People _____ them,
                    32. (neg. / last)   33. (see)

and they _____ them, but then they _____
                  34. (enjoy)   35. (have)

an end. That _____ life. Everything _____ an
                    36. (be)   37. (have)

end. Mia _____ that her art _____ the same. It
                  38. (believe)   39. (be)

_____ forever.
        40. (neg. / last)

3 Read the conversation aloud with two classmates.

4 [APPLY] Close your book. Work with a partner. One person is an interviewer, and one
person is a woman from Gee's Bend. Ask and answer questions about the women and
their quilts. After each person speaks six times, switch roles. Remember to use the simple
present tense in your conversation.

▶ Go to **MyEnglishLab** for more grammar practice.

PRONUNCIATION

Using Correct Intonation in Questions

At the end of a question, we use special *intonation*. This means that our voice may go up to a higher
pitch or note ("rising" intonation), or it may go up and then down ("rising-falling" intonation).

Wh- Questions

To ask a *Wh-* question (information question), your voice rises (goes up) and then it falls (goes
down) to a low sound (rising-falling intonation). *Wh-* question words include **who, what, where,
when, why, how, how much,** and **how many.**

What do you mean?

What's going to happen to this sculpture?

Who are the Gee's Bend women?

Yes / No Questions

To ask a *yes / no* question, your voice rises on the last word or syllable (rising intonation).

Is that why her sculptures are so big?

Do you see that window?

1 ▶ **Listen to the intonation at the end of these questions. Does the speaker use rising or rising-falling intonation? Circle the correct answer.**

a. What's going to **happen**? (*rising / rising-falling*)

b. Is it going to a different **museum**? (*rising / rising-falling*)

2 Look at the questions in Exercise 1. Circle the correct answer.

a. Use rising-falling intonation in (**Wh-** *questions* / **yes / no** *questions*).

b. Use rising intonation in (**Wh-** *questions* / **yes / no** *questions*).

3 Read the interview silently. Draw an arrow on the line at the end of each question. Show if the speaker uses rising intonation ↗ or rising-falling intonation ⌒↘.

WRITER: How does Mia Pearlman make her sculptures? _____
1.

GUIDE: Well, first she goes to the museum or gallery.

WRITER: Why does she do that? _____
2.

GUIDE: She needs to know a few things, like, "How big is the space?" _____
3.

"Are there any windows?" _____
4.

"Is there any sunlight?" _____
5.

WRITER: Why are those things important? _____
6.

GUIDE: Well, because the space is part of the sculpture. Mia makes each one of her sculptures for only one specific space.

WRITER: That's very unusual. What does she do next? _____
7.

GUIDE: Next, she goes back home, and she starts to draw.

WRITER: What materials does she use for that? _____
8.

GUIDE: She just uses long pieces of white paper and black ink. She draws all kinds of black lines on the paper.

WRITER: Before she starts, does she have a specific plan? _____
9.

Does she know what she wants to draw? _____
10.

GUIDE: No, she just draws what she feels at that time.

4 Compare your arrows with your partner's and the teacher's. Then practice reading the conversation aloud with your partner. Pay special attention to use the correct intonation for information (Wh-) questions and yes / no questions.

Expressing Opinions

When we give our opinion in a discussion, we often begin with a phrase such as *I think* . . . Here are some other useful phrases:

In my opinion, . . .   *I believe (that)* . . .

If you ask me, . . .   *I feel (that)* . . .

Read the example opinions below:

I feel (that) *Mia Pearlman's art is beautiful.*

In my opinion, *the Gee's Bend women are true artists.*

If you ask me, *eggshell sculpture is not real art.*

I believe (that) *art is a good way to express your ideas about the world.*

Work with a partner. Express your opinions about the types of art below. Then switch roles.

Example

Mia Pearlman's art

A: In my opinion, Mia Pearlman's paper art is beautiful. I really like it. What do you think?

B: I feel that it's very unusual, but I like it a lot.

1. modern art

   A: If you ask me, _____ . What do you think?

   B: _____ .

2. the eggshell sculpture

   A: In my opinion, _____ . What do you think?

   B: _____ .

3. the Gee's Bend quilts

   A: I feel _____ . What do you think?

   B: _____ .

4. Mia Pearlman's sculpture *Inrush*

   A: I believe _____ . What do you think?

   B: _____ .

 Go to **MyEnglishLab** for more skill practice and to check what you learned.

You are going to role-play a discussion about what kind of art to buy for a modern art museum. You will be playing the role of museum curators. A curator is the person who finds art to put in a museum.

STEP 1

Meet in three groups. Each group wants to buy one type of art for their modern art museum:

Group 1: Mia Pearlman's paper sculpture

Group 2: a Gee's Bend quilt

Group 3: an eggshell sculpture

STEP 2

1 **With your group, look carefully at the photo and description of your piece of art.**

2 **Discuss the questions below with your group. Take notes as you discuss. You will use these notes to support your opinion during the role-play in STEP 3.**

   a. Is this art beautiful? Is it interesting? Why?

   b. Is it difficult to make this art?

   c. Does this art have a special meaning? What is it?

   d. Does the artist use unusual or interesting material?

   e. How do you feel when you see this art?

   f. Why is this art important or special?

   g. Why is this a good piece of art for your museum?

Group 1:
Mia Pearlman's
paper sculpture

"Eddy,"[1] a paper
sculpture by Mia
Pearlman

Group 2:
Gee's Bend quilt

A quilt made by a
woman from Gee's
Bend, Alabama
using old clothing
and curtains

Group 3:
Eggshell sculpture

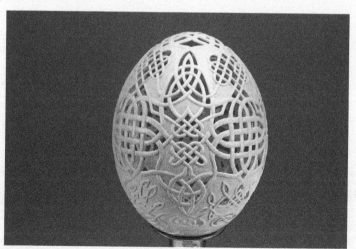

"1000 Celtic Dreams,"
an eggshell sculpture
by Gary LeMaster

LeMaster used one
continuous line to
make the traditional
Celtic design on this
egg. It took him over
1000 hours to finish
this sculpture. That's
why he called it "1000
Celtic Dreams."

[1] An "eddy" is air or water that moves in a circle. Mia Pearlman cut paper to make this sculpture. It looks like something in the
weather. When it's in the museum, the shadows of the sculpture make a new drawing all around it.

3 **APPLY** Use the vocabulary, grammar, pronunciation, and speaking skills from the unit. Use the checklist to help you.

☐ **Vocabulary:** Read through the list of vocabulary on page 51. Which words can you include in your role-play to make it clearer and more interesting? Choose at least three words or phrases and add them to your notes.

☐ **Grammar:** Scan your notes for simple present verbs. Are you using the correct form of the verb?

☐ **Pronunciation:** What questions can you ask the other people in your role-play? Add them to your notes. Practice asking those questions with correct final intonation.

☐ **Speaking Skill:** What phrases for expressing opinions and expressions for likes and dislikes can you use in your role-play? Add them to your notes.

STEP 3

1 Now, form new groups of three, with one person from each "art" group. You and your new partners all work for the same modern art museum. You need to decide which piece of art to buy for your museum. You can buy only one piece of art.

2 Take turns speaking about the piece of art you discussed in STEP 2. Tell your partners why your museum needs to buy that piece of art. If anyone says, "That is not art," explain to them why it *is* art. As you listen to the other people in the group, ask questions about the art they describe.

3 Decide together which piece of art to buy for your museum.

4 Compare your answers with the other groups. Choose one person from each group to explain your choice.

ALTERNATIVE SPEAKING TOPICS

APPLY **Discuss one of these questions in small groups. Use the vocabulary, grammar, pronunciation, and speaking skills you learned in the unit.**

1. In your country, do students take art classes in school?

   a. If they do, at what age? (elementary school, junior high school, high school) Do the students make art, learn about art, or study famous art?

   b. If students don't take art classes in school, is this OK? Why or why not?

   c. Is it important to have art classes in school? Why or why not?

2. Does your country have a traditional type of art (paper or other type)? What materials do people use to make it?

3. Do you have any art in your room or home? What kind of art is it (paintings, posters, sculptures, etc.)? What kind of art do you like to have in your home?

CHECK WHAT YOU'VE LEARNED

Check (✔) the outcomes you've met and vocabulary you've learned. Put an X next to the skills and vocabulary you still need to practice.

Learning Outcomes
- ☐ Infer why a listener is surprised
- ☐ Use initials to reference people in your notes
- ☐ Identify main ideas and details
- ☐ Use the simple present
- ☐ Use correct intonation in questions
- ☐ Express opinions

Vocabulary
- ☐ control (v.)
- ☐ cut (v.)
- ☐ draw (v.)
- ☐ expensive
- ☐ inside
- ☐ last (v.)
- ☐ material
- ☐ outside
- ☐ specific AWL

Multi-word Units
- ☐ part of
- ☐ put together
- ☐ throw away

🔊 Go to **MyEnglishLab** to watch a video about art, access the Unit Project, and take the Unit 2 Achievement Test.

LEARNING OUTCOMES

> Infer a speaker's beliefs
> Draw pictures in your notes
> Recognize and understand a speaker's excitement

> Use the simple present with adverbs of frequency
> Pronounce -s endings
> Invite others to speak

▶ Go to **MyEnglishLab** to check what you know.

Special Possessions

1 FOCUS ON THE TOPIC

1. Look at the photograph of dream catchers. What do you think a dream catcher is? What do you think people do with them? Where do you think they come from?

2. A dream catcher is a special possession[1] to some people. Do you have or own any things that are important to you? What are some other special possessions that people have?

---

[1] **special possession:** something you keep because it is important to you

LISTENING ONE | The Story of Dream Catchers

VOCABULARY

1 ▶ **Read and listen to the web page about the Mille Lacs people of the Ojibwe Nation. Notice the boldfaced words. Try to guess their meanings.**

Welcome to the culture page of

THE MILLE LACS PEOPLE

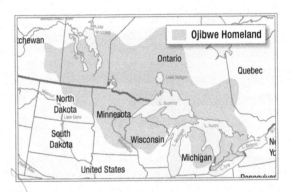

We are a group of Ojibwe people living in the Mille Lacs area of Minnesota. Many years ago, the Ojibwe people lived in the Great Lakes area. Our **traditional** way of life was **peaceful** as we hunted, fished, and farmed. Then people moved to our land from Europe and the United States. They came to our land with **modern** ways, and our life changed. These changes lasted for many years—they were not **temporary**. Some Ojibwe people became sick from European diseases and died. The United States government made us move from our homes to other lands. During this time, many Ojibwe people died because it was too cold or there was not enough food. Also, our traditional **style** of government changed, and the young Ojibwe could not go to our schools anymore. They went to English-speaking schools. Many important things were taken from the Ojibwe people. We lost our language and traditional stories. Many of us lost our life and **breath**!

Today, things are different. We **protect** our culture in many ways. We send our older people into schools to teach children about Ojibwe life. At our Culture Center, we have **popular** classes on our language, history, and music. In the summer, we have our powwow tradition. This is a time for people to dance and sing together. We believe that dancing and singing are good for the **mind** and body. Body, mind, and music—a powwow brings everything together.

Please visit our Culture Center to learn more about the Mille Lacs people. We appreciate your interest.

2 Match the words with the definitions. Write the correct word on the line.

popular	breath	modern	style	protect

1. _popular_ : liked by many people
2. _style_ : new
3. _____ : pattern or design
4. _protect_ : to keep safe
5. _breath_ : air coming into or out of the mouth or nose

appreciate	mind	peaceful	temporary	traditional

6. _traditiou_ : coming from the past
7. _appreciate_ : understand that something is good and important
8. _mind_ : the thinking part of humans
9. _peaceful_ : not fighting or worrying
10. _temporart_ : not lasting

Go to the **Pearson Practice English App** or **MyEnglishLab** for more vocabulary practice.

PREVIEW

1 How do you think people make dream catchers? Discuss this question with a partner.

2 ▶ Listen to the excerpt from "The Story of Dream Catchers." Read the sentences. Check (✓) Yes, No, or I Don't Know. Discuss your answers with a partner.

	Yes	No	I Don't Know
1. A dream catcher has a web.	✓	☐	☐
2. The web has holes at the top.	☐	✓	☐
3. The meaning of the web is "life."	☐	☐	✓

A spider web

Feathers on a dream catcher

1 ▶ **An Ojibwe man is speaking to a class. He is telling the story of dream catchers. Listen to the entire talk with your books closed.**

2 **What did you understand from the talk? Discuss with a partner.**

3 **Now practice taking notes. Create a chart like the one below to take notes. Write down any information you remember. Put big ideas or general pieces of information under Main Ideas. Put important names, words, or smaller pieces of information under Details.**

TAKE NOTES **The Story of Dream Catchers**

Main Ideas	Details
Ojibwe people believe Spider Woman (SW) gave life to world	• made web to catch sun • people moved away → hard for SW to take care of everyone • women made dream catchers to help SW, for babies

4 ▶ **Listen again. As you listen, add information to your notes.**

5 **Discuss the talk again with a partner. What else did you understand this time? What information did you add to your notes?**

↖ Go to **MyEnglishLab** to view example notes.

MAIN IDEAS

Put the sentences in order from 1 to 7. The first one has been done for you.

_3_ a. The traditional dream catcher comes from the story of Spider Woman's web.

_5_ b. Young Native Americans still learn about the dream catcher tradition.

_2_ c. The Ojibwe people move away from Spider Woman to other parts of North America.

_1_ d. The Ojibwe people tell traditional stories about Spider Woman.

_7_ e. The traditional place to put a dream catcher is over your bed.

_4_ f. Mothers, sisters, and grandmothers start making dream catchers for babies.

_6_ g. A dream catcher keeps out bad dreams and lets good dreams enter the mind.

1 ▶ **Listen again and add to your notes. Then circle the correct answer to complete each sentence. Use your notes to help you.**

1. Traditional dream catchers have a little ___b___ in the center.

   a. plant

   b. feather

2. Traditional dream catchers are made from parts of plants and ___b___ .

   a. materials

   b. trees

3. Today, modern dream catchers are ___a___ traditional ones.

   a. different from

   b. the same as

4. Modern dream catchers have beautiful colors and ___a___ .

   a. styles

   b. holes

5. Letting in good dreams through a dream catcher helps the ___b___ .

   a. breath

   b. mind

6. People today give dream catchers as gifts for ___a___ .

   a. friends

   b. babies

7. Big dream catchers that are sold in stores are not ___b___ .

   a. popular

   b. traditional

Handwritten note: The traditional dream catcher story comes from the Ojibwe people. They are different.

2 With a partner, take turns summarizing your notes. Then discuss how your notes and your answers in Preview helped you understand the listening.

▶ Go to **MyEnglishLab** for more listening practice.

MAKE INFERENCES 🔍

Inferring a Speaker's Beliefs

An inference is a guess about something that is not said directly. To make an inference, try to understand more than the words the speaker says.

We can make inferences about a speaker's beliefs. To do this, we listen for important words that show what a speaker believes about something. Words with a strong meaning, positive or negative, help us to understand a speaker's beliefs.

▶ **Listen to an excerpt from the lecture. What does the speaker believe about dreams?**

Example

Speaker's belief: Bad dreams are _____a_____ .

a. powerful — *Poderoso*

b. very important

Explanation

The correct answer is *a*. The word **protect** helps us understand the speaker's belief that bad dreams have power. He believes they have the power to hurt us, and that the dream catcher stops them from entering the mind.

▶ **Listen to the excerpts from the interview. Pay attention to the speaker's words and think about the speaker's beliefs. Circle the correct word or phrase to complete the sentence.**

Excerpt One

1. The speaker believes: Good dreams are important because they change our way of _____ .

   a. living   b. feeling

Excerpt Two

2. The speaker believes: It is beautiful to share our _____ with each other.

   a. dreams   b. stories

Excerpt Three

3. The speaker believes: It is important to use dream catchers in a _____ way.

   a. traditional   b. lucky

DISCUSS 🔍

Work in a small group. Read the questions. Discuss your ideas.

1. How do dream catchers protect people? Why is this important?

2. Do you agree that dream catchers are good gifts? Why? Give one reason from the listening.

3. What are three differences between traditional dream catchers and modern ones?

> **USE YOUR NOTES**
>
> **APPLY** Find information in your notes to use in your discussion.

▶ Go to **MyEnglishLab** to give your opinion about another question.

VOCABULARY

1 **Read the conversation and notice the boldfaced words and phrases. Try to guess their meanings.**

A: Why are you wearing a red baseball cap?

B: It's my **good luck charm**. It helps me pass tests.

A: That's **cool**. I have a lucky ring. See? It was my grandmother's ring. She had it for a long time and then she passed it down to me. I wear it all the time because I love her so much. It has a lot of **sentimental value** to me.

A: Nice. I think my sister has our grandmother's old ring. She keeps everything! Old books, old toys, everything. She's **a pack rat**.

B: My brother is **a pack rat**, too. He keeps all his old clothes, but he never wears them!

A: My sister's like that, too . . .

2 **Draw a line to connect the beginning of the sentence with the end of the sentence.**

1. If you are a pack rat, . . .
2. Things with sentimental value . . .
3. If someone passes a ring down, . . .
4. A good luck charm is . . .
5. Something "cool" is . . .

a. nice or good.
b. you always save your old things.
c. an object that makes good things happen.
d. help us remember family and friends.
e. it goes from older to younger family members.

3 **Compare your answers with a partner's. Now take turns performing the conversation.**

Go to the **Pearson Practice English App** or **MyEnglishLab** for more vocabulary practice.

Jet

ivel

Newborn Children

evil eyes

Small black fist on a red strip

Drawing Pictures in Your Notes

Drawing pictures in your notes is a helpful way to remember new vocabulary. For example, if you are listening to someone talk about a piece of jewelry or a toy, drawing a picture of it in your notes will help you to remember it later. You can also write the name of your drawing, along with any words to help you understand it.

Example

Imagine listening to George Wolf's talk about dream catchers. He is showing you one and talking about how to make it. In your notes, you can draw a picture of the dream catcher, like the one below, and you can add new vocabulary or important words.

web —————— hole

feather

Dream catcher

Drawing pictures is also a fast and easy way to add information to your notes. For example, you can draw a heart to show love or a sun to show good weather.

1 ▶ **Listen to a college student talk about a four-leaf clover. Many people believe this is a special plant. As you listen, take notes in the chart. Imagine what a four-leaf clover looks like, and draw a picture in your notes. Add any other words or symbols to your notes.**

Main Ideas	Details

2 **With a partner, compare notes and drawings. Then turn to page 72 to see a photo of a four-leafed clover. How similar is it to your drawing?**

🔘 Go to **MyEnglishLab** for more note-taking practice.

COMPREHENSION

1 ▶ Listen to three college students have a conversation as they move into an apartment.
Sara and Amber are in the apartment before Lauren arrives. When Lauren arrives with
her big teddy bear named Lucy, they all begin to talk about their special possessions.
Create a chart like the one below to take notes. Try to include drawings in your notes.

TAKE NOTES Toys in College	
Main Ideas	**Details**

2 Are the statements below true or false? Write *T* (true) or *F* (false). Correct the false
statements. Use your notes to help you.

___F___ 1. At the beginning, both Sara and Amber are happy about the teddy bear.

___T___ 2. Lucy the bear has sentimental value.

___F___ 3. Lucy is a new teddy bear.

___F___ 4. Amber doesn't keep old things.

___F___ 5. Sara has a lucky dream catcher to help her
pass tests.

USE YOUR NOTES

Compare your notes with
a partner's. How can you
improve your notes next time?

A teddy bear

1 ▶ **Listen to the two speakers. Who is louder and more excited?**

_____ Speaker A _____ Speaker B

Recognizing and Understanding a Speaker's Excitement

Excitement is one emotion you hear while listening. When speakers are very excited about a topic, they often speak louder. They sometimes pronounce words more slowly or with a higher voice. When speakers are not excited about a topic, their voices do not change very much. They say all the words in the same way.

Understanding a speaker's excitement is part of understanding how he or she feels about the topic. When we understand a speaker's feelings, we can have a better conversation because we understand the other person's opinion and point of view.

▶ **Listen to the example. Is the speaker excited? How do you know?**

Example

1. Is the speaker excited?

_____ a. Yes _____ b. No

2. How do you know? Which words are louder, higher, or spoken more slowly?

Explanation

The correct answers are: 1. *a*, 2. The speaker says *a long time* louder and more slowly. She says *to me* in a higher and louder voice.

When Lauren uses a louder voice and pronounces words more slowly, she emphasizes the importance of Lucy, the teddy bear. She is excited that her grandmother and mother gave her something so important and with such sentimental value.

2 ▶ **Listen to these excerpts. Is the speaker excited? Listen to the speaker's voice. Is it loud? Is it high? Does the speaker pronounce some words more slowly than others?**

Excerpt One

1. Is the speaker excited? Circle one: Yes / No.

2. How do you know? Which words are louder, higher, or spoken more slowly?

_____

Excerpt Two

1. Is the speaker excited? Circle one: Yes / No.

2. How do you know? Which words are louder, higher, or spoken more slowly?

_____

Excerpt Three

1. Is the speaker excited? Circle one: Yes / No.

2. How do you know? Which words are louder, higher, or spoken more slowly?

_____

🔊 Go to **MyEnglishLab** for more skill practice.

CONNECT THE LISTENINGS

ORGANIZE

USE YOUR NOTES

APPLY Review your notes from Listening One and Two. Use the information in your notes to complete the chart.

Look at the list of reasons why special possessions are important. Complete the chart by writing three reasons for keeping dream catchers (Listening One) and old toys (Listening Two).

help you feel happy and peaceful   lucky   part of families for many years

keeping old traditions   many beautiful styles   sentimental value

Why It Is Important to Keep Dream Catchers	Why It Is Important to Keep Old Toys
Reason 1: _____	Reason 1: _____
Reason 2: _____	Reason 2: _____
Reason 3: _____	Reason 3: _____

SYNTHESIZE

Work with a partner. You are both students in a psychology[2] class. Student A, interview Student B for a report on special possessions. Ask Student B questions about dream catchers. Student B, answer the questions with reasons from the chart. Then talk about another special possession that people like to keep.

Example

A: I hear that you have a lot of dream catchers. Why do you have so many?

B: I really like dream catchers. Lots of people do. They keep them in their homes and cars.

A: Why?

B: I think one reason is . . .

A: Really? Is there another reason?

B: Yes. Another reason is . . .

A: That's so interesting. What else can you tell me about dream catchers?

B: Well, I think people also like to keep dream catchers because . . .

A: I see. What other special possessions do people like to keep?

B: *[Answer with another example. Give reasons why it is important.]*

A: Thank you!

---

[2] **psychology:** the study of how people think and what people do

Now switch roles. Student B, interview Student A. Ask Student A questions about old toys. Student A, answer the questions with reasons from the chart. Then talk about another special possession in your own life.

Example

B: I hear that you have a lot of old toys. Is that true?

A: Yes, it is. Many people love their old toys. They keep them for a long time.

B: Why?

A: I think one reason is . . .

A: Really? Is there another reason?

B: Yes. Another reason is . . .

A: That's so interesting. What else can you tell me about old toys?

B: Well, I think people also like to keep old toys because . . .

A: I see. What other special possessions do people like to keep?

B: *[Answer with another example. Give reasons why it is important.]*

A: Thank you!

Go to **MyEnglishLab** to check what you learned.

VOCABULARY

REVIEW

A professional organizer helps people make their homes more organized. In an organized home, it is easy to find things. Read the Web page of a professional organizer and fill in the blanks with the words from the box. You will not use all of the words.

appreciate	good luck charms	pack rat	sentimental value
breath	mind	peaceful	style
cool	modern	popular	traditional

Get Organized!

Are you a _____ with too many things?

        1.

Do you want to feel more _____ in

        2.

your home? Do you want to think with a clear

_____? I can help. I am a professional

    3.

organizer for this busy _____ world. I

        4.

can make your house a very _____

        5.

place for you and your friends. They will love it! (And it's

sometimes true—a nice, organized house will make you

more _____ with friends.)

   6.

Get help organizing your closet today!

Listen—I know that organizing is hard. I understand that some of your things have

_____, and you want to keep them. That's fine with me. You can keep your

   7.

special possessions and _____. I will not tell you what to do. That's not my

        8.

_____. But I will organize your home—and you will

  9.

_____ the changes. Contact me today to schedule a visit!

   10.

EXPAND

1 Work with a partner. Read the conversation between a professional organizer and a pack rat. Notice the boldfaced words and phrases. Try to guess their meaning.

ORGANIZER: OK, let's get started. What is something that you don't need anymore? What do you want to **get rid of**?

PACK RAT: I'm not sure. I don't like to throw things away. Maybe I will need them later. Then what will I do?

ORGANIZER: Don't worry about that. Let's think about today. What about this old bike? Do you want to keep it?

PACK RAT: Yes. It's my first bike. It's very important to me.

ORGANIZER: OK. You want to **hold on to** it. That's fine. What about these old math books? Do you still need them?

PACK RAT: Not today, but maybe in the future . . .

ORGANIZER: I really don't think you will need them in the future. They **clutter up** the room. Why don't we **give** them **away**?

PACK RAT: To who?

ORGANIZER: I'm sure we can find someone—maybe a teacher or an old book **collector**. Or maybe somebody wants to **recycle** them. Let's keep going . . .

2 Match the words and phrases with their definitions.

_____ 1. recycle

_____ 2. collector

_____ 3. get rid of something

_____ 4. give something away

_____ 5. hold on to something

_____ 6. clutter up

a. keep something instead of losing it

b. use something again

c. a person who gets and keeps interesting things (books, stamps, jewelry)

d. fill a space with too many things

e. give something you don't want or need to another person

f. to throw something away because you don't want or need it

CREATE

APPLY Discuss these questions with a partner. Student A, ask questions 1–3. Student B, ask questions 4–6. Use the boldfaced words and phrases in your answers. Prepare to share interesting answers with the class.

1. Are you a **collector**? What do you **collect**?

2. Are you **a pack rat**? Is it hard for you to **get rid of** things? Explain.

3. How often do you **give** things **away**? What do you give away?

4. Do you **clutter** your home? Do you want a professional organizer to help you at home? Why or why not?

5. Do you have any **good luck charms**? Do they help you?

6. What kinds of things have **sentimental value** in your life?

 Go to the **Pearson Practice English App** or **MyEnglishLab** for more vocabulary practice.

GRAMMAR FOR SPEAKING

1 Read the sentences. Then answer the questions.

    a. The book collector often shops online.

    b. Old traditional ways always change.

    c. I never keep old things.

    d. She usually puts a dream catcher near her bed.

    e. It is always **expensive**[2] to collect cars.

    f. Professional organizers are sometimes very busy.

1. Which words tell us how often these things happen? Underline them.

2. Look at the sentences with the verb **be**. Where are the words you underlined—before or after **be**?

3. Look at the other sentences. Where are the words you underlined—before or after the verb?

---

[2] **expensive:** costing a lot of money

Using the Simple Present with Adverbs of Frequency

1. Adverbs are words that change or add to the meaning of verbs. **Adverbs of frequency** tell you how often something happens, or how often people do things.	*Always: 100% of the time* *Usually: 90% of the time* *Often: 70% of the time* *Sometimes: 30% of the time* *Never: 0% of the time*
2. When the verb is **be**, put the adverb of frequency after the verb.	*A teddy bear is **always** cute.* *The style of a dream catcher is **sometimes** modern.*
3. With all other verbs, put the adverb of frequency before the verb.	*He **often** keeps his old books.* *She **usually** looks for rings online.* *I **never** forget to bring my lucky charm.*
4. For *yes / no* and *wh-* questions, put the adverb before the verb. You can also ask about frequency by using *How often . . . ?*	*Does she **often** buy toys?* *Is a dream catcher **always** expensive?* *What do they **usually** collect?* ***How often** do you remember your dreams?*
5. In negative statements, put ***don't*** and ***doesn't*** before the adverb of frequency. Use ***ever*** instead of ***never***. In negative statements with the verb **be**, put the adverb of frequency after the verb **be**.	*They don't **often** go shopping.* *He doesn't **always** keep old things.* *She doesn't **ever** take off her ring.* *We aren't **usually** late to class.* *Clothing isn't **always** expensive.*

2 Alexandra and Sofia are in a college psychology class. They are listening to a professor speak about special possessions. Complete the sentences with the correct adverb of frequency.

PROFESSOR: We know that people _____ have special possessions, but why? For
1. (often / never)
example, an 80-year-old grandmother loves her old ring. She _____
2. (never / sometimes)
shows it to her grandson, but he doesn't think the ring is important. Why do

people _____ like different kinds of things? Can anyone tell me why?
3. (never / often)

ALEXANDRA: Is it because of male and female[3] differences? I know that males and females
_____ have different likes and dislikes.
4. (usually / sometimes)

PROFESSOR: That is an interesting idea. However, think about the grandmother's history

with the ring. The grandmother has many memories about her ring. She

_____ wears it. That's why she doesn't _____ want
5. (always / never)   6. (never / ever)
to give her ring away. It has a lot of sentimental value. However, the boy has no

special memories of the ring, so it isn't important to him.

SOFIA: I think the grandson has memories connected to possessions, but he probably

likes different things because he is so much younger than his grandmother.

PROFESSOR: That's a great point, Sara. The grandmother is much older than the grandson, so

they _____ put value on different kinds of possessions. An older
7. (usually / never)
person may keep something like a ring or a photo album, but a younger person's

special possession is _____ something like a favorite game or a toy.
8. (usually / always)

ALEXANDRA: I agree with you, Professor, but I think we need to remember that every person

is different. My little brother is young, but he doesn't like games. He would

_____ want to keep one as a special possession.
9. (never / always)

PROFESSOR: Another excellent point! We can talk about people in general, but we

_____ need to see each person as a unique individual.
10. (always / sometimes)

3 Read the lecture aloud with two classmates.

---

[3] **male and female:** boy and girl, man and woman

4 APPLY **Work with a partner. Take turns describing a special possession. Use adverbs of frequency.**

Partner A (ask B): What does your special possession look like? Where does it come from? Is it useful or beautiful? Does it have any sentimental value?

Partner B (ask A): What is your special possession? Where do you keep it? How do you take care of it? How often do you use it or show it to others?

Example

I **always** keep my grandmother's ring in a box. I **often** wear it on my birthday because it **always** helps me remember my grandmother. To take good care of it, I **often** clean it. I **sometimes** show the ring to my children, and I **never** want to lose it.

Go to the **Pearson Practice English App** or **MyEnglishLab** for more grammar practice. Check what you learned in **MyEnglishLab**.

PRONUNCIATION

1 ▶ **Listen to the underlined verbs in the conversation. The present tense ending *-s* has three different pronunciations.**

A: Your mother has a beautiful ring!

B: She <u>loves</u> that ring. She only <u>takes</u> it off to clean it.

A: Clean it? How do you clean a ring?

B: With toothpaste! She <u>brushes</u> her ring with toothpaste.

Look at the three underlined verbs in the conversation. Answer this question for each verb: Does the *-s* ending add a new sound, /s/ or /z/? Or does it add a new syllable (a new vowel sound, /əz/)?

In the present tense, the pronunciation of the third-person singular ending depends on the last sound of the *base form* of the verb.

Pronouncing *-s* Endings

In the present tense, the pronunciation of the third-person singular ending depends on the last sound of the *base form* of the verb.

1. Pronounce the *-s* ending /əz/ or /ɪz/ after /s/, /z/, **sh** and **ch** and **j**. (See the phonetic alphabet on page 233.) After these sounds, the *-s* ending adds a new syllable.	*use* (one syllable) → *uses* (two syllables) She **uses** *toothpaste to clean her ring.* *Tom* **washes** *his new car every day.* *The professor* **teaches** *the students on Mondays.*
2. Pronounce the *-s* ending /s/ after /p, t, k, f/. The *-s* ending is a final sound.	*She* **keeps** *her rings in a special box.* *He* **wants** *to keep his old guitar.* *The ring* **looks** *beautiful.* *The child* **laughs** *as she plays with her toys.*
3. Pronounce the *-s* ending /z/ after **all other sounds**. The *-s* ending is a final sound.	*She never* **wears** *rings.* *The student* **stays** *at school all day.* *The professor* **arrives** *at 8:00 a.m.*

2 ▶ **Listen to the conversation and repeat the lines. Make sure to pronounce the -s sound correctly. Then practice the conversation with a partner.**

A: My roommate is a jewelry collector. Tonight she **wants** to watch a video about Native American jewelry. Do you want to see it with us?

B: Sure. What time? My class **ends** at 7:30, but the professor never **finishes** on time. Sometimes she **teaches** until 8:00!

A: No problem. We're going to watch it online. Just come when she **lets** you out.

B: OK. Is the video long? I have an early class in the morning.

A: I don't think it's long. It probably **lasts** about an hour.

B: Good. I'll see you tonight.

3 **Circle the pronunciation of the -s ending of the underlined words. Then check your answers with a classmate's and take turns reading the sentences. The first one has been done for you.**

1. Lauren <u>wears</u> her ring all the time. It <u>looks</u> expensive.

    əz / s / ⓩ   əz / s / z

2. George <u>buys</u> and <u>sells</u> expensive jewelry. He <u>travels</u> all over the world.

    əz / s / z əz / s / z   əz / s / z

3. My roommate really <u>likes</u> toy animals. She <u>gets</u> something new every week.

    əz / s / z   əz / s / z

4. The movie about dream catchers <u>starts</u> at 2:00. It <u>takes</u> about an hour to get there,

    əz / s / z   əz / s / z

    so let's leave before 1:00.

5. The book store <u>opens</u> at 10 A.M. and <u>closes</u> at 6:00 P.M.

    əz / s / z   əz / s / z

4 **APPLY** **Work with a partner. Student A, you want to learn more about dream catchers. Student B, you want to learn more about the Ojibwe people. Student A, go to page 202. Student B, go to page 206. Ask your partner for the missing information in your chart. Then write the information.**

Example

B: Do you know the hours of the Ojibwe Museum?

A: Yes, <u>it opens at 10:00 A.M. and closes at 6:00 P.M.</u>
          /z/   /əz/

Student A	Times		Student B	Times	
The hours of the Ojibwe Museum (verbs: *open, close*)	10:00 A.M.	6:00 P.M.	The hours of the Ojibwe Museum	10:00 A.M.	6:00 P.M.

Inviting Others to Speak

A good speaker knows how to include others in a conversation or a discussion by asking questions. These questions allow others to share their thoughts and opinions. Giving other people a chance to speak, keeps a conversation going.

Read the example.

Example

> LAUREN: Lucy isn't just a stuffed animal. She's a part of my life—and a part of my family, too. **What about you? Don't you have any special possessions?**

The first question invites the other person to speak. The second question begins with **don't.** This means that the speaker expects the other person to say "yes." Questions that begin with a negative auxiliary (*don't, doesn't, isn't, aren't,* etc.) mean that the speaker expects the other person to agree or say "yes." Look at these examples:

A: Don't you think teddy bears are cute?
B: Yes, I do.

A: Isn't this pen lucky?
B: Yes, it is.

Other questions begin with affirmative auxiliaries (*do, does, is, are,* etc.) and invite others to speak. These questions mean that the speaker wants information. The speaker does not expect the other person to agree or say "yes." Look at these examples:

A: Do you have a teddy bear?
B: No, I don't. But I have an old guitar that I love!

A: Is this pen lucky?
B: I don't know. But I have a lucky penny!

In addition to *yes / no* questions, there are several *Wh-* questions you can use to invite others to speak. Here are some examples:

- *What do you think, [name]?*
- *What about you, [name]?*
- *How about you, [name}?*

- *What's your opinion, [name]?*
- *What's your point of view, [name]?*
- *What's your take on this, [name]?*

Remember: When inviting others to speak in a group discussion, it's a good idea to use their names so it's clear who you are talking to.

1 ▶ **Read and listen to the examples from Listening Two. Underline the questions in each one. Then say the questions out loud. Which questions ask for more information? Which questions expect the listener to say "yes"?**

1. Old things really aren't that important to me. How about you, Sara?

2. It stops the bad dreams. It only lets the good dreams come into your mind. Isn't it beautiful?

3. Is it a good luck charm? Does it help you to pass tests?

4. When I take notes with my lucky pen, I usually get As! What about you, Lauren—do you ask the big bear for help with your tests?

2 **What do you know about good luck charms in North America? Look at the photos. Complete the discussion by writing questions in the blanks. Then read the conversation with a partner. Change roles and repeat the conversation. Notice how the questions invite the other person to speak.**

- Isn't that a little plant with four leaves?
- Do you have a lot of tests, too?
- Don't you agree?

- Can you think of other good luck charms?
- Isn't that lucky?

A: I want to buy a rabbit's foot.

B: Why?

A: It's good luck.

B: Really? A rabbit's foot?

A: Not a real one—a fake[4] one.

B: Oh, I see. Well, I need some good luck, too. I'm really busy at

school. _____
1.

A: Yes—too many!

B: What other good luck charms do you know about?

A: Well, there's a little plant . . .

B: A clover? _____
2.

A: Yes. It brings good luck. What about you?

_____
3.

B: How about a horseshoe? _____
4.

A: You're right—it is. Maybe we can buy one. We need to pass our

tests! _____
5.

B: Yes—I do.

a horseshoe

a rabbit's foot

a four-leaf clover

---
4 **fake:** made by humans; not natural

⬙ Go to **MyEnglishLab** for more skill practice and to check what you learned.

In this task, you will choose a special possession to keep. Then you will work in a small group to discuss your reasons for keeping it. One student from your group will report to the whole class about your group's reasons for keeping possessions.

STEP 1

1 Imagine that there is a fire in your home. You need to leave very quickly. You only have time to take one special possession with you. First, make a list of several special possessions in your home. Then look at the list of questions. Use the questions to decide which special possession you will keep.

- Is it useful?
- Is it beautiful?
- Is it a traditional part of the family?

- Is it a good luck charm?
- Does it have sentimental value?
- Is it expensive?

2 **Plan your discussion. Use the outline below:**

What I will keep

_____

My reasons for keeping it

1. _____
2. _____
3. _____

STEP 2

1 **Work in groups of four or five students. Choose one reporter for the group. The reporter will listen and complete the chart as you discuss your special possessions and the reasons for taking them with you. The reporter will write your names and possessions and check (✓) all of the reasons you give.**

Reasons for Keeping It	Name: _____ Possession: _____	Name: _____ Possession: _____	Name: _____ Possession: _____	Name: _____ Possession: _____
It's useful.				
It's beautiful.				
It's a traditional part of the family.				
It's a good luck charm.				
It has sentimental value.				
It's expensive.				
Other				

2 **APPLY** Use the vocabulary, grammar, pronunciation, and speaking skills from the unit. Use the checklist to help you.

☐ **Vocabulary:** Read through the list of vocabulary on page 75. Which words can you include in your discussion to make it clearer and more interesting? Choose at least three words or phrases to use and add them to your outline.

☐ **Grammar:** Think about how often you use, take care of, or enjoy your possession. Use at least three adverbs of frequency in your discussion.

☐ **Pronunciation:** Listen to your classmates as they describe their special possessions. Are they pronouncing the –s endings of simple present verbs correctly?

☐ **Speaking Skill:** After you discuss your reasons, use the questions you learned to invite other students to speak. Try to keep the discussion going.

STEP 3

The reporter for your group will tell the class about the two most important reasons for keeping a special possession. The reporter will also tell the class which possessions the students in your group want to hold on to.

Example

- It's useful. __✓✓✓✓__
- It's beautiful. __✓✓__
- It's a traditional part of the family. __✓__

- It's a good luck charm. __∅__
- It has sentimental value. __∅__
- It's expensive. __✓✓✓__

Based on this example, the reporter tells the class:

In our group, the two most important reasons are "expensive" and "useful." These are the things we want to keep: phones, watches, jewelry, and laptops.

LISTENING TASK

Now, listen to the reporters from each group. What are the reasons for each decision? Which reasons did students choose most often? Which reasons do you agree and disagree with? Discuss your opinions with a partner.

ALTERNATIVE SPEAKING TOPIC

APPLY **Discuss one of these topics in small groups. Use the vocabulary, grammar, pronunciation, and speaking skills you learned in the unit.**

1. What are some good luck charms in your home culture? Do you believe that they bring good luck to people? How often do you use them? Explain.

2. Imagine that you have the chance to collect anything. What will you collect? Why?

3. Antique furniture can be hundreds of years old. Some people like it and spend a lot of money on it. What kind of furniture do you like—antique or modern? Explain.

4. Pack rats usually hold on to everything, not only their special possessions. What is your advice to pack rats? How can they learn to get rid of things or give them away?

CHECK WHAT YOU'VE LEARNED

Check (✔) the outcomes you've met and vocabulary you've learned. Put an X next to the skills and vocabulary you still need to practice.

Learning Outcomes
- ☐ Infer a speaker's beliefs
- ☐ Draw pictures in your notes
- ☐ Recognize and understand a speaker's excitement
- ☐ Use the simple present with adverbs of frequency
- ☐ Pronounce -s endings
- ☐ Invite others to speak

Vocabulary
- ☐ appreciate AWL
- ☐ breath
- ☐ cool
- ☐ mind
- ☐ modern
- ☐ pack rat
- ☐ peaceful
- ☐ popular
- ☐ style AWL
- ☐ traditional AWL

Multi-word Units
- ☐ good luck charms
- ☐ sentimental value

⏺ Go to **MyEnglishLab** to watch a video about a stolen wedding dress, access the Unit Project, and take the Unit 3 Achievement Test.

LEARNING OUTCOMES

> Make inferences about contrasting ideas
> Take notes with the equal sign
> Identify signal words for main ideas

> Use *there is / are / was / were*
> Pronounce *th* sounds
> React to information

(•) Go to **MyEnglishLab** to check what you know.

Creativity in Business

1 FOCUS ON THE TOPIC

1. Look at the photo and the title. How old do you think the girl in the photo is? What is she doing? How does the title relate to the photo?

2. Children are usually creative when they play. They have new ideas, and they create, or make, new things. When you were a child, what creative things did you do? Did you ever make or sell anything?

3. What kinds of businesses need creative workers?

LISTENING ONE | KK Gregory, Young and Creative

VOCABULARY

1 ▶ Many big companies are teaching their employees to be more creative. Read and listen to this article from an online business magazine. Notice the boldfaced words. Try to guess their meanings.

Business information, insight and resources

Can Employees Learn to Be More *Creative*?
Many Business Owners Say "YES!"

Big companies, like American Express®, Microsoft®, FedEx Office®, and Disney®, want their **employees** to be **creative**—to think in new and interesting ways. These companies pay billions of dollars for **creativity** classes for their employees.

In some creativity classes, employees play games together in a classroom. In other classes, they do **exciting** sports together outside. For example, at the Joyful Company, a **successful** advertising company, employees go whitewater rafting and rock climbing together. All of these activities help employees to think in new ways.

In creativity classes, teachers also give employees important **advice**:

• Relax. When people relax, they can think better.

• Don't be **afraid** to **make mistakes**. No one is perfect. Just try to do your best. Great ideas sometimes come from mistakes.

• Think young! Children are very creative, so sometimes we need to think like children.

When employees have creative ideas, companies become more successful. One successful business owner said, "One creativity class helped my employees more than many years of work **experience**." Many other big business **owners** agree. Creativity classes are helping their companies.

This work is produced by Pearson Education and is not endorsed by any trademark owner referenced in this publication.

2 Circle all of the choices that correctly complete the sentence. Then check your answers with your teacher.

The article says that when employees relax and play games, they can _____ .

a. make a lot of money

b. get creative ideas for work

c. be more active

d. lose their jobs

e. think in new ways

f. feel afraid to make mistakes

3 Take turns with a partner. Student A, read the sentence and choose the correct meaning of the word from the magazine article. Student B, say if you agree.

Example

Employees are (*people who work for a company* / *people who don't have jobs*).

A: Employees are *people who don't have jobs.*

B: No, I don't think so. I think employees are people who work for a company.

1. **A:** A **creative** person has (*new and interesting ideas* / *the same ideas as other people*).

   B: (Yes, I agree. / No, I don't think so. I think a creative person has . . .)

2. **A:** Business **owners** are people who (*work for a business* / *have their own business*).

   B: (Yes, I agree. / No, I don't think so. I think they are people who . . .)

3. **A:** **Creativity** means having ideas that (*can make a lot of money* / *are new and different*).

   B: (Yes, I agree. / No, I don't think so. I think it means having ideas that . . .)

4. **A:** **Exciting** things (*are a lot of fun* / *cost a lot of money*).

   B: (Yes, I agree. / No, I don't think so. I think they . . .)

5. **A:** A **successful** company (*makes a lot of money* / *has many employees*).

   B: (Yes, I agree. / No, I don't think so. I think it is a company that . . .)

6. **A:** When you give **advice**, you give information (*to help another person* / *about yourself*).

   B: (Yes, I agree. / No, I don't think so. I think it means you give information . . .)

7. **A:** To be **afraid** means to be nervous and scared because something is (*very boring* / *difficult or different*).

   B: (Yes, I agree. / No, I don't think so. I think it means to be nervous and scared because something is . . .)

8. **A:** When you **make mistakes**, you do something (*the right way* / *the wrong way*).

   B: (Yes, I agree. / No, I don't think so. I think it means you do something . . .)

9. **A:** When you have work **experience**, it means you (*worked at a job* / *got a new job*).

   B: (Yes, I agree. / No, I don't think so. I think it means you . . .)

🔊 Go to the **Pearson Practice English App** or **MyEnglishLab** for more vocabulary practice.

▶ **Listen to the beginning of "KK Gregory, Young and Creative." Then circle your idea.**

Professor Jason Chandler teaches an MBA (Master's in Business Administration) class at a California university. He invited KK Gregory to speak to his class. KK is a high school student. She has her own business. It is called Wristies.

Why do you think Professor Chandler wants KK to speak to his business students?

a. The business students will enjoy listening to KK's talk.

b. The business students can learn from KK's experience.

c. The business students can get jobs at KK's company.

GRADUATE SCHOOL OF BUSINESS
SPECIAL LECTURE!

"Increasing Creativity in Business"

Guest speaker: KK Gregory

Room 121 • Prof. J. Chandler • 9:00–11:00

LISTEN

1 ▶ **Listen to KK's entire talk with your books closed.**

2 **What did you understand from the talk? Discuss with a partner.**

3 **Now practice taking notes. Create a chart like the one below to take notes. Write down any information you remember. Put big ideas or general pieces of information under Main Ideas. Put important names, words, or smaller pieces of information under Details.**

◤ **TAKE NOTES   Increasing Creativity in Business**

Main Ideas	Details
KK = successful business owner	• 17 yrs old • makes Wristies

4 ▶ Listen again. As you listen, add information to your notes.

5 Discuss the interview again with a partner. What else did you understand this time? What information did you add to your notes?

▶ Go to **MyEnglishLab** to view example notes.

MAIN IDEAS

Answer the questions. Use your notes to help you.

1. What makes KK's business different from other businesses?

   _____

   _____

2. What are Wristies?

   _____

   _____

3. How did KK get the idea for Wristies?

   _____

   _____

4. Why did KK start a business?

   _____

   _____

1 ▶ **Listen again and add to your notes. Two answers are correct. Cross out the incorrect answer. Use your notes to help you. Then read the correct sentences aloud with a partner. The first one has been done for you.**

1. When you wear Wristies, _____ .

   a. ~~your thumbs are covered~~

   b. your wrists are warm

   c. you can move your fingers

2. KK made the first pair of Wristies by _____ .

   a. cutting material she found in her house

   b. cutting up new material she bought at a store

   c. wrapping material around her wrist

3. KK's friends _____ .

   a. really liked their Wristies

   b. wanted to sell their Wristies

   c. wore their Wristies every day

4. When KK started the Wristies company, _____ .

   a. her mother helped her

   b. her mother had a store

   c. she had a few problems

5. KK's mother _____ .

   a. had a lot of business experience

   b. asked for advice about running a business

   c. had no business experience

6. People can buy Wristies _____ .

   a. in many stores

   b. on the Internet

   c. at the supermarket

7. When KK went on a TV shopping show, _____ .

   a. she was very successful

   b. she was angry

   c. she was nervous and excited

8. KK's advice to the business students is to _____ .

   a. be creative

   b. do new things

   c. start your own business

2 **With a partner, take turns summarizing your notes. Then discuss how your notes and your answers in Preview helped you understand the listening.**

⏵ Go to **MyEnglishLab** for more listening practice.

MAKE INFERENCES 🔍

Making Inferences About Contrasting Ideas

An inference is a guess about something that is not said directly.

In English, when we stress a word, we say it louder, longer, and with higher pitch. When we want to show that there is an important difference, or contrast, between two things or ideas, we give the two contrasting (different) words the strongest stress in the sentence. These words are stressed more than the other stressed words.

▶ **Listen to the sentence. All the stressed words are in boldfaced letters. The words with contrastive stress are in BOLDFACED CAPITALS.**

Example

KK: It's **really exciting** to be here, in a **BUSINESS** school class, because I'm **still** in **HIGH** school!

Which two words is KK contrasting? _____ and _____

Why? KK wants to explain that:

a. It is scary for her to speak to a class full of business students.

b. It's very unusual for a high school student to speak to business school students.

Explanation

KK is contrasting the words **BUSINESS** and **HIGH**.

Why? The correct answer is **b**. It's very unusual for a high school student to speak to business school students.

By using contrastive stress on the words **BUSINESS** and **HIGH**, KK is explaining that these two kinds of schools are very different. Notice that we do not place extra stress on the word that is the same: *school*.

▶ **Listen to each excerpt from the talk. Write down the two words that KK is contrasting in each sentence. Then choose the sentence that explains the idea she is trying to express.**

Excerpt One

1. Which two words is KK contrasting? _____ and _____

2. What does KK want to explain?

   a. She is young now, but when she started her company, she was much younger.

   b. KK has worked at her company for a very long time.

1. Which two words is KK contrasting? _____ and _____

2. What does KK want to explain?

   a. The gloves are very long.

   b. Most gloves have fingers, but Wristies do not have fingers.

1. Which two words is KK contrasting? _____ and _____

2. What does KK want to explain?

   a. Most people only wear gloves outside, but people can wear Wristies inside, too.

   b. Wristies are not only good for sports, but also for work.

1. Which two words is KK contrasting? _____ and _____

2. What does KK want to explain?

   a. Her warm clothes and gloves did not cover her wrists.

   b. KK's wrists were always cold in the winter.

DISCUSS 🔍

USE YOUR NOTES

APPLY Find information in your notes to use in your discussion.

Work with a partner. Answer the questions.

1. What did KK tell the business class about trying something new? Is this good advice? Why or why not?

2. Do you agree or disagree with the following statement? "KK's mother made an excellent decision. It's very good for a child to have a business." Explain your opinion.

3. What do you need to start your own company like KK did? Do you think it would be easy or difficult? Why?

🡢 Go to **MyEnglishLab** to give your opinion about another question.

LISTENING TWO | A Business Class

VOCABULARY

1 Work with a partner. Student A, read the first sentence. Student B, complete the second sentence with the word or phrase from the box so your sentence has the same meaning. Then switch roles.

came up with	for the first time	made her feel good
completely new	increase their creativity	

1. **A:** KK **thought of** a new idea—to make Wristies.

   B: That means she _____ the idea to make Wristies.

2. **A:** KK started a business, **but she had absolutely no business experience**.

   B: So, starting a business was a _____ experience for her.

3. **A:** People can learn to **become more creative**.

   B: That means they can _____ .

4. **A:** When KK was 17, she spoke at a business school. **She had never done that before.**

   B: So, when she was 17, she spoke at a business school _____ .

5. **A:** When people liked KK's new idea, it **gave her a happy feeling**.

   B: OK, so in other words, it _____ .

2 APPLY Talk with a partner about a time when you did or tried something for the first time as a child. Use the new vocabulary. Then share your stories with the class.

➤ Go to the **Pearson Practice English App** or **MyEnglishLab** for more vocabulary practice.

NOTE-TAKING SKILL

Taking Notes with the Equal Sign

You are probably familiar with the equal sign (=) from math class. You use it to show the result of the equation: 2 + 2 = 4.

We also use the equal sign when taking notes:

1. Use the equal sign in your notes for definitions. It signals that the information on both sides of the equal sign means the same thing.

   Wristies = gloves, cover wrists, not fingers

2. Use the equal sign as a way to note people's jobs or explain who they are.

   KK = successful business owner

3. Use the equal sign in your notes instead of writing the word "is" or "are." When you hear sentences like, "The problem is. . ." or "My advice to you is. . .," you can write phrases like *Problem =* or *Advice =* in your notes.

4. Use an equal sign with a slash through it (≠) to note that two things are not the same.

   Wristies ≠ normal gloves

1 Read the sentences below. Rewrite them as notes with the equal sign.

1. Children are very creative.

   _____

2. The problem is adults are afraid to make mistakes.

   _____

3. Being a child and thinking like a child are not the same thing.

   _____

2 ▶ Listen to these sentences. Take notes using the equal sign.

1. _____

2. _____

3. _____

4. _____

3 Compare your notes with a partner's. How are they similar? How are they different?

➤ Go to **MyEnglishLab** for more note-taking practice.

COMPREHENSION

1 ▶ Listen to Professor Chandler's business class. He is telling his students why KK's experience is important for them. Create a chart like the one below to take notes. Try to use the equal sign in your notes.

TAKE NOTES Professor Chandler's Business Class	
Main Ideas	**Details**

2 Read the sentences. Write *T* (true) or *F* (false). Correct the false sentences. Use your notes to help you.

_____ 1. KK made something that many people needed.

_____ 2. KK listened only to her mother.

_____ 3. Adults understand that it's OK to make mistakes.

_____ 4. If you want to be creative, don't be afraid to make mistakes.

_____ 5. A relaxation exercise can help the students remember their childhood.

_____ 6. The students will remember a time when they were afraid.

LISTENING SKILL

1 Which phrases tell you that the speaker is going to introduce a main idea? Check (✓) your guesses. Then compare with a partner.

☐ As I was saying, . . .

☐ I agree . . .

☐ One example is . . .

☐ The second part is . . .

☐ Some people think . . .

☐ Next, let me introduce . . .

☐ To begin today, . . .

☐ The next step is . . .

☐ First, . . .

Identifying Signal Words For Main Ideas

A lecture often has a general topic (big main idea). We can usually understand this idea from the title of the lecture. There are also subtopics (smaller main ideas) in the lecture. After the subtopics, there are details and examples. Many university professors also use these ways to be clear in their lectures:

• Divide all the information into clear parts.

• Use a signal word to introduce the main idea of each part of the lecture.

A *signal word* is a word (or phrase) that gives a clue to the listener about what is coming next. When you hear the signal word, you will know that the speaker is going to say something important. Some examples of signal words are: *first, second, next.* These words usually signal that the speaker is going to tell you the main idea of the next part of the lecture. What other signal words do you know?

Try to notice signal words when you listen to a lecture. They will help you to understand how the information in the lecture is organized.

2 ▶ **Read the questions and the outline. Then listen to the beginning of Professor Chandler's lecture again and fill in the missing information.**

1. Professor Chandler wants his students to understand that KK became successful because

   she did _____ important things.

   <u>(how many?)</u>

2. How did Professor Chandler organize the information about what KK did?

Signal Words	**Main Ideas**
a. _First_____	a. _KK came up with a creative idea._____
b. _____	b. _____
c. _____	c. _____

▶ Go to **MyEnglishLab** for more skill practice.

USE YOUR NOTES

APPLY Review your notes from Listening One and Two. Use the information in your notes to complete the story.

CONNECT THE LISTENINGS 🔍

ORGANIZE

Professor Chandler told his students that KK had three important lessons to teach them.

1. Find something that people need.

2. Listen to other people.

3. Don't be afraid to do something new.

Read the sentences below. For each sentence, decide which lesson the business students can learn from KK. Write 1, 2, or 3 in the blank. Sometimes there is more than one lesson.

KK'S STORY

a. KK was wearing gloves, but her wrists were very cold. That's when she had an idea. __1__

b. Her friends wore their Wristies every day. They liked them a lot. _____

c. KK's friends told her, "You can sell your Wristies." _____

d. KK's mother had no business experience, but she thought a business was a great idea.

   _____

e. KK and her mother talked to a lot of people, asked a lot of questions, and learned a lot.

   _____

f. KK went on a TV shopping show to sell Wristies. She was nervous, but it was very exciting. She sold 6,000 pairs of Wristies. _____

SYNTHESIZE

Nathan, a student in Professor Chandler's business class, took notes during class, but he made some mistakes. He didn't understand what lessons he could learn from KK. After class, he speaks to another student to check his information.

Role-play with a partner.

Student A, you're Nathan. Read the notes you summarized to your classmate.

Student B, you're Nathan's classmate. Correct Nathan's mistakes. Then explain what lesson we can learn from KK's experience.

Use information from Organize in your conversation. Change roles after sentence 3.

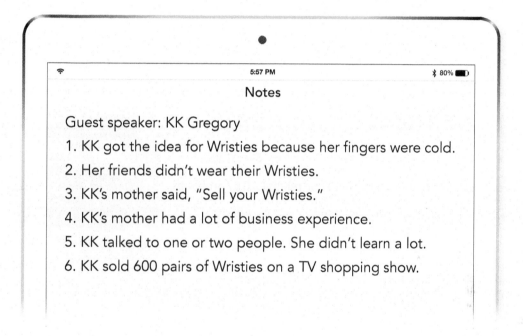

5:57 PM   ✱ 80% ▭

Notes

Guest speaker: KK Gregory

1. KK got the idea for Wristies because her fingers were cold.
2. Her friends didn't wear their Wristies.
3. KK's mother said, "Sell your Wristies."
4. KK's mother had a lot of business experience.
5. KK talked to one or two people. She didn't learn a lot.
6. KK sold 600 pairs of Wristies on a TV shopping show.

Example

NATHAN: Well, KK got the idea for Wristies because her fingers were cold, right?

CLASSMATE: Sorry, that's not right. KK was wearing gloves, so her fingers were not cold. Her wrists were cold, and she needed something to make them warm. That's how we learn that to have a successful business, you have to find something that people need.

🔵 Go to **MyEnglishLab** to check what you learned.

VOCABULARY

REVIEW

Work in pairs. Read the story about another young and creative business owner, Brent Simmons. Complete the sentences with words from the box. Then take turns reading the paragraphs aloud.

advice	completely	exciting	increases	owner
afraid to	creative	experience	makes me feel (+ adj.)	successful
came up with	employees	for the first time	made mistakes	

BRENT SIMMONS, "COMPUTER DOC"

When Brent Simmons was 10 years old, he knew everything about computers. Whenever his friends or relatives had problems with their computers, they came to Brent to ask for his

_____. Sometimes, computer store
    1.

_____ said, "It's impossible to fix this
    2.

computer. It is _____ broken." But Brent was never
                      3.

_____ look for a new way to fix it. Sometimes he _____
    4.   5.

and he had to start again. But in the end, he usually _____ a new, very
                                                                          6.

_____ way to fix the computer.
    7.

Brent Simmons

Brent loved to fix computers, and he had a lot of _____. So, when he was
                                                                    8.

14, he started his own business. Brent is the _____ of the "Computer Doc"
                                                            9.

company. When people meet Brent _____, they often think, "He's just a
                                              10.

kid. He can't fix my computer." But after they see his work, they are surprised.

Now Brent is 18 years old. He made more than $50,000 a year when he was in high school, and

the number of people he helps _____ every year. His business is very
                                          11.

_____. But Brent doesn't do this work just to make money. Brent says, "It's
    12.

_____ to do work that I love and to help people, too. Sometimes people
    13.

come to me with very difficult computer problems. When I can find the problem and fix it, they

are so happy. Helping people with their computer problems _____ great.
                                                                            14.

EXPAND

1 ▶ **Read and listen to the paragraph about creativity and stress.**

. . . where the experts go for business advice.

Creativity experts say that when people feel **stressed out**, they can't be creative. These experts have some unusual advice about how to help employees **reduce** their **stress**.

One idea is to give free massages and yoga classes at work. These can help employees to **relax**. They also say that companies should give their employees time to **exercise** and **do sports**. When employees exercise and do sports, they **have fun**, and it also helps them to **stay healthy**. Creativity experts say that all these unusual **perks** can help employees to be more creative in their work.

Reduce stress at work with our helpful tips!

2 **Work with a partner. Student A, read a sentence in the left column. Student B, read the correct response from the right column. Switch roles for Conversation 2.**

Conversation 1: The Creative Ideas Company

1. The employees at Creative Ideas Company can have free massages every day at work.

2. The company also gives them time to exercise.

3. Yeah, so the employees at Creative Ideas say that they never feel stressed out at work.

a. They're really lucky! Their company helps them to reduce their stress in many ways. And then they can be more creative.

b. Well, everyone knows that that's the number one way to stay healthy.

c. Wow, what an unusual perk! It's such a great way to relax and clear your mind.

Conversation 2: The Imagine Ads Company

4. Listen to this. The employees at Imagine Ads play basketball every afternoon!

5. Yeah, and I think it's also a good way to reduce their stress.

6. The owner of Imagine Ads wants to help her employees increase their creativity.

d. Well, doing sports together is a great way for employees to have fun!

e. That's why she gives her employees these great perks!

f. I agree. When you feel stressed out, it's hard to be creative.

CREATE

APPLY Interview two classmates with the following questions. When it is your turn to answer the questions, use the words from Review and Expand.

1. When do you usually feel **stressed out**? How do you try to **reduce** your **stress**? Does it always help?

2. In your opinion, is it a good idea for **employees** to **relax** at work? Is it a good idea for them to **have fun**? Why or why not?

3. When people **do sports** (like playing soccer or basketball), does it usually **reduce** their **stress** or increase it? What are some other good ways to **stay healthy**? Explain.

4. Do you know of any companies that give their employees unusual **perks**? What are they?

5. Do you know a successful business **owner**? How did he or she become successful?

6. Are you ever afraid to **make a mistake**? In what situations? Why?

7. "Great ideas sometimes come from mistakes." Do you agree with this statement? Explain why or why not.

8. Did you ever solve a problem in a **creative** way? How did you **come up with** the **creative** idea?

Go to the **Pearson Practice English App** or **MyEnglishLab** for more vocabulary practice.

GRAMMAR FOR SPEAKING

1 Read the conversation. Follow the directions.

PROF. CHANDLER: Are there any more questions?

STUDENT: Yes. Were there any problems in the beginning?

KK: Yeah, there were a few problems. For example, business was very slow at first because there weren't any other people in my company. There was only one person—me! Now there are three employees.

1. Find and underline *there are, there was, there were,* and *there weren't* in the conversation.

2. Which ones talk about the present? Which ones talk about the past?

3. Which one (*there was / there were*) talks about only one thing (singular)? Which one (*there was / there were*) talks about more than one thing (plural)?

4. Find and underline *Are there* and *Were there.* Do you use this word order in a statement or in a question?

Using *There Is / Are / Was / Were*

1. Use **there is** or **there are** to describe a situation in the present.

There is + **a** + singular count noun (a noun like *table*, *book*, and *pencil*)	There is a website.
There is + non-count noun (a noun like *money*, *water*, and *food*).	There is information about Wristies on the website.
Use the contraction (short form) **There's** in speaking or informal writing.	There's a website.
	There's information about Wristies on the website.
There are + plural count noun (nouns like *tables*, *books*, and *pencils*).	There are many places where you can wear Wristies.

2. Use **there was** or **there were** to describe a situation in the past.

There was + **a** + singular count noun	**There was** a problem in the beginning.
There was + non-count noun	**There was** snow on the ground.
There were + plural count noun	**There were** problems in the beginning.

3. To form a negative statement, add the contraction **n't** (short form of **not**).

	There isn't any snow.
	There aren't any more questions.
	There weren't many employees.

4. For questions, put **is / are** or **was / were** before **there**.

	Are there any questions?
	Was there a problem yesterday?
	When **was there** a problem?

In *yes / no* questions, use **a** with singular nouns, and **any** with plural nouns and non-count nouns.

	Is there a problem?
	Were there any problems?
	Was there any snow?

2 Read the interview with Raj Singh, founder of the Joyful Company. Fill in the blanks using *there* + a form of the verb *be*. Use the contraction *there's* when possible.

RAJ: Welcome to Joyful! Please come in.

INTERVIEWER: Wow! This office is very unusual.

RAJ: Yes, when people come to our office for the first time, they're usually surprised.

INTERVIEWER: Is this your meeting room?

RAJ: No, _____ any meeting rooms at Joyful. This is a "playroom."
　　　　　　　1. (neg.)

INTERVIEWER: A playroom?

RAJ: Sure. We learn to be creative from children, and children play. So this playroom is where we come up with all our new ideas. _____ a meeting in
　　　　　　　　　　　　　　　　　　　　　　　　　　　　　2.
this playroom one hour ago. Let's look around.

INTERVIEWER: But . . . _____ any tables or chairs in this room. _____
　　　　　　　　　3. (neg.)　　　　　　　　　　　　　　　　　　　　　　　4.
really a business meeting here? Are you sure? It looks like children were

playing here. _____ balls and children's toys on the floor, and
　　　　　　　　5.
_____ pictures and pieces of paper on the floor and walls.
　　6.

RAJ: Those are some ways that we try to increase our creativity. Boring meetings give people boring ideas. Joyful meetings are exciting! In Joyful meetings, the employees play. And _____ a table in the room because we
　　　　　　　　　　　　　　　　　7. (neg.)
don't need one. We write our ideas on special material on the walls. Do you

see that? _____ a special camera in each playroom. The camera
　　　　　　　8.
photographs everything that we write on the walls. OK, now look over there.

On that wall, _____ a list of all the new ideas from the meeting.
　　　　　　　　　　9.

Let's see . . . _____ ten people in this room for one hour, and now
　　　　　　　　　　10.
_____ 50 new ideas on this list.
　　11.

INTERVIEWER: This is really an unusual place to work.

RAJ: Yeah. Working here is fun, and we're also very successful!

3 Now read the interview aloud with a partner. Switch roles and read it again.

4 APPLY Think of an office you have seen, visited, or worked in. Was it similar to or different from the Joyful Company? Take turns describing this office to your partner. Use *there* + a form of the verb *be*.

🄰 Go to **MyEnglishLab** for more grammar practice.

PRONUNCIATION

Pronouncing *th* Sounds

Put the tip of your tongue between your teeth.

This is the most important part of the pronunciation of the "th" sound.

Blow out air to make the sound. Be careful: Keep the tip of your tongue between your teeth while you blow out the air.

The "th" sound in *they, them, there, then, these,* and *mother* is a voiced sound. This means that the vocal cords (a part of your throat that makes sound) vibrate (move up and down or back and forth quickly).

The "th" sound in *thumb, thought, things, anything, think,* and *thousand* is a voiceless sound. The vocal cords do not vibrate.

The tip of the tongue is between the teeth for both sounds.

1 ▶ **Underline every word that has a "th" sound. Then read the sentences aloud to a partner. Be sure to pronounce all the "th" sounds correctly. Then listen to the sentences to check your pronunciation.**

1. They're long gloves with no fingers.

2. There's a hole for the thumb.

3. Some people wear them outside; others wear them inside.

4. They all wore them every day.

5. So then I thought, "I can sell these things!"

6. My mother didn't know anything about business.

7. A lot of stores sell them, and there's also a website.

2 **Work with a partner. Student A, ask the first question. Student B, answer the question using a word from the box. Student A, listen to your partner's answer. Say, "That's right" or "I don't think that's right." If you don't think it's right, discuss why. Take turns being A and B.**

anything	mother	thinks	thought	~~thousand~~	thumb

Example

A: How many Wristies did KK sell on TV?

B: She sold six _____*thousand*_____ !

A: _____*That's right*_____ .

1. **A:** Why does KK like business?

   B: She _____ it's exciting.

   A: _____

2. **A:** Who helped KK a lot?

   B: Her _____ did.

   A: _____

3. **A:** Did KK know a lot about business when she was 10?

   B: No, she didn't know _____!

   A: _____

4. **A:** Did KK's mother like the idea of selling Wristies?

   B: Yes, she _____ it was a good idea.

   A: _____

5. **A:** Why do Wristies have a little hole?

   B: That's for the _____ .

   A: _____

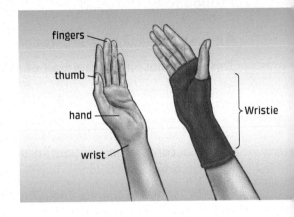

fingers
thumb
hand
wrist
Wristie

SPEAKING SKILL

Reacting to Information

When people tell us new information, we usually show our interest. The expression we use to react depends on how new the information is to us and whether or not we find it interesting, surprising, or unusual.

REACTING TO NEW AND INTERESTING INFORMATION		
	KK:	And that's how I made the first pair of Wristies.
That's (so) interesting.	**Prof. Chandler:**	That's so interesting.
Uh-huh . . .	**KK:**	So, I asked my mother about it, and she thought it was a great idea. And she helped me to start my company.
Really . . . (*falling intonation*)	**Prof. Chandler:**	Really . . .

REACTING TO NEW AND SURPRISING / UNUSUAL INFORMATION		
Wow!	**KK:**	I'm 17 now, but when I started my company, I was 10.
That's amazing! / incredible! / unbelievable!	**Student:**	Wow! That's unbelievable!
Really?! (*rising intonation*)	**KK:**	I sold six thousand pairs of Wristies in 6 minutes!
That's great! / wonderful!	**Student:**	That's great!

Practice reading the reactions in the chart on the previous page. Then role-play the conversation about Google® World Headquarters with a partner. Student A, read the sentence. Student B, respond with the best expression from the chart. Take turns being A and B. Try to use all of the expressions.

1. **A:** Did you know that Google employees can wear jeans to work?

   B: _____

2. **A:** Listen to this! There is a real dinosaur skeleton[1] on the first floor of Google's office!

   B: _____

3. **A:** Google employees play roller hockey[2] twice a week in the parking lot.

   B: _____

4. **A:** Did you know that Google employees can bring their dogs to work?

   B: _____

5. **A:** Google bought its building in California for $319 million.

   B: _____

6. **A:** There are giant red and blue rubber balls all over Google's office.

   B: _____

7. **A:** At Google, three or four employees work together in one space with no walls.

   B: _____

   _____

8. **A:** In the Google office, there's an exercise room that is open 24 hours a day.

   B: _____

   _____

---

[1] **skeleton:** all the bones in an animal or person

[2] **roller hockey:** a sport played on the street; players use long curved sticks to hit a ball into a goal; the players wear Rollerblades®

🔵 Go to **MyEnglishLab** for more skill practice and to check what you learned.

You are going to role-play a business meeting at an advertising company called the Joyful Company. The Joyful Company's business in California is very successful, so now they want to build a new office in New York. They want to design an office that will increase their employees' creativity.

The company has decided to have a competition to see which employee can come up with the best plan. The winner will get four weeks of vacation. Today, two office designers from the Joyful Company are meeting with two vice presidents (VPs) of their company. The VPs will ask the designers questions about their plans. Then the VPs will decide which ideas from each plan are the best.

The plan with the most ideas for the new office is the winner of the competition!

STEP 1

1 **Form three large groups and follow the directions:**

Vice Presidents: Read the example questions in Student Activities on page 202. Write at least five more questions to ask the office designers.

Office designers of Plan A: Read the list of ideas for your plan in Student Activities on page 203. Discuss the ideas in your plan. Choose eight ideas that are the most important for increasing creativity at work. Take short notes to use in your role-play on why you chose these ideas.

Office designers of Plan B: Read the list of ideas for your plan in Student Activities on page 203. Discuss the ideas in your plan. Choose eight ideas that are the most important for increasing creativity at work. Take short notes to use in your role-play on why you chose these ideas.

2 **APPLY** Use the vocabulary, grammar, pronunciation, and speaking skills from the unit. Use the checklist to help you.

☐ **Vocabulary:** Look at the list of vocabulary on page 101. Which words can you use in your questions and answers? Choose at least six words and add them to your notes.

☐ **Grammar:** Look at your notes. Did you use *there is, there are, there was,* or *there were*? Try to add this grammar where it is possible.

☐ **Pronunciation:** Circle any words that have the "th" sound in your notes (including "there" from the grammar). Practice pronouncing the "th" words with your partners.

☐ **Speaking Skill:** Choose two ways to react to interesting information and two ways to react to surprising or unusual information when you discuss, present, and hear all the ideas.

STEP 2

1 **Work with the partners in your group.**

VPs: Practice reading your questions aloud.

Office designers: Practice explaining the ideas in your plan aloud. Use your notes to help you.

2 **Listen to your partners and give feedback. Use the checklist to help you.**

☐ Did they use the new language correctly?

☐ Did they explain their ideas clearly?

☐ Do they need to change anything?

STEP 3

1 Form three new groups. Each group will have two VPs, one designer of Plan A, and one designer of Plan B.

2 The two VPs will take turns asking questions, and the Plan A and Plan B designers will answer. Read the example below. Notice the new language in boldface:

Example

    VP: In your plan, **is there** a way for **employees** to **relax**?

  PLAN A: Yes, **there is** a massage room with free massages, so when **employees** are **stressed out**, they can get a massage.

    VP: **That's great!** A massage is a good way to **relax**.

  PLAN B: In our plan, there is a meditation room, so when **employees** want to **relax**, there is a quiet place for them to go.

    VP: **That's interesting** . . .

3 After the VPs hear the two answers to each question, they will have one minute to decide which idea is better for their new office. One VP will take notes on their decisions. Then they will continue with the next question.

4 Discuss the decisions and determine the winner.

  VPs: After hearing all the answers, take turns announcing which ideas you chose from Plan A and Plan B.

  Office designers A and B: Listen to the VPs' decisions and look at your notes. Check off which ideas the VPs chose from your plan, and tell your group the number. The office designer with the most ideas for the new office is the winner!

  Announce the winner from each group to the class.

ALTERNATIVE SPEAKING TOPIC

APPLY Many companies want their employees to be more creative. These companies have unusual activities for employees. Here are some of the activities. Which are good ways to increase creativity? Which are not? Check (✓) the boxes. Then explain your reasons to a small group of classmates. Use the vocabulary, grammar, pronunciation, and speaking skills from the unit.

	It's a good idea.	It's not a good idea.	I'm not sure.
Doing exciting outdoor sports together (rock climbing, whitewater rafting, etc.)			
Studying music (alone or with co-workers)			
Sometimes working at home			
Learning how to meditate or do yoga			
Playing with children's toys (electric trains, giant rubber balls, air hockey, etc.)			
Writing new ideas on the walls			
Getting a massage during work time			
Exercising in the gym during work time			

CHECK WHAT YOU'VE LEARNED

Check (✔) the outcomes you've met and vocabulary you've learned. Put an X next to the skills and vocabulary you still need to practice.

Learning Outcomes
- ☐ Make inferences about contrasting ideas
- ☐ Take notes with the equal sign
- ☐ Identify signal words for main ideas
- ☐ Use *there is / are / was / were*
- ☐ Pronounce *th* sounds
- ☐ React to information

Vocabulary
- ☐ advice
- ☐ creative AWL
- ☐ creativity AWL
- ☐ employees
- ☐ exciting
- ☐ experience
- ☐ successful

Multi-word Units
- ☐ be afraid
- ☐ come up with
- ☐ completely new
- ☐ for the first time
- ☐ increase their creativity
- ☐ make mistakes
- ☐ make you feel good

🔘 Go to **MyEnglishLab** to watch a video about selling hot dogs, access the Unit Project, and take the Unit 4 Achievement Test.

LEARNING OUTCOMES

- > Infer the meaning of exaggerations
- > Take notes with bullets and dashes
- > Recognize contradictions

- > Use the simple past
- > Pronounce *-ed* endings
- > Give orders, advice, and encouragement

🡒 Go to **MyEnglishLab** to check what you know.

Understanding Fears and Phobias

1 FOCUS ON THE TOPIC

1. Look at the photo. What is happening? How does it make you feel? Would you do this? Why or Why not?

2. What are some things that many people are afraid of? Why do you think they are afraid of these things?

3. How does having a fear change a person's life?

VOCABULARY

1 ▶ **A phobia is a very strong fear. Read and listen to the blog about arachnophobia, the fear of spiders. Notice the boldfaced words. Try to guess their meanings.**

PHOBIAS: You Are Not Alone

Arachnophobia

There are many different kinds of phobias. One is arachnophobia, the **fear** of spiders. People with arachnophobia are very scared of spiders. Their hearts beat fast when they see a spider, and sometimes they cry or **shake**. Other people laugh at them. They say, "Why are you so afraid of a little spider?" But remember—many people have this problem. Having arachnophobia is not your fault.

Comments

(1) Thanks for explaining this. I am very scared of spiders. Sometimes, I can't sleep at night because I worry about spiders in my house. My friends say that I'm really not **in danger**, but spiders are **still** a big problem for me. I feel like they're going to kill me! (**Just kidding.**)

—*Fatima*   4hrs ago   Reply

(2) I worry about spiders, too. This is **a serious issue** in my life. Do you know that some spiders can **hurt** you? That's why I look for them in my house. And I worry about spiders outside the house, too. Spiders are everywhere. You can't always see them—but they're there. I don't know what to do. I'm **confused** about this, and sometimes I'**m angry with** myself.

—*David*   2hrs ago   Reply

2 **Match the words and phrases with the definitions. Write the correct word or phrase on the line.**

be angry with   in danger   not your fault   just kidding   shake

1. _____ : you didn't make a problem happen

2. _____ : I'm joking; I'm not serious.

3. _____ : in a situation that may hurt or kill you

4. _____ : move back and forth quickly

5. _____ : feel mad or upset because something is not OK

a serious issue	confused	fear	hurt	still

6. _____ : up to now

7. _____ : make a person feel pain

8. _____ : not understanding

9. _____ : feeling of being in danger

10. _____ : a big problem

Go to **MyEnglishLab** for more vocabulary practice.

PREVIEW

You are going to listen to *Human Minds,* a call-in radio show. The host of the show is Doctor Jones. She is a psychologist, someone who helps people understand their feelings.

▶ **Listen to an excerpt from the radio show. Answer the questions.**

1. According to Doctor Jones, what is a phobia? (Circle one.)

   a. a shaking body

   b. a real danger

   c. a strong fear

2. What happens to people with phobias? (Circle one.)

   a. They feel that they are in danger, but they are not.

   b. They are in real danger.

   c. They get hurt.

3. What words will you probably hear in this radio show? (Check (✓) three.)

   ☐ afraid   ☐ problem   ☐ scared

   ☐ happy   ☐ money   ☐ serious

1 ▶ Listen to the entire radio show with your books closed.

2 What did you understand from the radio show? Discuss with a partner.

3 Now practice taking notes. Create a chart like the one below. Write down any information you remember. Put big ideas or general pieces of information under Main Ideas. Put important names, words, or smaller pieces of information under Details.

TAKE NOTES Human Minds	
Main Ideas	**Details**
What is a phobia?	• very strong fear
	• body shakes + heart beats fast

4 ▶ Listen again. As you listen, add information to your notes.

5 Discuss the radio show again with a partner. What else did you understand this time? What information did you add to your notes?

◑ Go to MyEnglishLab to take notes.

MAIN IDEAS

Choose the best answer to each question. Use your notes to help you.

1. What does Doctor Jones say about phobias?

   a. A phobia can't hurt you.

   b. A phobia changes your life

2. What happened to Anna because of her phobia?

   a. She was excited in Paris.

   b. She was scared in Paris.

3. What was difficult in Anna's life after Paris?

   a. taking elevators and riding cars

   b. working in low buildings

4. How did Anna get help for her phobia?

    (a) doctors and books

    b. good friends

5. Why is Anna's life better today?

    a. She worked hard to learn about phobias.

    b. She learned to use stairs, not elevators.

6. What is Anna's advice about phobias?

    a. Don't be angry with yourself.

    b. Don't take a job for a million dollars.

DETAILS

1 ▶ **Listen again and add to your notes. Then read the sentences. Write *T* (true) or *F* (false). Correct the false information. Use your notes to help you.**

_____ 1. Arachnophobia is the fear of spiders.

_____ 2. A phobia is being afraid of danger.

_____ 3. Anna cared about the kids in the Eiffel Tower.

_____ 4. Claustrophobia is the fear of small spaces.

_____ 5. After Anna returned from Paris, her phobia got better.

_____ 6. Anna was scared of elevators and cars.

_____ 7. It was hard for Anna to visit her good friends.

_____ 8. Writing helps Anna feel less afraid.

_____ 9. Anna wanted to understand more about phobias.

_____ 10. Anna's life is easy today.

2 **With a partner, take turns summarizing your notes. Then discuss how your notes and your answers in Preview helped you understand the listening.**

↖ Go to **MyEnglishLab** for more listening practice.

The Eiffel Tower in Paris, France

Inferring the Meaning of Exaggerations

An inference is a guess about something that is not said directly.

Speakers sometimes use an exaggeration, which is a way of saying something that makes something sound better, larger, etc. than it really is, to talk about strong feelings. One example of an exaggeration is saying, "I am so hungry—I can eat a horse." Exaggerations describe things that are bigger than things in real life. Speakers use exaggerations to make what they are saying sound stronger or more interesting.

▶ **Listen to the example. Answer the question. Choose *a* or *b*.**

Example

The speaker says she felt like she "was going to die." What does this mean?

a. She was in real danger inside the Eiffel Tower.

b. She felt very afraid inside the Eiffel Tower.

Explanation

The correct answer is *b.* Usually, people do not die when they go inside high towers. This is an exaggeration. The meaning of the exaggeration is that the person had a very strong fear of high places. She wasn't really going to die, but she felt that way because her fear was very strong.

▶ **Listen to the excerpts from the radio show. Think about the exaggeration. What do you think the speaker really means?**

Excerpt One

Why does the speaker use the word *forever*?

a. To explain that she spent a long time climbing stairs

b. To explain that she wasted time because of her phobia

Excerpt Two

Why does the speaker use the phrase "twenty books a week"?

a. To express how much she loves reading books

b. To express how much she wants to understand her phobia

Excerpt Three

Why does the speaker use the phrase "a million dollars"?

a. To express that money cannot make people with elevator phobias work in high buildings

b. To explain that it costs a lot of money for people with phobias to work in high buildings

Discuss the questions with a partner.

USE YOUR NOTES

APPLY Find information in your notes to use in your discussion.

1. How did Anna's phobia change her life? In your opinion, which change was the most difficult? Why?

2. Think back. Were there signs or technology to help Anna in the Eiffel Tower? Should there be this kind of help? Explain.

3. How much did doctors and books help Anna with her phobia? What other things can help people with phobias? Explain.

🡒 Go to **MyEnglishLab** to give your opinion about another question.

LISTENING TWO | Crossing A Bridge

VOCABULARY

Read the conversation and notice the boldfaced phrases. Match the phrases on the left with the definitions on the right. Write the letter of the correct definition on the line.

YOUNG MAN: I can't ride this motorcycle. I'm going to fall!

FRIEND: **Calm down.** You can do it.

YOUNG MAN: I don't know how. **What's wrong with me?**

FRIEND: **Come on,** you can do it. You need to **believe in yourself.**

YOUNG MAN: How can I do that? I'm going to fall!

FRIEND: Just **keep going.** Don't **give up.** 🖝

___ 1. believe in yourself   a. why do I have this problem?

___ 2. calm down   b. don't stop doing something

___ 3. come on   c. stop feeling scared

___ 4. keep going   d. have a good opinion of yourself

___ 5. what's wrong with me?   e. stop trying

___ 6. give up   f. something we say to help others feel stronger

🡒 Go to the **Pearson Practice English App** or **MyEnglishLab** for more vocabulary practice.

Taking Notes with Bullets and Dashes

Details help you understand more about something important. If something is important, a speaker will give details. A good listener pays attention to details to understand important ideas.

You can organize details in your notes in different ways. Two common ways to list details include using bullets (•) or dashes (–).

Look at these two sample notes from Listening One.

Response to phobia
- body shakes
- heart beats fast
- feel danger

Response to phobia
– body shakes
– heart beats fast
– feel danger

Notice how the bullets and dashes help to organize short pieces of related information in a list, which makes them easier to write, read, and review.

1 ▶ **Listen to an excerpt from Listening Two. Use bullets or dashes to take notes on the things Allen does well. Then compare your notes with a partner.**

Main Ideas	Details
P encouraging Allen *sbor music very good*	*Allan is afraid a bridg afraid*

2 Review your notes from Listening One. How did you note your details? Rewrite a section of your notes using bullets or dashes. Then compare with a partner.

↖ Go to **MyEnglishLab** for more note-taking practice.

COMPREHENSION

Driving across a bridge is very difficult for people with bridge and driving phobias. In this listening, Allen is a man with these problems. He is driving across a bridge with the help of a psychologist.

1 ▶ **Listen to the conversation between Allen and the psychologist. Create a chart like the one below to take notes. Try to use bullets and dashes when noting details.**

TAKE NOTES	Crossing a Bridge
Main Ideas	Details

2 Use the information in your notes to circle the correct answer to complete each sentence.

1. Allen is afraid _____ .

   a. a truck will hit him

   b. of driving a truck

2. The psychologist tells Allen to believe _____ .

   a. in a book

   b. in himself

3. The psychologist tells him to _____ .

   a. look straight ahead

   b. look at the trucks

4. In the end, Allen feels _____ .

   a. very happy that he crossed the bridge

   b. unhappy because he didn't cross the bridge alone

USE YOUR NOTES

Compare your notes with a partner's. How can you improve your notes next time?

1 Read the conversation below. Do the mother and daughter agree? How do you know?

DAUGHTER: I'm tired of driving. Let's stop for lunch.

MOTHER: It's not that far. Let's keep driving.

DAUGHTER: It *is* far! Too far for me!

Recognizing Contradictions

When speakers disagree strongly with each other, they sometimes contradict each other. To contradict, you say the opposite of what the other person says. You often repeat the other person's words in a contradiction. To understand a contradiction, pay attention to words that speakers stress.

▶ **Listen to the example.**

Example

Who is disagreeing with whom? How do we know?

Explanation

In this example, the psychologist is disagreeing with Allen. He is saying the opposite of what Allen says. We know this because he puts stress on the word *not* to make the meaning clear. This contradiction shows that the psychologist disagrees with Allen about the trucks.

2 ▶ Listen to two excerpts from "Crossing a Bridge." Pay attention to contradictions. Who is disagreeing with whom? What are the two speakers disagreeing about? Which words do they stress?

Excerpt One

Who is disagreeing with whom? How do we know?

a. Allen disagrees with the psychologist.

b. The psychologist disagrees with Allen.

How do we know? He stresses the word _____.

Excerpt Two

Who is disagreeing with whom?

a. Allen disagrees with the psychologist.

b. The psychologist disagrees with Allen.

How do we know? He stresses the word _____.

⬆ Go to **MyEnglishLab** for more skill practice.

ORGANIZE

Work with a partner. Complete the chart with details about phobias.

USE YOUR NOTES

APPLY Review your notes from Listening One and Two. Use the information in your notes to complete the chart.

	Type Of Phobia	Where They Got Help	How They Feel About Phobias	How Phobias Changed Their Lives
Anna	a. fear of _elevators_ b. fear of high places _small space in_	a. books b. _Doctor_	a. A phobia is a _____. b. Don't be _stressed_. c. Does she feel OK? (Circle one.) Yes / **No**	a. After Paris, her phobia got _____. b. She took the _____ instead of elevators. c. She did not visit friends or work in _Paris_. d. She did not travel by _____.
Allen	a. fear of bridges b. fear of _high_	a. _Books_ b. doctors	a. He _____ crossing bridges. b. He feels that something is _____ with him. c. Does he feel OK? (Circle one.) **Yes** / No	a. He needed a _____ to help him cross a bridge. b. He was still afraid of _____. c. He did not think that _psychologist_ or _books_ helped him.

SYNTHESIZE

Work in groups of three to create an interview. Student A is Anna. Student B is Allen. Student C is a reporter. Complete the interview with information from the chart in Organize. Then read the conversation aloud.

REPORTER: What kind of phobias do you have?

ANNA: I have claustrophobia. This means _____ .

ALLEN: I have a phobia, too. I can't _____ .

REPORTER: Does anything help you with this?

ANNA: Yes! I think _____ .

ALLEN: I disagree. I don't think _____ .

REPORTER: Tell me more. How do you feel about having a phobia?

ALLEN: I feel _____ .

ANNA: Not me. I feel _____ .

> Go to **MyEnglishLab** to check what you learned.

VOCABULARY

REVIEW

A psychologist is speaking to a young person. This young person is worried about having a phobia. Read the conversation and fill in the blanks with the words from the box.

come on	fear	in danger	issue	wrong with

PSYCHOLOGIST: So, why are you here today? How can I help?

YOUNG MAN: Well, I'm 25 years old, and some of my friends are getting married. I have a girlfriend, but when I think about getting married, I get a really strong feeling of _____ . Do you think I have a phobia?
1.

PSYCHOLOGIST: I don't think so. Many people feel scared about getting married.

YOUNG MAN: Really? Are you sure I don't have a phobia? How do you know?

PSYCHOLOGIST: First of all, people with phobias feel like they are _____ when they
2.
are not. There's really no reason to be scared. But you have a good reason. I think you're scared because you're not ready to get married.

YOUNG MAN: But my friends are ready. They're getting married. What's _____ me?
3.
Why am I so scared? Am I just a big baby?

PSYCHOLOGIST: Oh, _____ now. Don't be angry with yourself. This is a serious
4.
_____ for many people—not feeling ready to get married.
5.

| calm down | confused | hurt | shake | still |

Young Man: Maybe you're right. But when I think about getting married, my heart beats fast

and my hands _____ . My whole body feels bad. Are you sure I don't

           6.

have a phobia?

Psychologist: I'm sure you don't. There are good reasons to feel scared of getting married.

Young Man: What are they?

Psychologist: Well, first of all, marriage is not easy. Married people sometimes fight and

_____ each other. Sometimes they're very unhappy. This is a big

         7.

decision. Don't get married if you're not sure about it. Don't do it if you feel

_____ .

      8.

Young Man: But what if I never get married? What about my parents? They really want me to

get married, but I'm _____ not sure. My parents will be so angry!

         9.

Psychologist: Please, _____ . Don't get so upset. When you are ready to get

       10.

married, you'll know it. You'll be happy, not scared.

EXPAND

1 **Read the advertisement for an e-book, *Power of Speaking in Public*.[2] Notice the boldfaced words.**

Hardcover $28.99   Paperback $18.99   Audiobook $6.99

Power of Speaking in Public

★★★★☆ 148 customer reviews

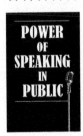

Do you know the #1 fear of Americans? Speaking in public! Are you afraid of speaking in public? You are not alone. This is a very **common** problem. You can **deal with** your fear today. You can become more **confident**. Our e-book, *Power of Speaking in Public*, will really give you **power**. You will speak better and better. You will lose all your fear of speaking in front of others. Try the *Power of Speaking in Public*!

ADD TO CART

---

[2] **speaking in public:** speaking in front of a large group of people

2 Complete the sentences by matching each sentence beginning on the left with the correct ending on the right. Write the letter of the correct ending on the line.

_____ 1. If a problem is **common,** . . .

_____ 2. When you **deal with** a problem, . . .

_____ 3. **Confident** people . . .

_____ 4. If you have **power,** . . .

a. you find a way to solve it.

b. believe they can do things.

c. you can change a situation.

d. many people have it.

CREATE

APPLY **Look at the list of fears. Discuss the questions with a partner. Use these words from Review and Expand:** *fear, hurt, in danger, shake, common, confident, deal with.*

| darkness | dogs | driving | elevators | insects | public speaking |

1. Why are these fears serious issues for people?

2. What's the best way to deal with these fears?

3. Which one of these fears do you think is common? Why?

Go to the **Pearson Practice English App** or **MyEnglishLab** for more vocabulary practice.

GRAMMAR FOR SPEAKING

1 Read the excerpts. Then answer the questions.

Excerpt One

ANNA: So I started running down the stairs really fast. I was so scared—I had to get out.

Excerpt Two

PSYCHOLOGIST: There! You did it! You crossed the bridge.

ALLEN: We crossed the bridge.

1. What are the verbs? Underline them.

2. How are the verbs similar? How are they different?

Use the simple past to describe finished actions or situations.

1. We use the simple past to talk about a specific time in the past: *last year, last month, yesterday,* and so on.	*Anna **started** running down the stairs.* *Allen **talked** to his psychologist yesterday.*
2. Some simple past verbs are regular. Add *-ed* to the verbs (*walked, wanted*).	*Allen **walked** to work. He **wanted** to stay away from cars.*
3. Some simple past regular verbs have spelling changes. If the verb ends in *-e*, only add *-d.* If the verb ends in *-y,* change it to *-i* and add *-ed.*	*Allen and Anna **decided** to learn more about their phobias.* *Allen and Anna **studied** books to help manage their phobias.*
4. Some simple past verbs are irregular (*got, became*). Common irregular past tense verbs include *did, came, gave, heard, knew, made, ran, saw, told, took,* and *understood.*	*Allen **got** scared of the trucks.* *Anna's life **became** easier.*
5. To make the negative form of the simple past, use ***didn't*** plus the base form of the verb.	*Anna **didn't take** the elevator.* *Allen **didn't cross** the bridge alone.*

2 **Complete the sentences with the simple past tense of each verb. Then read each sentence aloud with a partner.**

THE FEAR OF CLOWNS

Many children and adults react with fear to clowns. A few years ago,

British psychologists _____ the reaction of more than
1. (study)

250 children. They _____ the children about pictures
2. (ask)

of clowns in a children's hospital. All the children _____
3. (show)

strong fear. They _____ that the clown pictures
4. (say)

_____ scary. Also, in 2017, many adults _____ scared when they
5. (be)   6. (get)

_____ the remake of the movie *It*. In this movie, a clown _____
7. (watch)   8. (make)

some friends and then _____ them. After watching this movie, some people
9. (hurt)

_____, and their hearts _____ fast. Recently, one psychologist in
10. (cry)   11. (beat)

Canada _____ that clowns are scary because they wear a lot of makeup. In her
12. (explain)

opinion, people need to see faces. She believes that people have a strong reason to be afraid

of clowns. It is because they cannot see their real faces.

3 **APPLY** Use the simple past to discuss fears or phobias that you or someone else had in the past. (Remember: a phobia is a very strong fear.) Student A, interview Student B. Then switch roles.

Interview Questions

1. What kind of fear did you (or someone else) have?

2. How old were you (or someone else)?

3. Why did you (or someone else) have this fear? Was there a real reason for this fear?

4. How did you (or the other person) feel? Were you angry or confused?

5. How strong was this fear? How did this fear change you (or the other person's life)?

Example of a Report to the Class

My partner is Manuel. When Manuel **was** 10 years old, he **was** very afraid of dogs. He **had** a reason for this fear. One time, a big dog **hurt** his older brother. After this, he started shaking when he **saw** dogs. His heart **beat** faster, and he **cried**. He **stayed** home often. Sometimes, when friends **invited** him to their houses, he **didn't go**. He **didn't want** to see their dogs.

Go to the **Pearson Practice English App** or **MyEnglishLab** for more grammar practice. Check what you learned in **MyEnglishLab**.

PRONUNCIATION

Pronouncing -ed Endings

The **-ed** ending is sometimes pronounced as a new syllable. A syllable is a part of a word with a vowel sound. For example, there is one syllable, or vowel sound, in "want." There are two syllables, or vowel sounds, in "wanted."

▶ **Listen to Allen's explanation of an accident.**

Example

Allen: The driver in front of me <u>stopped</u> quickly. I don't know why he <u>needed</u> to stop. I tried to stop, too, but it was too late. When I <u>stopped</u>, the driver behind me <u>crashed</u>[3] into my car!

Look at the underlined verbs. Read each one out loud. Which verb has a new syllable?

Pronounciation of -ed Endings	
1. If the last sound in the base verb is /d/ or /t/, **-ed** is pronounced as a new syllable: /ɪd/ or /əd/.	/ɪd/ The other driver **wanted** to stop. /ɪd/ I **decided** to stop, too.
2. With other verbs, the **-ed** ending is pronounced as a new sound, not a syllable: a. If the last sound in the base verb is /p/, /f/, /k/, /s/, /ʃ/, or /tʃ/, **-ed** is pronounced /t/. These voiceless sounds are followed by /t/, which is also voiceless. (See the phonetic alphabet on page 233.) b. After all other verbs, the **-ed** ending is pronounced /d/. (See the phonetic alphabet on page 233.)	/t/ The car **stopped** quickly. /t/ The driver **watched** other cars. /d/ Allen **explained** the accident. /d/ Allen **changed** his way of driving.

1 ▶ **Listen to the words. Circle the pronunciation of the -ed ending that you hear.**

1. wanted   /t/   /d/   /ɪd/
2. changed   /t/   /d/   /ɪd/
3. tried   /t/   /d/   /ɪd/
4. needed   /t/   /d/   /ɪd/

5. walked   /t/   /d/   /ɪd/
6. decided   /t/   /d/   /ɪd/
7. stopped   /t/   /d/   /ɪd/
8. started   /t/   /d/   /ɪd/

2 ▶ **Listen to the sentences about Dr. Jones, the psychologist in Listening One. Repeat each sentence and look at the underlined verbs. Is -ed pronounced /t/, /d/, or /ɪd/? Write your answers above the verbs.**

        / /

1. She <u>wanted</u> to help others with their problems.

---

[3] **crash:** to hit very hard

2. She <u>studied</u> at New York University. ^{/ /}

3. After she <u>graduated</u>, she became a psychologist. ^{/ /}

4. She <u>worked</u> at a hospital for three years. ^{/ /}

5. She <u>talked</u> to many people about their problems. ^{/ /}

6. Then she <u>decided</u> to start a radio show. ^{/ /}

7. She <u>helped</u> many people with fears and phobias. ^{/ /}

8. She also <u>earned</u> a lot of money for her work. ^{/ /}

9. After many years of working, she <u>stopped</u>. ^{/ /}

10. She <u>decided</u> to enjoy life at the beach. ^{/ /}

3 **Work in small groups. Take turns telling the story of Allen's phobia. One person will start the story, and the other members will continue it. Remember to use the simple past and pronounce the -ed endings correctly.**

Example

When Allen was a young man, he

a. (start) to be afraid of many things.

The correct response is: ***When Allen was a young man, he started to be afraid of many things.***

1. When he was a young man, he

   a. (stop) driving his car.

   b. (walk) to work every day.

   c. (decide) to see a psychologist.

   d. *your own idea:* _____

2. While working with the psychologist, he

   a. (learn) a new way of thinking about himself.

   b. (change) his old ideas about driving.

   c. (try) to cross the bridge in his car.

   d. *your own idea:* _____

3. After working with the psychologist, he

   a. (want) to try new things.

   b. (study) planes and flying.

   c. (start) flying a small plane.

   d. *your own idea:* _____

Giving Orders, Advice, and Encouragement

Speakers often use imperatives to give orders and advice. They sometimes use imperatives to give encouragement, which means helping people to feel better. An imperative is the command form of a verb. It is always in the present tense. *Don't* is used in the negative form. The subject is "you" since the speaker is giving a command to other people. However, the word *you* is not included in the imperative.

▶ **Listen to the examples from Listening One and Listening Two. Underline the imperative in each one. Then listen again and repeat the imperative verb.**

Examples

1. Believe me, a phobia is a very serious issue.

2. Don't be angry with yourself.

3. Think of all the other things you do well.

4. Don't look at the trucks. Just look at the road.

Work with a partner to complete a conversation between two friends on a plane. Student A, you are scared of flying. Student B, use imperatives to give orders, advice, and encouragement to help Student A. Then switch roles. Use the words in the box to help you.

be	believe	calm	don't	keep	think

A: I'm so scared—I hate flying!

B: Don't _____ scared. You can do it.
        1.

A: No, I can't. I always think about crashing.

B: _____ think about that. _____ about happy things.
        2.   3.

A: I still feel scared. What's wrong with me? I'm shaking.

B: You're OK. _____ breathing, OK? Just _____ down.
                  4.   5.

A: But maybe there's something wrong with the plane.

B: _____ worry. Please, _____ me. The plane is OK.
        6.   7.

🎧 Go to **MyEnglishLab** for more skill practice and to check what you learned.

In this task, you will create and perform a one- to three-minute role-play about phobias.

STEP 1

1 **Look at the story strip. Use it to create a real conversation between the two women about a water phobia. Write down notes that will help you make a conversation.**

2 **Work in pairs. Student A, you are a person with a water phobia. Student B, you have the same phobia, but your life is better today. As you prepare for your role-play, follow these points:**

- **Student A**, explain your problem. Talk about your water phobia and all your problems—all the things you can't do in your life.

- **Student B**, talk about your life in the past. You had a difficult life with your water phobia. But your life is better today. Give some advice to Student A.

3 APPLY **Use the vocabulary, grammar, pronunciation, and speaking skills from the unit. Use the checklist to help you as you review your notes.**

☐ **Vocabulary:** Read through the list of vocabulary on page 125. Which words can you include in your role-play to make it clearer and more interesting? Choose at least three words or phrases to use.

☐ **Grammar:** What verbs will you use to share any stories or problems from your past? Are they regular or irregular verbs?

☐ **Pronunciation:** How do you pronounce the *-ed* endings of those simple past verbs?

☐ **Speaking Skill:** What kind of orders, advice, and encouragement will you give? How do you form imperatives with those words?

STEP 2

1 Practice your role-play. Make sure you are using the vocabulary and grammar from this unit. Use the correct pronunciation of past tense endings.

2 Give feedback to your partner.

☐ Did your partner use the new vocabulary correctly?

☐ How well did your partner use correct past tense forms? How well did your partner pronounce past tense endings?

☐ What did your partner do well? How can you both improve the role-play?

STEP 3

Perform your role-play for the class. Act like your character and speak naturally.

LISTENING TASK

As you listen to each role-play, think about these questions:

☐ Does it seem real?

☐ Does it show strong emotion?

☐ Does it include good advice?

Be prepared to give feedback to each pair.

ALTERNATIVE SPEAKING TOPICS

APPLY **Work in small groups. Discuss one of these topics. Use the vocabulary, grammar, pronunciation, and speaking skills from this unit.**

1. Tell the story of someone you know—a person with a serious issue in his or her life. (Serious issues include problems with health, money, fears, or other people.) Is this person happy or unhappy? How does this person deal with his or her issues? What can we learn from this person?

2. Do you believe that psychologists can really help people with their issues? Why or why not? What are some other ways to help people with their problems in life?

CHECK WHAT YOU'VE LEARNED

Check (✔) the outcomes you've met and vocabulary you've learned. Put an X next to the skills and vocabulary you still need to practice.

Learning Outcomes	Vocabulary	Multi-word Units	
☐ Infer meaning from exaggerations	☐ confused	☐ a serious issue **AWL**	☐ give up
☐ Take notes with bullets and dashes	☐ fear (*n.*)	☐ be angry with	☐ just kidding
☐ Recognize contradictions	☐ hurt	☐ be in danger	☐ keep going
☐ Use the simple past	☐ shake	☐ believe in yourself	☐ not your fault
☐ Pronounce *-ed* endings	☐ still	☐ calm down	☐ What's wrong with me?
☐ Give orders, advice, and encouragement		☐ come on	

ⓝ Go to **MyEnglishLab** to watch a video about phobias, access the Unit Project, and take the Unit 5 Achievement Test.

LEARNING OUTCOMES

- Infer the meaning of rhetorical questions
- Take notes on cause and effect
- Recognize and understand negative questions

- Use the present progressive
- Pronounce vowels /iy/ and /ɪ/
- Describe photos and visuals

 Go to **MyEnglishLab** to check what you know.

Risks and Challenges

1 FOCUS ON THE TOPIC

1. What's happening in this photo? Is it dangerous? Why or why not?

2. What are some dangerous jobs people have, or dangerous sports people play? What makes them dangerous?

3. Why do people choose to have a dangerous job or play a dangerous sport?

VOCABULARY

1 ▶ **Read and listen to the article about Diana Nyad. Notice the boldfaced words. Try to guess their meanings.**

Diana Nyad

Diana Nyad grew up in south Florida, near the ocean. When she was only eight years old, she **decided** to be the first person to swim from Cuba to Florida, a **distance** of 103 miles (166 km). Diana joined her school swim team in fifth grade. After her coach watched her for 15 minutes, he said, "Kid, one day, you're going to be the best swimmer in the world." He was right! Diana Nyad became an **amazing** swimmer, and she **set** many **world records**. From 1969 to 1979, she was the best long-**distance** swimmer in the world.

At age 28, Diana tried to reach her childhood goal for the first time. She started swimming from Cuba to Florida. **Unfortunately**, after 42 hours, the weather became very bad. There was a lot of rain and wind. Diana saw that it was impossible to reach Florida, so she had to stop. One year later, Diana set a new record. She swam the longest distance of any swimmer (man or woman) in history—102.5 miles (164 km) from the Bahamas to Florida.

Then, Diana Nyad did not swim again for 30 years.

For 30 years, Nyad worked as a TV and radio sports reporter. She was very successful, but, as she got older, she wasn't happy. She felt that she needed a new **challenge** in her life. That's when she started thinking again about her old dream. She decided to try to swim from Cuba to Florida again.

"Maybe it's impossible to reach my goal."

At the age of 60, Diana began the very difficult training. For more than a year, she swam 8 to 14 hours every day. When people asked Diana why she wanted to try the difficult swim again, she just said, "It is never too late to start your dream." The ocean between Cuba and Florida is full of **dangerous** jellyfish and sharks, but Diana **was determined** to swim **without** a shark cage to protect her.

Over the next four years, Diana started the swim from Cuba to Florida three times, but **unfortunately**, each time, the jellyfish bites and very bad weather stopped her. After the last time, Diana thought, "Maybe it's impossible to **reach my goal**," but a few days later, she changed her mind. On August 31, 2013, eleven days after her 64th birthday, Diana Nyad jumped into the ocean near Cuba and began to swim to Florida again.

▲ swimming inside a shark cage

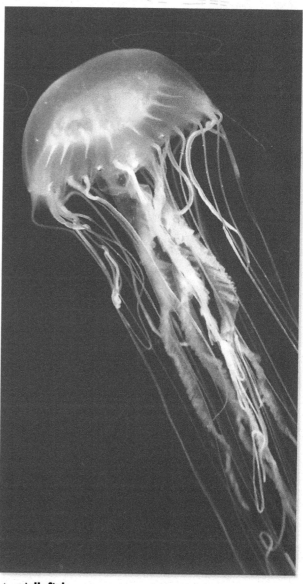

▲ a jellyfish

2 Take turns with a partner. Look at the boldfaced words in the text. Then choose the best meaning. Your partner will tell you if she or he agrees or not. The first one has been done for you.

1. **A:** **Distance** is the amount of (*space* / *time*) between two places or things.

   B: (Yes, I agree. / No, I don't think so. I think it is the amount of . . .)

2. **A:** An **amazing** swimmer means "(*an excellent* / *a good*) swimmer."

   B: (Yes, I agree. / No, I don't think so. I think it means . . .)

3. **A:** She **decided** means "She thought about something and (*made a choice* / *changed her mind*)."

   B: (Yes, I agree. / No, I don't think so. I think it means she . . .)

4. **A:** She **set world records** means "She did things (*all over the world* / *better than any other person in the world*)."

   B: (Yes, I agree. / No, I don't think so. I think it means she . . .)

5. **A:** She tried to **reach her goal** means "She tried to do something that was (*her dream* / *very important*)."

   B: (Yes, I agree. / No, I don't think so. I think it means she . . .)

6. **A:** **Unfortunately** means "This is (*lucky* / *sad*) information."

   B: (Yes, I agree. / No, I don't think so. I think it means this . . .)

7. **A:** A **challenge** is something you enjoy doing because it is (*easy* / *difficult*).

   B: (Yes, I agree. / No, I don't think so. I think it is . . .)

8. **A:** Jellyfish and sharks are **dangerous** because they (*can kill people* / *are in the ocean*).

   B: (Yes, I agree. / No, I don't think so. I think they are dangerous because they . . .)

9. **A:** She is **determined** means "No one (*can stop her* / *is better than she is*)."

   B: (Yes, I agree. / No, I don't think so. I think it means no one . . .)

10. **A:** **Without** a shark cage means "(*outside a shark cage* / *with no shark cage*)."

    B: (Yes, I agree. / No, I don't think so. I think it means . . .)

▶ Go to the **Pearson Practice English App** or **MyEnglishLab** for more vocabulary practice.

PREVIEW

▶ Two sports reporters are talking about Diana Nyad on a sports broadcast. Listen to the beginning of their news report. Check (✓) the things they are going to talk about next.

☐ Diana's world records   ☐ sharks

☐ the weather   ☐ singing songs

☐ Diana's childhood   ☐ Diana's age

☐ jellyfish   ☐ life in Cuba

1 ▶ **Listen to the entire sports broadcast with your books closed.**

2 **What did you understand from the broadcast? Discuss with your partner.**

3 **Now practice taking notes. Create a chart like the one below to take notes. Write down any information you remember. Put big ideas or general pieces of information under Main Ideas. Put important names, words, or smaller pieces of information under Details.**

TAKE NOTES   The Amazing Swimmer, Diana Nyad

Main Ideas	Details
Diana Nyad (DN) swimming Cuba → Florida, but not going well	• 4th try ⊙ 51 hrs in ocean

4 ▶ **Listen again. As you listen, add information to your notes.**

5 **Discuss the interview again with a partner. What else did you understand this time? What information did you add to your notes?**

↪ Go to **MyEnglishLab** to view example notes.

MAIN IDEAS

Choose the best word or phrase to complete each sentence. Use your notes to help you.

1. Long distance swimming is difficult because the swimmer (*is alone in the water* / *doesn't have a team of helpers*).

2. To swim long distances, Diana trains her body and her (*mind* / *breathing*).

3. Diana uses a kind of meditation[1] to help her to (*enjoy swimming more* / *continue swimming for a very long time*).

4. Diana doesn't give up easily because she enjoys (*doing dangerous things* / *having a challenge*).

5. Diana is very (*determined* / *afraid*) to reach her goal.

6. Diana is a great example for many people who want to (*set a new goal in their life* / *become amazing swimmers*).

---

[1] **meditation:** spending time in quiet thought in order to clear your mind or relax

1 ▶ **Listen again and add to your notes. Then read the false sentences below. Use your notes to help you correct them.**

1. Diana is swimming from Cuba to Florida for the fifth time.

2. Diana started swimming 31 hours ago.

3. The wind is helping Diana.

4. Diana has shark bites all over her body.

5. Long-distance swimming is very exciting.

6. Diana clears her mind by thinking about her life.

7. Diana can count to 100 in four languages.

8. Diana thinks long-distance swimming is easier for young people.

9. Diana's doctor is waiting for her in Florida.

2 **With a partner, take turns summarizing your notes. Then discuss how your notes and your answers in Preview helped you understand the listening.**

↖ Go to **MyEnglishLab** for more listening practice.

MAKE INFERENCES 🔍

Inferring the Meaning of Rhetorical Questions

An inference is a guess about something that is not said directly.

One reason people use *rhetorical questions* is to show that they have very strong feelings about something. Rhetorical questions are not real questions, so listeners do *not* answer them.

When people use rhetorical questions, they pronounce the stressed words with *extra strong stress*—much stronger stress than usual. It's important to notice the difference between real questions and *rhetorical* questions so you can understand a speaker's meaning.

▶ **Listen to Examples One and Two and answer the questions.**

Example One

What does Jim's question mean?

a. How can Diana swim in these terrible conditions?

b. It's amazing that Diana can continue swimming even in these terrible conditions!

Explanation

The correct answer is *b.* It's amazing that Diana can continue swimming even in these terrible conditions!

This is a rhetorical question. Jim wants to show how strongly he feels that Diana is an amazing swimmer. He uses extra strong stress on the question word **How** and the main verb **do.** Jim does

(continued on next page)

not expect an answer from Sue because this is not a real question. Notice that Sue responds by agreeing with Jim's strong feeling.

What does Jim's question mean?

a. How does Diana clear her mind?

b. I can't believe that Diana knows how to completely clear her mind!

Explanation

The correct answer is *a.* How does Diana clear her mind?

Jim asks the same question as in Example One, but here he is asking a real question, not a rhetorical one. He pronounces the question word **How** and the main verb **do** with regular stress. Jim asks this question because he wants Sue to explain something. Because this is a real question, Sue answers by giving him information.

▶ **Listen to the excerpts from the news report. Choose the best answer.**

Excerpt One

Is Sue's question real or rhetorical? _____

What does Sue's question mean?

a. Do you really believe that Diana counts to 1,000 in four languages and sings songs 1,000 times?

b. It's very difficult to count to 1,000 in four languages and sing songs 1,000 times! It's unbelievable that Diana can do this!

Excerpt Two

Is Jim's question real or rhetorical? _____

What does Jim's question mean?

a. How many people are as determined to reach their goal as Diana Nyad is?

b. Diana Nyad is an extremely determined person! There aren't many people like her!

Excerpt Three

Is Sue's question real or rhetorical? _____

What does Sue's question mean?

a. Can you see if Diana is having breathing problems?

b. I don't think Diana is having trouble breathing. She is too strong for that!

DISCUSS 🔍

Work in small groups. Discuss each question.

1. Why is Diana Nyad so determined to swim from Cuba to Florida? Is it always good to be so determined to reach a goal? Explain your opinion.

2. Why does Diana swim in the ocean without a shark cage? Do you agree or disagree with her decision to do this? Explain your opinion.

3. Can athletes like Diana be a good example for older people? Explain your opinion.

🔴 Go to **MyEnglishLab** to give your opinion about another question.

USE YOUR NOTES box

> **USE YOUR NOTES**
>
> **APPLY** Find information in your notes to use in your discussion.

LISTENING TWO | An Outward Journeys Experience

VOCABULARY

Work with a partner. Read the conversation and fill in the blanks with one of the words or phrases from the box. Then read the conversation aloud.

careful	discover	prove something	strong	take a risk

A: Why do people like to do dangerous sports like rock climbing and race car driving?

B: I think those people enjoy doing dangerous things. They think it's exciting to _Take a risk_ .
    1.

A: Yeah, but I think some people want to show the world that they can do something very

dangerous and be successful.

B: Maybe you're right. A lot of risk-takers are trying to _Prove Something_ to other people. They
    2.

want to be the first person in the world to do something dangerous.

A: Yeah, like the guy who walked across Niagara Falls on a tightrope. He comes from a famous

family of tightrope walkers. So they always try to _Discover_ new ways to show
    3.

people the dangerous things they can do.

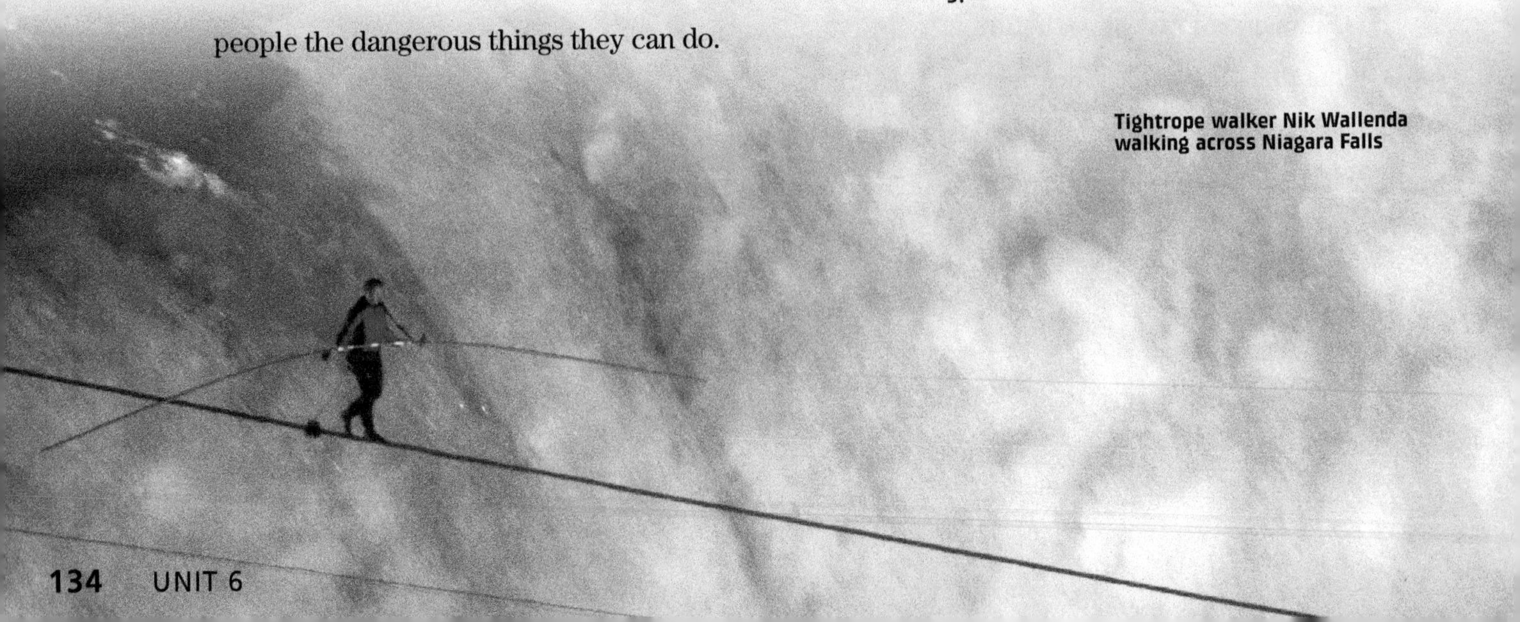

Tightrope walker Nik Wallenda walking across Niagara Falls

page 134 UNIT 6

B: Well, that's their job, right? But I think some people want to do dangerous things because they're really afraid, and they want to stop feeling that way. After they do something dangerous, they feel _Strong_ .

4.

A: That's OK if they're successful. But what if they're not _Careful_ and they make a

5.

mistake? They can really get hurt, or even die! I think it's a little crazy.

B: I know. I'm not interested in doing dangerous things at all!

▶ Go to **MyEnglishLab** for more vocabulary practice.

NOTE-TAKING SKILL

Taking Notes on Cause and Effect

Sometimes, speakers tell you about something that happened, and then they explain what happened next, as a result of the first event.

- What happened first? This action is called the **cause.**

Sometimes, speakers tell you about something that happened, and how a person felt after that.

- What happened after the cause? This is called the **result** or **effect.**

You can show the connection between causes and effects in your notes by using arrows (→). An arrow is a symbol that shows that one thing leads to another thing. Point the head of the arrow at the result or effect. If that effect causes something else to happen, you can draw another arrow after it. Look at the example below.

Example One

▶ **Listen to this excerpt from Listening One. Notice how the arrows in the notes help to show the connection between the causes and effects.**

windy → off course → longer swim

If one cause has multiple effects, you can separate the effects with commas, or you can draw several arrows coming from the same word or phrase in your notes.

Example Two

▶ **Listen to another excerpt from Listening One. Notice that the arrows show several (4) effects from the same cause.**

jellyfish bites → sick, slow, shaking, problems breathing
OR
jellyfish bites → sick
→ slow
→ shaking
→ problems breathing

1 Listen to two more short excerpts from Listening One. On a separate sheet of paper, takes notes on the causes and effects using arrows.

2 Compare your notes with a partner's. Did you identify the same causes and effects? Whose notes are simpler and clearer? Why?

Go to **MyEnglishLab** for more note-taking practice.

COMPREHENSION

Jeremy Manzi is a teenager from New Jersey. He is spending three weeks in the mountains of Wyoming with a group called Outward Journeys. In Outward Journeys, teenagers learn how to live in nature without beds, TVs, computers, or cell phones. They also experience exciting activities outside, like whitewater rafting.

1 Listen to the interview with Jeremy. Create a chart like the one below to take notes. Try to link any causes and effects in your notes with arrows.

TAKE NOTES Jeremy Manzi's Outward Journeys Experience

Main Ideas	**Details**

2 Circle the two correct answers to complete each sentence. Use your notes to help you.

1. Jeremy joined Outward Journeys _____ .

   a. to meet new people

   b. to experience new things

   c. to prove that he's not a "baby"

2. Jeremy wants to prove to _____ that he can do hard things.

   a. himself

   b. his family

   c. his group leaders

3. Jeremy thinks Outward Journeys is great because _____ .

   a. he's doing a lot of hard things

   b. he has new challenges

   c. he walks in the mountains every day

4. Before he went rock climbing, Jeremy _____ .

   a. was afraid to do it

   b. was sure that he could do it

   c. thought it was impossible to do it

5. After he went rock climbing, Jeremy _____ .

   a. felt that it was really dangerous

   b. felt excited that he did it

   c. felt more confident

6. Jeremy discovered that _____ .

   a. he's a strong person

   b. it's exciting to take risks

   c. it's dangerous to take risks

> **USE YOUR NOTES**
>
> Compare your notes with a partner's. How can you improve your notes next time?

LISTENING SKILL

1 ▶ **Listen to an excerpt from Listening Two. Why does the interviewer asks the question this way?**

Recognizing and Understanding Negative Questions

We usually ask a *yes / no* question with an affirmative verb because we are trying to get new information. We don't know if the answer will be yes or no. For example:

Did you know *how to do those things before you came here?*

Is Jeremy *excited?*

However, sometimes we feel sure that the speaker will agree with us. In these cases, we ask the question with a *negative* verb. We often ask negative questions after the speaker says something that is very surprising.

▶ **Listen to the example and answer the question.**

Example

Why does the interviewer ask "But aren't some of the things you're doing a little dangerous?" with a negative question?

Explanation

The interviewer knows that whitewater rafting and rock climbing can be dangerous and are often done by adults and not kids, so he is very surprised that Jeremy is doing those things. He asks his question with a negative verb (***aren't***) because he feels sure that Jeremy will agree with him and say "yes." Jeremy may say "no," but the interviewer thinks he will say "yes."

Compare

(affirmative question) *Are some of the things you do a little dangerous?*

In this question, the interviewer doesn't know if Jeremy will say "yes" or "no." He wants Jeremy to tell him the answer.

Note

With negative questions, we always use a contraction:

Aren't you afraid? Didn't he go rock climbing?

With the subject *I*, we use the negative form of *are* (not *am*):

Aren't I your partner?

2 ▶ **Listen carefully to the questions in each excerpt and choose the correct answer.**

Excerpt One

The interviewer thinks he _____ Jeremy's answer to his question.

a) knows

b. doesn't know

The interviewer thinks he _____ Jeremy's answer to his question.

a. knows

(b.) doesn't know

The interviewer thinks he _____ Jeremy's answer to his question.

a. knows

(b.) doesn't know

The interviewer thinks he _____ Jeremy's answer to his question.

(a.) knows

b. doesn't know

⬆ Go to **MyEnglishLab** for more skill practice.

CONNECT THE LISTENINGS 🔍

ORGANIZE

> **USE YOUR NOTES**
>
> **APPLY** Review your notes from Listening One and Two. Use the information in your notes to complete the chart.

Diana Nyad, the long-distance swimmer, and Jeremy Manzi, the teenager in Outward Journeys, both took risks. How else are they similar? How are they different?

	Diana Nyad	Jeremy Manzi
1. How old is she / he?	64	14
2. What risk did she / he take?	long-distance swimming in the ocean without _____ _____	whitewater rafting and _____ _____
3. What was her / his goal?	to be the first person to _____	to have _____ and to learn _____
4. What is she / he trying to prove?	64 is not too old to _____ _____	He's not _____
5. How dangerous was the risk?	0 5 10 not at all so-so very	0 5 10 not at all so-so very
6. How afraid was she / he during the experience?	0 5 10 not at all so-so very	0 5 10 not at all so-so very

SYNTHESIZE

Two teenagers on Outward Journeys are talking about Diana Nyad's swim to Florida. Use the information in Organize to continue their conversation. Say at least six more sentences each. Begin like this:

KEIKO: Did you hear about Diana Nyad?

EMILIA: Yeah, I think she's amazing. Can you believe she is 64 years old?

KEIKO: I know! It's pretty unbelievable. You know, we're similar to her in some ways.

EMILIA: Similar to Diana Nyad? What do you mean?

KEIKO: Well, she likes to do things that are dangerous. She swam in the ocean without a shark cage. And we're doing some dangerous things, too.

EMILIA: I don't think rock climbing with Outward Journeys is so dangerous. We're very careful, and our leaders help us.

KEIKO: Well, Diana Nyad said that she loves having new challenges.

EMILIA: OK , we . . .

But she isn't afraid of anything, and . . .

 Go to **MyEnglishLab** to check what you learned.

VOCABULARY

REVIEW

Read the homepage of the Adaptive Outdoors website. Complete the text with the words and phrases in the box. Then take turns reading the text aloud with a partner.

careful   decided   proved   take a risk
challenges   determined   reach her goals unfortunately
dangerous   discovered   strong

(handwritten notes: widious, retos, peligroso, decicion)

ADAPTIVE OUTDOORS

Adventure programs for children and adults with disabilities

Many people with physical disabilities[2] think that they cannot do any sports. However, at Adaptive Outdoors, we believe that everyone can do sports! We teach disabled people whitewater rafting, skiing, snowboarding, and many other exciting outdoor sports. Many disabled people don't do any sports because they think it's too __dangerous__ for them; they are afraid that they will get hurt. However, for the past

1.

12 years, we have __proved__ to our students again and again that this is not true. Our excellent

2.

instructors are very __careful__ when they teach disabled people, so our students are always safe.

3.

In fact, many of our instructors have disabilities, too, so they really understand how their students feel.

They also know that many people with disabilities need new __challenges__ in their lives. When people

4.

with disabilities __decided__ by trying something new, and they are successful, it is an exciting

5.

experience for them! Many students tell us that after they learned how to do a new sport, they

__discovered__ that they felt much more self-confident, not only about doing sports, but about all parts

6.

of their life. Here is what the father of one of our students said about us:

> *My wife and I both love to ski, so when our daughter was born with a disability, we thought that*
>
> *_____ she could never enjoy the sport that we love so much. When she was six, we heard*
>
> 7.
>
> *about Adaptive Outdoors, and we __take a risk__ to take her to your ski school for one week. This was*
>
> 8.
>
> *the best decision we ever made! We learned that when your child has a disability, you have to keep*
>
> *teaching her to do new, more difficult things. This teaches her how to __reach her goals__. Being*
>
> 9.
>
> *successful helps her to become a __strong__ and happy person. Now our daughter says that*
>
> 10.
>
> *skiing is easy, and she is __determined__ to learn how to snowboard! Thank you, Adaptive Outdoors!*
>
> 11.

2 **physical disabilities:** problems with one's body

EXPAND

Adjectives that end in *-ing* describe people, things, or situations. Adjectives that end in *-ed* describe people's feelings. We often use them with the verbs *be* or *feel*.

*Diana Nyad is an **amazING** swimmer* → *I was **amazED** when I heard about her.*
    (cause)   (effect)

The *-ing* adjective causes the feeling in the *-ed* adjective.

Here are some common *-ed* and *-ing* adjectives:

amazed	challenging	excited	interested	surprising
amazing	determined	exciting	interesting	tired
bored	disappointed	frightened	scared	tiring
boring	disappointing	frightening	surprised	worried

Note:
The adjective *scared* is never used with *-ing*. *Determined* and *worried* are rarely used with *-ing*.

Complete the sentences using any of the adjectives from the list. More than one answer may be possible. Be sure to use the correct form. Compare your answers with a partner's.

1. Diana Nyad thinks that long-distance swimming is _boring / challenging / tiring_ .

2. In my opinion, long-distance swimming is very _amazing_.

3. Jeremy thought that rock climbing was _frightened_

4. After he climbed up the mountain, Jeremy felt _Tired_.

5. If my son or daughter goes rock climbing, I will feel _worried_ .

6. Doing new things for the first time can be _interested_ .

7. Doing the same thing again and again is _boring_ .

8. People who never stop trying to reach their goal are very _surprised_ .

9. People were very _interesting_ when they heard Diana Nyad's story.

10. When Diana couldn't finish her swim the fourth time, she probably felt very _disappointed_

CREATE

APPLY **Work in small groups. Ask and answer the questions. Use the vocabulary from Review and Expand.**

1. Did you ever **take a risk**? What kind of **risk** was it? (Risks are not always physical. They can be financial or cultural, or involve relationships with other people.) Were you successful? How did you feel?

2. Did you ever do anything **dangerous**? What was it? Were you **careful**? How did you feel?

3. Did you ever feel very **determined** to do something? What was it? Were you successful? How did you feel?

4. Did you ever **discover** something about yourself? What was it? How did you **discover** it?

🔊 Go to the **Pearson Practice English App** or **MyEnglishLab** for more vocabulary practice.

GRAMMAR FOR SPEAKING

1 Read the excerpts from Listening One and Listening Two. Follow the directions.

a. We're speaking to you from a boat.

b. She is still swimming, but things are not going very well right now.

c. They're pulling her out of the water.

d. I'm doing a lot of new things.

e. You're discovering some new things about yourself.

1. Underline the verbs in sentences a–e.

2. What are the two parts of the verb?

   _____ + _____

3. What form of *be* is used after each subject?

   I _____   We _____

   You _____   They _____

   He / She / It _____   Things _____

4. Which sentences (a–e) tell about an action right now (at this moment)? Which sentences tell about a change that is happening these days (but not at this moment)?

   Right now / at this moment: _____

   These days / not at this moment: _____

1. Use the present progressive tense to describe actions or situations that are happening:

   a. right now, at this moment, or

   a. *She **is** still **swimming**, but things **are not going** very well.*

   b. now, as in this week, this month, this semester, this year, or these days.

   b. *You**'re discovering** some new things about yourself.*

---

2. To form the present progressive, use the present tense of *be* + the *-ing* form of the main verb.

*I**'m doing** a lot of new things.*

   a. If the main verb ends in -e, like *have,* drop the -e and add *-ing.*

***Is** she **having** problems breathing?*

   b. The verb *swim* has a consonant (*w*) / vowel (*i*) / consonant (*m*) pattern at the end. Double the final consonant (*mm*) before *-ing.* Similar verbs include *get*(ting), *begin*(ning), *put*(ting), *run*(ning), and *stop*(ping).

*Diana Nyad **is swimming** from Cuba to Florida.*

---

3. For negative sentences, use the **be verb + not** (or **n't**) + **the main verb.**

*She **is not giving** up.*
*Things **aren't going** very well.*

---

4. For **yes / no** questions, put the **be verb before the subject.**

You can answer **yes / no** questions with a **short** answer: **subject + be verb.**

***Is** she **swimming**?*
*Yes, **she is.***
*No, **she isn't.** / No, **she's not.***

---

5. For **wh-** questions, use the **question word + be verb + subject + main verb.**

***Where is** she **swimming**?*
***What are** you **doing**?*

---

6. Stative (non-action) verbs are **not** used in present progressive, even though the action is happening right now.

Stative verbs usually describe something that you are, believe, think, or feel. They do not describe an action that will end.

   a. Some common verbs that are **always** stative (non-action) are: *be, believe, hate, know, like, love, mean, need, understand,* and *want.*

*Diana **knows** how to clear her mind.*

*She **likes** challenges!*

   b. Some verbs have two meanings: a *non-action* meaning and an *action* meaning. Some common verbs with both meanings are: *feel, have, look, see, smell, taste,* and *think.*

*Everyone **thinks** I'm the "baby."*

*Diana is counting. She **isn't thinking** about anything.*

   c. When the verb **have** is used in some expressions, it has an **action meaning,** and it **can** be used in present progressive.

*She **is having** difficulty breathing.*
*We**'re having** a good time.*

Some common expressions are: *have trouble, have difficulty, have problems, have fun, have a good time,* and *have a party.*

2 It's August, 2013, and Diana Nyad is on television. Work with a partner. Fill in the blanks with the correct form of the verb in parentheses. Use present progressive for action verbs and simple present for non-action verbs. Then read the dialog aloud.

A: Hi. What _____ ?
1. (you / do)

B: I _____ Diana Nyad, the famous swimmer.
2. (watch)

A: _____ from Cuba to Florida again?
3. (she / swim)

B: Yes! This is her fifth time, and this time she's finally going to make it. She _____ the last few feet right now. This _____ so exciting!
4. (swim)   5. (be)

A: Look, she _____ up and _____ out of the water. She did it!
6. (stand)   7. (get)

B: I _____ . I can't believe it. And look at all the people on the beach. They _____ and _____ .
8. (know)   9. (cheer)   10. (scream)

A: But look at Diana's face. Wow, she _____ terrible. She's really sunburned, and she _____ standing up. Her friend _____ her to walk.
11. (look)   12. (have trouble)   13. (help)

B: Well, that's because she's so tired. She just swam for 53 hours!

A: But she _____ now. It looks like she _____ to say something. A reporter _____ over to talk to her.
14. (smile)   15. (want)   16. (go)

REPORTER 1: Sixty-four-year-old Diana Nyad has just finished her historic swim from Havana, Cuba, to Key West, Florida. She is the first person in the world to do this without a shark cage, and she is also the first person in the world to swim for 53 hours!

REPORTER 2: Diana, congratulations! Millions of people all over the world _____ you on TV right now, and they _____ all so excited that you reached your goal! Do _____ something to say to all the people who _____ you and _____ you right now?
17. (watch)   18. (be)   19. (you / have)   20. (love)   21. (watch)

DIANA: I've got three messages. One is "we should never, ever give up." Two is "you _____ never too old to chase your dreams." And three is "it _____ like a solitary³ sport, but it's a team effort."
22. (be)   23. (look)

³ **solitary:** for only one person

3 APPLY Look around your classroom. With a partner, use the present progressive to describe what is happening right now. Remember you can use verbs like *think* and *feel* when you are using the action meaning.

Go to the **Pearson Practice English App** or **MyEnglishLab** for more grammar practice. Check what you learned in **MyEnglishLab.**

Pronouncing Vowels /iy/ and /ɪ/

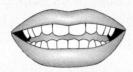 

To pronounce /iy/ (as in *eats*), the front of your tongue is very high in your mouth. Your lips are spread and tense, like a smile.

To pronounce /ɪ/ (as in *it's*), the front of your tongue is slightly (a little bit) lower. Your lips are relaxed.

1 ▶ **Listen and repeat these words with the sound /iy/.**

be, we, she, see, eat, even, easy
keep, mean, meet, teach, reach, dream
here, clear, years
we'll, feel, deal
people, really, leader, breathing
agree, believe

2 ▶ **Listen and repeat these words with the sound /ɪ/.**

if, in, is, it, it's
did, big, give, wind, with, this, sick, fish, swim, think, things
will, still
didn't, giving, distance, different, middle
finishes, difficult
conditions, continue

3 ▶ **Listen and repeat these pairs of words with /iy/ and /ɪ/.**

	A	B		A	B
1.	eat	it	6.	we'll	will
2.	eats	it's	7.	feel	fill
3.	ease	is	8.	deed	did
4.	reach	rich	9.	seek	sick
5.	leave	live	10.	these	this

4 Take turns with a partner. Read one of the words from each pair in Exercise 3. Your partner will tell you if you pronounced the word from Column A (/iy/) or Column B (/ɪ/).

5 Work with a partner. Student A, read the beginning of each sentence in Column A. Student B, fold the page or cover Column A. Listen to Student A and choose the best ending in Column B. Change roles after number 5. Notice the syllables with /iy/ and /ɪ/. Be careful to pronounce them clearly.

<table>
<tr><th>A</th><th>B</th></tr>
<tr><td>1. *Did* Diana *swim* to Florida com*pletely* alone?</td><td>some*thing* to *eat*.</td></tr>
<tr><td>2. There were thirty *people* . . .</td><td>because many jel*lyfish bit* her.</td></tr>
<tr><td>3. Every hour, the *team* gave Diana . . .</td><td>on Diana's *team*.</td></tr>
<tr><td>4. One person on the *team* used a special ma*chine* . . .</td><td>She swam alone, but *she* had a *team* on a boat.</td></tr>
<tr><td>5. Diana had trouble *swimming* . . .</td><td>to *keep* the sharks away from Diana.</td></tr>
</table>

Switch roles.

Switch roles.

<table>
<tr><td>6. When the jel*lyfish bit* Diana,</td><td>Diana *did* not *leave* the water once.</td></tr>
<tr><td>7. Diana had *difficulty breathing*,</td><td>*it* made her *feel* very *sick*.</td></tr>
<tr><td>8. For *fifty-three* hours,</td><td>"You're help*ing me* to *reach* new goals."</td></tr>
<tr><td>9. Just before Diana *reached Key* West,</td><td>but *she* con*tinued swimming*.</td></tr>
<tr><td>10. Many men and *women* write to Diana to say,</td><td>*she* stopped *swimming* for a few *min*utes and said thank you to her *team*.</td></tr>
</table>

SPEAKING SKILL

Describing Photos and Visuals

In presentations, speakers often use visuals, such as charts, graphs, diagrams, or photos to show their listeners what they are talking about. This makes a presentation more interesting. It's important for a speaker to describe a visual well so listeners can understand it and how it is connected to the rest of the presentation.

There are some common phrases we use to show a photo or visual to a group. Here are some examples:

To show a photo or visual

Please look at (this / the first / the second / the third) photo.

In this photo, X is . . .

As you can see, X is . . .

If you look at (this / the first / the second / the third) photo, you can see that X is . . .

Note: Make sure to use the present progressive tense to describe the action in the photo or visual.

APPLY Work with a partner. Imagine you have just returned from a trip. Tell your partner about it. Use your personal photos (on your phone or computer) or the photos below. Make sure to use the phrases on page 147 to describe the photos.

STUDENT A: London, England

Tower Bridge

Shakespeare's Globe Theater

LONDON

Covent Garden

STUDENT B: Toronto Canada

TORONTO

Hockey Hall of Fame

Toronto Jazz Festival

A boat tour

🅟 Go to **MyEnglishLab** for more skill practice and to check what you learned.

FINAL SPEAKING TASK: Interview 🔍 APPLY

In this activity, you are going to role-play an interview between a risk-taker and a TV news reporter. Each student will have the chance to play both the TV news reporter and the risk-taker.

STEP 1

Work in two groups: Group A and Group B. First, prepare to play the role of the TV news reporter. Here are three questions to ask the risk-taker during the interview to find out more about his or her life. With your group, add three more questions.

1. Where are you from?

2. What did you do? (What was your goal?)

3. Why did you want to take risks?

4. Weren't you _____

5. Didn't you _____

6. _____

STEP 2

1 Now prepare to play the role of the risk-taker. Group A, look at page 204. Group B, look at page 205.

   a. Take notes on the important information that you will tell the reporter about yourself and the risks you take.

   b. Look at the photos of yourself having an adventure. Prepare note cards to help you describe your photos during the interview.

2 **APPLY** Use the vocabulary, grammar, pronunciation, and speaking skills from the unit. Use the checklist to help you.

☐ **Vocabulary:** Read through the list of vocabulary on page 151. Which words can you include in your risk-taker note cards to make them clearer and more interesting? Choose at least six words or phrases to use, and add them to your notes.

☐ **Grammar:** Remember to use the present progressive tense to describe your photos. Did you include this in your note cards?

☐ **Pronunciation:** Be sure to pronounce the vowel sounds /iy/ and /I/ correctly. Notice which words in your notes and / or questions have those sounds, and practice pronouncing them.

☐ **Speaking Skill:** Be sure to describe your photos clearly and completely. Make sure to use appropriate phrases, the correct action words, and the present progressive tense.

STEP 3

Finally, form pairs with one person from Group A and one person from Group B. Role-play the interview.

- **TV news reporter:** Ask the risk-taker your questions.
- **Risk-taker:** Answer the questions that the TV news reporter asks you. Show the reporter the photos of you doing something very challenging or dangerous. Describe the photos.

When you finish, change roles.

ALTERNATIVE SPEAKING TOPICS

APPLY Discuss one of these topics. Use the vocabulary, grammar, pronunciation, and speaking skills from this unit.

1. There are many famous sayings about challenges and determination. In your own words, explain each quote. Give an example. Then say whether you agree with it, or not. Explain your opinion.

    a. "If at first you don't succeed, try, try, try again."

    b. "I've failed over and over and over again in my life, and that is why I succeed." —Michael Jordan

    c. "Take risks: If you win, you will be happy; if you lose, you will be wise.[3]"

2. Explain this quote by Amelia Earhart. What does she mean? Do you agree with her? Why or why not?

    "Please know that I am aware of the hazards[4]. I want to do it because I want to do it. Women must try to do things as men have tried. When they fail, their failure must be a challenge to others."—Amelia Earhart, American (1897–1937)

3. Did you ever do any dangerous sports? Did you ever live in nature without a cell phone, computer, TV, etc.? Tell about your experiences. If you never did these things, do you want to? Why or why not?

---

[3] **wise:** intelligent; smart
[4] **hazards:** dangers

CHECK WHAT YOU'VE LEARNED

Check (✔) the outcomes you've met and vocabulary you've learned. Put an X next to the skills and vocabulary you still need to practice.

Learning Outcomes
- ☐ Infer the meaning of rhetorical questions
- ☐ Take notes on cause and effect
- ☐ Recognize and understand negative questions
- ☐ Use the present progressive
- ☐ Pronounce vowels /iy/ and /ɪ/
- ☐ Describe photos and visuals

Vocabulary
- ☐ careful
- ☐ challenge (*n.*) AWL
- ☐ dangerous
- ☐ decide
- ☐ discover
- ☐ distance (*n.*)
- ☐ prove (something)
- ☐ strong
- ☐ unfortunately
- ☐ without

Multi-word Units
- ☐ be determined
- ☐ reach a goal
- ☐ set world records
- ☐ take a risk

➦ Go to **MyEnglishLab** to watch a video about a heroic pilot, access the Unit Project, and take the Unit 6 Achievement Test.

LEARNING OUTCOMES

> Make inferences based on word choice
> Take notes with numbers
> Recognize and understand intonation in statements

> Use *be going to* for the future
> Pronounce *going to*
> Agree and disagree

🔊 Go to **MyEnglishLab** to check what you know.

Only Child— Lonely Child?

1 FOCUS ON THE TOPIC

1. Read the title of the unit and look at the photo. What is an *only child*? What will this unit be about?

2. In your country, how many children do *most* families have?

3. Why do some parents decide to have only one child? What are some advantages and disadvantages of being an only child?

LISTENING ONE | Changing Families

1 **Lisa and Jules Conner are the parents of an only child. They started a podcast for one-child families. Work with a partner. As you read, choose the correct words to complete the transcript of the podcast.**

Our Only Child:
A Podcast for One-Child Families

Lisa: Welcome to "Our Only Child!" "Our Only Child" is the first podcast for families like us—happy families with just one child. We started this podcast because we want to share information with other one-child families.

Jules: Many people think that only children are _____lonely_____
1. (intelligent / **lonely**)
because they don't have

_____. However,
2. (a baby / **siblings**)
we all know that this is not true!

Lisa: Of course it's not true! We can spend a lot of time with our children because we don't have to

_____ other
3. (afford / **take care of**)
children. Many parents with large families don't have enough time to do this, especially if both parents work full-time. Parents with one child don't have this problem.

Lisa, Jules, and Jonathan Conner

Jules: We also know that friends are very important to only children. Many of us move to neighborhoods with lots of young families, so our children can make a lot of friends.

Lisa: We also want to share information from the latest studies about one-child families. Here's some very interesting information: Only 3 percent of the American _____ says that a one-child family is
4. (population / personal)
the best family size. But recently, Time Magazine said that one-third (33 percent) of young Americans plan to _____ just one
5. (have / make)
_____ after they _____.
6. (child / money)   7. (get married / take care of)

Jules: Why is this? Of course, every family is different, so this is a very

_____ decision for every couple. But life in most
8. (personal / population)
American cities today is expensive. It costs between $286,000 and

$324,000 to _____ a child to age 18 in the U.S.—and
9. (raise / have)
that's before paying for college! Many parents today don't

_____ enough _____ at their jobs,
10. (have / make)   11. (children / money)
so they _____ to have a big family.
12. (can't afford / make money)

Jules: That's one reason that many Americans today are

_____ the responsible decision to have just one child
13. (having / making)
and to give their child the best life possible!

2 ▶ **Now listen to the podcast and check your answers. Then read the transcript aloud with a partner.**

3 **Match the vocabulary on the left with the correct definition on the right. Write the letter of the correct definition on the line.**

_____ 1. can't afford

_____ 2. get married

_____ 3. have a child

_____ 4. lonely

_____ 5. make a decision

_____ 6. make money

_____ 7. personal

_____ 8. population

_____ 9. raise

_____ 10. sibling

_____ 11. take care of

a. brother or sister

b. decide; choose

c. do everything that someone needs; watch over

d. become a husband or wife

e. bring up a child; give a child a home, food, clothing, and education until the age of 18

f. don't have enough money (to do something)

g. give birth to a baby

h. individual; different for every person

i. sad because you are by yourself

j. earn money from your job

k. the number of people in a city, country, the world

Go to **MyEnglishLab** for more vocabulary practice.

PREVIEW

Listen to the beginning of *Changing Families,* a TV talk show. The host, Maria Sanchez, is going to talk to two families. What do you think they are going to talk about? Check (✓) your ideas.

☐ feeling lonely

☐ decisions

☐ siblings

☐ population

☐ grandparents

☐ age

☐ culture

☐ having children

☐ teachers

☐ money

☐ friends

☐ big families

☐ expensive things

☐ having just one child

Maria Sanchez from *Changing Families*

1 ▶ Listen to the entire talk show with your books closed.

2 What did you understand from the talk show? Discuss with your partner.

3 Now practice taking notes. Create a chart like the one below to take notes. Write down any information you remember. Put big ideas or general pieces of information under Main Ideas. Put important names, words, or smaller pieces of information under Details.

TAKE NOTES Changing Families

Main Ideas	Details
More families have 1 child all over world, esp. in big cities	• show = Changing Families • host = Maria Sanchez (MS) • topic = only children

4 ▶ Listen again. As you listen, add information to your notes.

5 Discuss the interview again with a partner. What else did you understand this time? What information did you add to your notes?

◖ Go to **MyEnglishLab** to view example notes.

MAIN IDEAS

Complete the sentences with the words and phrases from the box. Use your notes to help you. You will not use all of the words and phrases.

a good life	difficult	a happy child	easy
a lot of money	lonely	busy	siblings

1. Today, many people don't believe that only children are _____lonely_____.

2. For Marion and Mark, raising a young child is _____difficult_____.

3. Marion and Mark think Tonia is _____a happy child_____.

4. Tom and Jenna decided to have only one child because they don't make _____, and raising a child is expensive.

5. Tom and Jenna can afford to give one child _____a good life_____.

DETAILS

1 ▶ **Listen again and add to your notes. Then read the statements below. Write *T* (true) or *F* (false). Correct the false information. Use your notes to help you.**

_____ 1. There are more only children in big cities.

_____ 2. Marion had a baby when she was 36.

_____ 3. Marion and Mark think they are too young to have another child.

_____ 4. Tonia spends time with her parents and friends.

_____ 5. Tonia is a very popular child.

_____ 6. Maria read that only children are more interesting than children with siblings.

_____ 7. In 2050, there are going to be more than 90 billion people in the world.

_____ 8. Jenna and Tom are both teachers.

_____ 9. School, music, and traveling are important to Jenna and Tom.

_____ 10. Jay is usually bored with his friends, sports, and music.

2 **With a partner, take turns summarizing your notes. Then discuss how your notes and your answers in Preview helped you understand the listening.**

↘ Go to **MyEnglishLab** for more listening practice.

MAKE INFERENCES 🔍

Making Inferences Based on Word Choice

An inference is a guess about something that is not said directly.

We can usually understand what people mean or how they feel even if they don't explain everything directly. Their word choices often help us to infer their meaning or feelings.

▶ **Listen to the example.**

Example

1. What can we infer / understand about Mark and Marion?

   a. After they had Tonia, they thought about having another child.

   b. After they had Tonia, they never thought about having another child.

2. Which word(s) helped you to understand this? _____

Explanation

The correct answers are: 1. *a*, 2. *decided*

Mark said, **"At some point, we just decided** that we couldn't take care of Tonia and a new baby." The word **decided** helps us to understand that he and Marion **thought about and discussed** having another baby (but then they decided not to have one).

▶ Listen to the excerpts from the TV talk show. Circle the correct answer to complete each sentence.

Excerpt One

1. What can we infer about Marion and Mark?

    a. They feel too old to raise a second child.

    b. They want to raise another young child.

2. Which word(s) helped you to understand this? _____

Excerpt Two

1. What does Maria want people to understand?

    a. There is new information about only children that many people don't know.

    b. Only children are often more popular than children with siblings.

2. Which word(s) helped you to understand this? _____

Excerpt Three

1. What does Jenna want to explain?

    a. Money is more important to them now than in the past.

    b. Their son needs a lot of expensive things.

2. Which word(s) helped you to understand this? _____

DISCUSS 🔍

USE YOUR NOTES

APPLY Find information in your notes to use in your discussion.

Discuss your answers to these questions with the class.

1. What information did Maria Sanchez tell the parents about only children? Do you think this is true? Why or why not?

2. Think about the reasons that the two families gave for having only one child. In your opinion, did Marion and Mark make the right decision? Why or why not? Did Tom and Jenna make the right decision? Why or why not?

3. Did either family think about the world's population problem when they made the decision to have only one child? Do you think that people today should think about this before they have children? Why or why not?

◐ Go to MyEnglishLab to give your opinion about another question.

LISTENING TWO | How Do Only Kids Feel?

Work in pairs. Student A, read your sentence aloud. Student B, read your sentence aloud and fill in the blank with the correct word from the box. Switch roles after each conversation.

| act | alone | have fun | mature | opportunities |

1. **A:** Why did Victor's family decide to move to Chicago?

   B: They wanted Victor to take classes in music and art, but their small town didn't have many _____ for that.

2. **A:** Ling is only 11, but she reads the newspaper every day, and she can discuss the news like an adult.

   B: I know. She is very _____. Most 11-year-old kids aren't interested in the news at all.

3. **A:** I'm worried about Rafael. His teacher said he was mean to one of his classmates today.

   B: Really? What did he do? How did he _____ ?

4. **A:** There is an international party at my school tonight. Do you want to come?

   B: Yes, thanks! That sounds great. I'm sure we will _____ .

5. **A:** I'm really sorry that I can't go to the soccer match with you tomorrow.

   B: Please don't worry about it. I can go _____ . It's not a problem for me.

↪ Go to **MyEnglishLab** for more vocabulary practice.

NOTE-TAKING SKILL

Taking Notes with Numbers

One way to make your notes shorter is to write numbers as digits (*0, 1, 2,* etc.), rather than words (*zero, one, two,* etc.).

A common number you may hear is someone's age. To help you remember that a number is someone's age, you can follow it with *yr. old* or *yrs old* (an abbreviation, or shortened version, of *years old*) in your notes: 15 yrs old.

Another common number you may hear is a year or date. Don't forget that each of the months of the year is associated with a number (1–12). So, for example, you can note *January 3, 2018* like this: 1/3/18 or 1/3/2018. In the U.S., the first number is the month; the second number is the day.

You may also hear large numbers. Rather than writing *million* or *billion* or trying to write down all of those zeroes, you can use abbreviations like a capital *M* or a capital *B*: $9M or 12B people.

Finally, you can use symbols with numbers. Look at these examples:

2+ (two or more)

> 2 (more than two)

< 2 (less than two)

1 ▶ **Listen to the excerpt from Listening One. Add numbers to complete the notes. Then compare with a partner.**

Main Ideas	Details
More families have _____ child	• _____ child ≠ lonely child • In big cities, _____ child popular w/ families

2 ▶ **Listen to the excerpt from Listening One. Take notes in the Details column using numbers. Then compare with a partner.**

Main Ideas	Details
World Population Problem → small families	• World pop. ↑ • •

↳ Go to **MyEnglishLab** for more note-taking practice.

COMPREHENSION

1 ▶ **Listen to Maria Sanchez interview two only children, Tonia Carter and Jay Mori. Create a chart like the one below to take notes. Try to use numbers to take shorter and clearer notes.**

TAKE NOTES	How do only kids feel?
Main Ideas	**Details**

2 Circle the best answer to complete each sentence. Use your notes to help you.

1. Tonia _____ being an only child.

   a. likes

   b. loves

   c. doesn't like

2. Most of Tonia's friends have _____ .

   a. siblings

   b. sisters

   c. older parents

3. Tonia's mother _____ her decision to Tonia.

   a. didn't explain

   b. explained

   c. isn't going to explain

4. How does Tonia feel about her parents' decision? She _____ .

   a. understands it and agrees with it

   b. understands it but isn't happy about it

   c. doesn't understand it

5. Jay and Tonia have _____ feelings about being only children.

   a. unusual

   b. the same

   c. different

6. When Jay spends time with his parents, he feels _____ .

   a. different

   b. special

   c. uncomfortable

7. Jay and his parents enjoy _____ .

   a. traveling

   b. living in Asia

   c. staying home

8. Many of Jay's friends don't like to _____ .

   a. do things alone

   b. spend time with their parents

   c. cry like a baby

Tonia

Jay

USE YOUR NOTES

Compare your notes with a partner's. How can you improve your notes next time?

1 ▶ **Listen to the excerpt. What do you notice about the intonation at the end of the speaker's sentence? What does this intonation mean?**

Recognizing and Understanding Intontation in Statements

At the end of a sentence or idea, we use rising-falling intonation. This is the same type of intonation that we use in *Wh-* questions (see Unit 2 Pronunciation). Our voice rises and then falls to a very low note. The very low note is important because it tells the listener that we are finished talking.

▶ **Read and listen to the examples.**

Example One

MARIA: And now, let's say hello to Tom and Jenna Mori from New York City.

Sometimes, we say a sentence or idea, but we are not finished talking. We want to add another idea before another person talks. When this happens, our intonation rises a little or stays the same without going up or down. This tells the listener that you are not finished. The listener will wait for you to continue speaking and will not interrupt you.

Example Two

JENNA: We want our son Jay to have a good life—you know—to go to a good school, take piano lessons, travel . . .

We often use this intonation when we want to add one more thought before we stop speaking.

2 ▶ **Listen to the excerpts. Pay attention to the final intonation. Is the speaker finished talking? Circle your answer.**

Excerpt One

Maria is (*finished / not finished*) talking.

Excerpt Two

Jay is (*finished / not finished*) talking.

Excerpt Three

Jay is (*finished / not finished*) talking.

Excerpt Four

Maria is (*finished / not finished*) talking.

▶ Go to **MyEnglishLab** for more skill practice.

ORGANIZE

What are the advantages and disadvantages of being an only child? Complete each sentence with a phrase from the box. Then compare your sentences with a partner's. Number 1 has been done for you.

USE YOUR NOTES

APPLY Review your notes from Listening One and Two. Use the information in your notes to complete the sentences below.

can afford	feel lonely	~~more time with their parents~~
children with siblings	feel more special	siblings to play with
feel different from	less time with their parents	spending time alone

Advantages of Being an Only Child

1. Most only children can spend _more time with their parents_ .

2. Some only children _____ .

3. Only children learn to enjoy _____ .

4. Only children are more mature than _____ .

5. Parents _____ to give only children special opportunities.

Disadvantages of Being an Only Child

6. Some only children really want to have _____ .

7. Some only children _____ children with siblings.

8. Some only children don't like to spend time alone, and they sometimes _____ .

9. Some only children want to spend _____ and more time with other children.

SYNTHESIZE

Work with a partner. Student A thinks it's good to be an only child. Student B thinks it's better to have siblings. Role-play. Complete the conversation orally with information from Organize. Add five more lines each. Begin like this:

A: Do you really believe that it's bad to be an only child?

B: Yes, for sure. There are a lot of disadvantages.

A: Like what, for example?

B: Well, some only children spend too much time with their parents and not enough time with other kids.

A: That's true, but I think most of the time, children like to spend time with their parents. It can make them feel special!

B: That is possible but, . . .

🔘 Go to **MyEnglishLab** to check what you learned.

VOCABULARY

REVIEW

Work in pairs. Student A, read your sentence aloud. Student B, read your sentence aloud and fill in the blank with the correct word from the box.

decision   had fun   lonely   personal   ~~raise~~   ~~took~~ care of   tired

A: Did both of your parents work when you were a child?

B: Yes, but my grandmother lived with us. She helped my parents _____*raise*_____ me.
1.

A: Really? That's unusual in the U.S.

B: I know, but my parents are both doctors. They worked a lot, and when they came home, they were really __tire__ .
2.

A: Sure . . .

B: So my grandmother ___took care of___ me during the week.
3.

A: Did you like that?

B: Yes, I loved it. She always had a lot of time to play with me, and we always __had fun__
4.

together. I was never __lonely__ .
5.

A: That's great.

B: Yeah, and we also talked a lot about so many things. My grandmother always helped

me if I had a __personal__ problem, and she taught me how to make the best
6.

__decision__ .
7.

A: You were lucky!

B: Yeah, I agree.

Now switch roles.

| can't afford | got married | have | make a lot of money | opportunities | take care of |

B: Did I tell you the news about my brother and sister-in-law[1]?

A: No. What's happening with them?

B: Well, you know that they ___got married___ a year ago, right?

8.

A: Yeah . . .

B: Well, now they're going to ___have___ a baby!

9.

A: That's great!

B: I know. I can't believe it!

A: It's very exciting. Is Joan going to stop working after she has the baby?

B: I think she's going to stay home for three months, and then she's going to go back to work. They ___can't afford___ to live on just one salary.

10.

A: Really? Doesn't your brother have a good job?

B: Well, he loves his job, and he has a lot of ___opportunities___ to travel, but, unfortunately, he doesn't ___make a lot of money___!

11. 12.

A: Oh, so I guess they're going to get a babysitter.

B: Yeah, and my mother is going to help them to ___take care of___ the baby, too.

13.

A: That's nice.

---

[1] **sister-in law:** your brother's wife or your spouse's sister

1 This is a page from the Conners' blog, "Our Only Child." Read Columns A and B.

A

Some people think that only children have a lot of problems. *They say:*

"Problem" #1: Only children are **selfish**.

Only children get all their parents' attention, so they think they are the most important people in the world. They never think about other people. These children are selfish. This means _____.

"Problem" #2: Only children are **spoiled**.

Parents of only children are sad that their child has no siblings. They think that toys, money, and other things can make their child feel happy. But the child keeps asking for more and more. These children are spoiled. This means _____.

"Problem" #3: Only children **don't get along well with** *other children.*

Only children live with adults, so they don't learn how to act like children. They act like "little adults." They don't learn how to play with other children, and they don't feel comfortable with them. Only children don't get along well with other children. This means _____.

B

Parents of only children know this is not true!

We say: _____ We and our children are happy with our families. We don't need to buy our children lots of toys to make them happy. But our children spend more time playing by themselves, so they learn how to be alone. They are more **independent** than children with siblings. This means _____.

Our children are usually more mature than other children their age, but we know that it's very important for them to have friends. We make sure that our children always have friends to play with. Our children are usually very popular with other children. They **have many close friends**. This means _____.

_____ We give our children a lot of attention. This makes our children feel good about themselves. They also care about other people. Our children are usually **self-confident**, not selfish. This means _____.

2 **Match the boldfaced words in Column A and Column B on page 167 with the definitions below. Write the letter of the correct definition in the blank at the end of each paragraph to complete the sentence. Then check your answers with a partner.**

Definitions:

a. . . . they have a lot of very good friends.
b. . . . they can do many things without help.
c. . . . they think only about themselves.
d. . . . they believe they are good people, with good abilities.
e. . . . they have problems with other children.
f. . . . they are never satisfied. They always want more and more things.

3 **Work with a partner. Match the problem in Column A with the best response by the "Our Only Child" bloggers in Column B. Write the number of the problem on the line in front of the best response.**

4 **Change partners. Take turns reading the problems and responses aloud with your new partner. Student A, read one problem. Then Student B, read the correct response. Check with your teacher if you have different responses to the problems.**

CREATE

APPLY **Work with a small group of students. Talk about each idea in the blog post. Which ideas do you think are true? Why? Use the vocabulary from Review and Expand.**

Example

Only children are selfish. / Only children are self-confident.

A: I think most only children are selfish. It's natural. Only children spend a lot of time alone. They don't learn how to think about other people's feelings. That's why they are selfish.

B: I'm not sure about that. In my opinion, . . .

C: I . . . because . . .

1. Only children are spoiled. / Only children are independent.

2. Only children don't act like children. / Only children are mature.

3. Only children don't get along well with other children. / Only children have many close friends.

Go to the **Pearson Practice English App** or **MyEnglishLab** for more vocabulary practice.

GRAMMAR FOR SPEAKING

1 **Read Maria's sentences. Look at the underlined verbs. Then answer the questions.**

MARIA: Today we're going to talk about only children.

MARIA: Next, I'm going to talk to the kids.

1. How many parts does each verb have?

2. What is the first part?

3. What is the second part? Does it change?

4. What's the form of the last part?

1. Use **be + *going to* + the base verb** to talk about an action in the future.	*I **am going to have** lunch later.* *He **is going to go** to his friend's house tonight.*
NOTE: Use contractions in speaking and in informal writing.	*I**'m going to have** lunch later.* *He**'s going to go** to his friend's house tonight.*
2. To make a negative sentence, put **not** before ***going to***.	*I'm **not going to** travel next week.* *She's **not going to** have a big family.*
NOTE: You can also use the negative contractions *isn't* and *aren't*.	*He **isn't going to** get married soon.* *We **aren't going to** have a big family.*
3. To make questions, put a form of **be** before **the subject**.	***Are you*** *going to visit us soon?* *Where **is he** going to go next year?*
4. To answer *yes / no* questions, you can use a short form: *Yes* + subject + *be* *No* + subject + *be* + *not*	 *Yes, I am / he is / you are / we are / they are.* *No, I'm not / he's not / you're not / we're not / they're not.*
NOTE: You can use contractions in negative answers, but not in affirmative ones	*No, he isn't. / No, they aren't.* *Yes, he is.* (Not "Yes, ~~he's.~~")
5. You can use these future time expressions with ***be going to***: later / tonight / tomorrow / soon in two days / in a week / in a month / in a year this Tuesday / week / month / year next Monday / week / month / year	 *I**'m going to** move to a different city **next year**.* *We**'re going to** have dinner together **this week**.*
Note: In the present progressive tense, you can use the verb ***going*** with the preposition ***to***. These sentences are about the present, **not** the future.	*Tonia and her friend are **going to** school.* *Jay is **going to** his music lesson.*

2 Tonia is talking about her plans for the future. Complete the conversation with the correct forms of *be going to*. Then read the conversation aloud with a partner.

MARIA: I know you don't like being an only child. So, _____ you

_____ have a big family when you grow up?
   1.

TONIA: Yes, definitely! I _____ have four or five kids! Maybe six!
   2.

MARIA: Well, then your children _____ be lonely!
   3.

TONIA: Right. They _____ have a lot of brothers and sisters to play with.
   4.

MARIA: But, you know, raising so many kids is very expensive!

TONIA: Well, I _____ work hard and save a lot of money. I _____
   5.   6.

be rich!

MARIA: You _____ be rich? That's amazing!
   7.

3 Work with a small group of students.

a. On a small piece of paper, write a question using *be going to* and a phrase from columns A and B. Put all the questions in a paper bag. Give your bag to another group.

b. Take turns. Choose a question from the bag. Read it aloud. The next student has to answer it using *be going to*. Ask and answer all the questions in the bag.

A	B
go shopping	this year
take a vacation	next week
move to a different city / country	in a month
move to the countryside	soon
see a movie	tonight
study another language	tomorrow
buy a car	in _____ years
have a big family	this weekend
get a new job	in the future

Examples

Are you going to move to a different city this year?

Are you going to see a movie tonight?

4 APPLY What plans do you have for your next trip or vacation? Talk about where you want to go and the activities you want to do. Remember to use *be going to* to talk about future plans.

Go to the **Pearson Practice English App** or **MyEnglishLab** for more grammar practice. Check what you learned in **MyEnglishLab**.

PRONUNCIATION

Pronouncing *Going to*

▶ **Native speakers pronounce *going to* in two ways. Listen to the sentences. How is *going to* pronounced?**

A: *I'm going to take a vacation next month.* (pronounced /gówɪŋtə/)

B: *I'm going to see you later!* (pronounced /gə́nə/)

- In formal or careful (slow) speech, use the full form: going to /gówɪŋtə/.

  In today's lecture, I'm going to speak about only children.

- In informal or fast speech, use the reduced (short) form: *gonna* /gə́nə/.

  I'm gonna ask my mom if you can come for dinner.

Notes:

1. We do not write *gonna* in formal (academic or business) English. *Gonna* is written only in very informal writing, such as text messages.

2. Pronounce *gonna* only when it means "future," and there is another verb. When **going** is the only verb in the sentence, you cannot use the reduced form.

   Example

   a. I'm **going to** see you later! ("gonna" is OK here.)

   b. I'm **going to** class now. ("gonna" is impossible here. You must pronounce it /gówɪŋtə/.)

3. You can use /gówɪŋtə/ (the careful pronunciation) when you speak if it's more comfortable for you.

1 ▶ **Listen to the sentences. Is *going to* pronounced in the full form or the reduced form (*gonna*)? Circle the correct answer. First, listen to the examples.**

   Example

   But my mom said, "_____ have another child."

   (a.) I am not going to

   b. I'm not gonna

   Today, _____ talk about only children.

   a. we are going to

   (b.) we're gonna

1. Today, _____ meet two families with only children.

   a. we are going to

   b. we're gonna

   (continued on next page)

2. First, _____ talk with Marion and Mark Carter.

    a. we are going to

    b. we're gonna

3. OK, next, _____ talk to the kids!

    a. I am going to

    b. I'm gonna

4. _____ speak to Marion and Mark's daughter, Tonia.

    a. I'm going to

    b. I'm gonna

5. And this winter, _____ go skiing in Europe.

    a. we are going to

    b. we're gonna

2 **Match the phrases in Column A and Column B to make true sentences about you and the people in your family. (You don't have to use all the phrases in Column B.) With a partner, take turns saying your sentences aloud. You can use *going to* or *gonna*. Then share some of your sentences with the class.**

Example

A: I'm not going to have a big family.

B: I'm gonna travel this year.

A

_____ 1. I'm (not) going to

_____ 2. My (wife / husband / best friend) is probably (not) going to

_____ 3. My (mother / father) is probably (not) going to

_____ 4. My (brother / sister / cousin) is probably (not) going to

_____ 5. My parents are (not) going to

B

a. travel this year.

b. have just one child.

c. have a big family.

d. take a vacation this year.

e. have a baby soon.

f. go skiing next winter.

g. get married in a few years.

h. be busy tonight.

Agreeing and Disagreeing

There are many ways to agree with another person's opinion and to disagree politely. Here are some common phrases you can use:

To Agree	To Disagree
I agree (with you).	I disagree.
(I think) You're right.	I don't agree (with you).
That's true. / That's for sure.	I don't think so.

When You're Not Sure (Uncertain)
I'm not sure about that.
That may be true, but . . .
Maybe . . .

Example One

MARION: *But . . . well, it's not easy to raise a young child at our age.*

MARK: **That's for sure***. We're always tired!*

MARIA: *I think many young parents feel the same way!*

MARK: *Mmm . . .* **Maybe***.*

Example Two

JENNA: *I'm sure you know, teachers don't make a lot of money!*

MARIA: **That's true***. Most teachers aren't rich!*

Work in groups of four. Two students will be Group A and two students will be Group B. One student from Group A, read the statement in number 1 that you think is true. Then one student from Group B, use a phrase to agree, disagree, or say you're not sure about Group A's statement. Explain why and state your opinion. Take turns agreeing or disagreeing and stating your opinions.

Example

A: Most only children feel very different from their friends.

B: I'm not sure about that. If their friends are only children, too, they don't feel different.

Statements

1. Most only children (*feel / don't feel*) very different from their friends.

2. Only children (*are / are not*) more popular than children with siblings.

3. Only children (*are / are not*) more mature than children with siblings.

4. Many only children (*are / are not*) spoiled.

5. It's (*good / not good*) to be the youngest child in a family.

(continued on next page)

6. It's (*good / not good*) to be the oldest child in a family.

7. (*All / Not all*) children need siblings.

8. Many only children (*have trouble / don't have trouble*) making friends.

9. It's (*fine / not a good idea*) to have more than one child.

10. Children (*need / don't need*) to learn how to enjoy being alone.

🔄 Go to **MyEnglishLab** for more skill practice and to check what you learned.

FINAL SPEAKING TASK: Role-play 🔍 APPLY

In this activity, you will role-play a conversation between Matt and Jessica. Matt and Jessica are married. They have a four-year-old daughter named Katie. They are talking about having a second child. Matt is 35 years old. He wants to have another child. Jessica is 34. She isn't sure if another child is a good idea.

Read about Matt, Jessica, and Katie Smith.

The Smith Family		
• apartment: nice but very small • rent: expensive		
Matt	**Jessica**	**Katie**

• job: engineer for a large company
• siblings: two brothers, and they're all very close
• thinks it's important to have a sibling
• wants another child
	• job:
	  – day: teaches music in high school
	  – some weekday and weekend evenings: sings at a jazz club
	• siblings: one brother, but they're not very close
	• doesn't think it's important to have a sibling
	• not sure if they should have another child
		• spends time with her grandmother or babysitter when Matt and Jessica are working
		• plays with a lot of friends in the neighborhood
		• likes to:
		  – read children's books in her room
		  – play with her toys
		  – watch children's videos
		  – play games on the computer

Follow the steps.

STEP 1

The teacher will divide the class into two groups. For this first task, work alone.

Group A: You are Matt. You want to have another child. Read the information about your family in the chart. Then look back at the unit and take notes on reasons to have another child. Include some reasons about the future. You may also add your own reasons.

Group B: You are Jessica. You aren't sure you want to have another child. Read the information about your family in the chart. Then look back at the unit and take notes on reasons NOT to have another child. Include some reasons about the future. You may also add your own reasons.

STEP 2

1 **Get together with your group (Group A or Group B). Share your reasons. Discuss which reasons are best. Write them in full sentences. For example:**

MATT: _Katie is going to feel lonely if she doesn't have a sibling._

JESSICA: _Katie is going to have a lot of friends to play with, so she isn't going to be lonely._

2 **APPLY** Use the vocabulary, grammar, pronunciation, and speaking skills from the unit. Use the checklist to help you.

☐ **Vocabulary:** Read the list of vocabulary on page 177. Which words can you use when you explain your reasons? Choose at least five words or phrases to use and add them to your list of reasons.

☐ **Grammar:** Read all of your reasons, and decide which ones you can say with *be going to*. Be sure to use the correct form of the verb *be* in *be going to* when you speak.

☐ **Pronunciation:** Practice pronouncing *be going to* in the full and reduced forms.

☐ **Speaking Skill:** Decide on two phrases of agreement, disagreement, and uncertainty that you will use in your role-play.

3 Practice reading your reasons aloud to each other. Be sure to practice the phrases for agreement or disagreement, too. Give each other feedback on the use of the language and skills from the unit. How can your partners improve?

STEP 3

1 Work with a partner from the other group. Role-play a conversation between Matt and Jessica. Try to make a decision about having another child. Use the reasons on your lists.

2 Share your decisions with the class.

LISTENING TASK

Listen to your classmates. Take notes on their decisions. Did every role-play end the same way? How many pairs made the same decision?

APPLY Look at the graph. What does it show about the number of American families with only one child? Is the same thing happening where you live? Do you know why? Discuss with a group. Use the vocabulary, grammar, pronunciation, and speaking skills you learned in the unit.

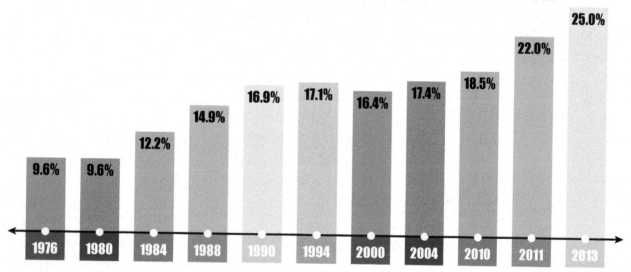

U.S. Women Age 40–44 with One Child

1976	1980	1984	1988	1990	1994	2000	2004	2010	2011	2013
9.6%	9.6%	12.2%	14.9%	16.9%	17.1%	16.4%	17.4%	18.5%	22.0%	25.0%

Source: U.S. Census Bureau

CHECK WHAT YOU'VE LEARNED

Check (✔) the outcomes you've met and vocabulary you've learned. Put an X next to the skills and vocabulary you still need to practice.

Learning Outcomes
- ☐ Make inferences based on word choice
- ☐ Take notes with numbers
- ☐ Recognize and understand intonation in statements
- ☐ Use *be going to* for the future
- ☐ Pronounce *going to*
- ☐ Agree and disagree

Vocabulary
- ☐ act (*v.*)
- ☐ alone
- ☐ lonely
- ☐ mature (*adj.*) AWL
- ☐ opportunity
- ☐ personal
- ☐ population
- ☐ raise (*v.*)
- ☐ sibling

Multi-word Units
- ☐ can't afford
- ☐ get married
- ☐ have a child
- ☐ have fun
- ☐ make a decision
- ☐ make money
- ☐ take care of

🔵 Go to **MyEnglishLab** to watch a video about birth order, access the Unit Project, and your health and take the Unit 7 Achievement Test.

LEARNING OUTCOMES

> Infer the meaning of comparisons
> Take notes with *e.g.* and *ex.*
> Identify signal words for reasons and results

> Use comparative adjectives
> Use contrastive stress
> Express results

⬤ Go to **MyEnglishLab** to check what you know.

Soccer: The Beautiful Game

1 FOCUS ON THE TOPIC

1. Look at the photo. What is the man doing?

2. Is soccer (football) a popular sport in your country? Why do you think so?

3. When is the last time you played or watched a sport? What sport was it? How did it make you feel?

LISTENING ONE | The Sports File

VOCABULARY

1 ▶ **Read and listen to a student's presentation about soccer. Notice the boldfaced words. Try to guess their meanings.**

SOCCER: THE WORLD'S MOST POPULAR SPORT

Soccer is the most popular sport in the world. Outside the U.S., people call it "football," and it's their **favorite** sport. Soccer is easy to learn because the **rules** of the game are **simple**, and the **players** don't need a lot of special things. They just need a ball to **kick** into the goal, and a **field** to play on. With a few friends, anyone can play soccer.

When a player makes a point, people in every country say, "Goal!" *Goal* is an international word. In 2018, the **teams** from France and Croatia played in the final **match** of the World Cup in Moscow, Russia. France **won** the match (4–2). It was their second World Cup title. Around 3.4 billion people watched matches during the 2018 World Cup—that is almost half of all the people living in the world.

2 Take turns with a partner. Read the sentences aloud. Choose the correct definition.

1. My **favorite** sport means (the sport I love the most / the most popular sport in my country).

2. The **rules** of a sport are (the things you must and must not do / the points you get for a goal).

3. If the rules are **simple**, the game is (easy / difficult) to understand.

4. The **players** are the people (in the game / watching the game).

5. When you **kick** a ball, you move it with your (head / foot).

6. A **field** is a place where you (play sports outside / watch the game on TV).

7. A **team** is a group of people who (watch / play) sports together against another group of players.

8. A **match** is a (game / ball).

9. My team **won** the match means my team (made more goals / played the game).

10. **Fans** are people who like to (play / watch) a sport.

▶ Go to **MyEnglishLab** for more vocabulary practice.

PREVIEW

▶ Listen to the beginning of a sports broadcast called *The Sports File*. Today's show is about soccer. What will you hear on the show? Check (✓) the items.

☐ People talking about soccer

☐ People talking about American football

☐ People discussing why soccer is so popular

☐ People describing how to become a professional soccer player

LISTEN

1 ▶ Listen to the sports broadcast with your books closed.

2 What did you understand from the broadcast? Discuss with a partner.

3 Now practice taking notes. Create a chart like the one below to take notes. Write down any information you remember. Put big ideas or general pieces of information under Main Ideas. Put important names, words, or smaller pieces of information under Details.

TAKE NOTES   The Sports File

Main Ideas	Details
Soccer = world's favorite sport	• not as popular in U.S. • in Brazil, soccer = life

4 ▶ Listen again. As you listen, add information to your notes.

5 Discuss the broadcast again with a partner. What else did you understand this time? What information did you add to your notes?

▶ Go to **MyEnglishLab** to view example notes.

MAIN IDEAS

Circle the correct answer. Use your notes to help you.

1. The main question that Jane Tuttle wants to answer is: _____ .

   a. Do people in the U.S. love soccer?

   b. Why are so many people watching soccer at Paolinho's?

   c. Why do people from most countries love soccer?

2. The four people Jane Tuttle talked to are all _____ .

   a. soccer fans from around the world

   b. sports fans from the U.S.

   c. soccer players on U.S. teams

DETAILS

1 ▶ **Listen again and add to your notes. Check (✓) two correct details about each person on *The Sports File*.**

   1. Gilberto

      ☐ is Brazilian.

      ☐ doesn't understand Jane's question.

      ✓ thinks soccer is beautiful.

   2. Ernesto

      ☐ thinks soccer brings people together.

      ✓ wants Mexico to win.

      ✓ is Anders's very good friend.

   3. Anders

      ☐ is from Italy.

      ✓ thinks people in the U.S. don't understand that soccer is great.

      ☐ likes soccer because it is a simple game.

   4. Marta

      ✓ thinks American football is hard to understand.

      ☐ has read books about football.

      ✓ thinks soccer is very exciting.

2 **With a partner, take turns summarizing your notes. Then discuss how your notes and your answers in Preview helped you understand the listening.**

🔵 Go to **MyEnglishLab** for more listening practice.

MAKE INFERENCES 🔍

Inferring the Meaning of Comparisons

An inference is a guess about something that is not said directly.

When people want to explain a difficult idea, they sometimes use a comparison. They say that two things are similar even though, at first, those things may seem very different. By thinking about how the two things are similar, you can understand the speaker's meaning.

People often use the phrase "be like" before a comparison. This means "be similar to." (It is not the same as the verb to *like*, which means "to enjoy or think something is good.")

Compare:

a. *I like my soccer coach.* (I think he's a good coach. I enjoy learning from him.)

b. *I'm like my soccer coach.* (We have similar personalities. We are the same in some ways.)

▶ **Listen to the example.**

Example

Why does Gilberto compare soccer to music?

  a. In Brazil, no one really understands why they enjoy soccer or music, so they can't explain it.

  b. In Brazil, soccer is not just a sport like other sports. Soccer is as important as music.

Explanation

The correct answer is *b.* In Brazil, soccer is not just a sport like other sports. Soccer is as important as music.

Most people enjoy listening to music because it's beautiful, or it makes them feel good. People don't need to ask, "Why do you like music?" because the reason is clear.

Most people in Brazil love soccer because it's very exciting and beautiful to watch. Brazilians never ask, "Why do you like soccer?" because almost everyone feels the same way. Gilberto is saying that both music and soccer are very important parts of life in Brazil.

▶ Listen to the excerpts from the radio show. Choose the best answer to each question. Then discuss your answer with a partner.

Why does Gilberto say that soccer players are like birds and dancers?

a. because the soccer ball flies through the air very fast

b. because soccer players are very beautiful to watch

Why does Ernesto say that soccer is like an international language?

a. because people from many different countries love soccer and can enjoy watching it together

b. because people from many different countries all speak English together when they watch a match

Why does Marta say that soccer is not like American football?

a. American football is more difficult to understand and play.

b. There are more books about American football.

DISCUSS 🔍

> **USE YOUR NOTES**
>
> **APPLY** Find information in your notes to use in your discussion.

Work in a small group. Read the questions. Discuss your ideas.

1. According to the listening, why is soccer so popular? How is soccer different from other sports?

2. Do you think another sport will ever become as popular as soccer in the future? If yes, which sport? If no, why not?

▶ Go to **MyEnglishLab** to give your opinion about another question.

LISTENING TWO | America Talks

VOCABULARY

Fill in the blanks with one of the words from the box. You will not use all the words. Then read the conversation aloud with a partner.

higher	lose	low	score (*n.*)	tie	win

A: Did you see the soccer match yesterday between Sweden and Korea?

B: No. Who won?

A: Sweden. The final _____ was 1–0, but there was a 0–0 _____ for
      1.   2.

most of the game.

B: One-nothing! I'm surprised that the final score was so _____ .
                                                              3.

A: Yeah, I expected a _____ score. And Korea had a very strong team. I didn't
                          4.

expect Korea to _____ !
                  5.

🔊 Go to the **Pearson Practice English App** or **MyEnglishLab** for more vocabulary practice.

NOTE-TAKING SKILL

Taking Notes with *e.g.* or *ex.*

Often while listening, you will hear people make a statement of opinion or fact and then follow it up with an example. An example helps to demonstrate a point or make an argument clearer to the listener. For that reason, examples are very useful to include in your notes. They will help you to better understand an opinion or fact when you review your notes later on.

A simple way to add an example in your notes is to write the abbreviation *e.g.* or *ex.* in front of the examples, as in these notes:

Many famous Brazilian soccer players, ex. Pelé, Neymar, Ronaldinho

E.g. is an abbreviation of the Latin phrase *exempli gratia*, which means "for the sake of example." You may also see this abbreviation in both academic and formal texts. *Ex.* is simply a shortened form of the word *example*. It is not used formally in published works, but it's fine to use it in your notes.

1 Write notes for the sentences using *e.g.* or *ex.* Then compare with a partner.

1. The U.S. Men's National Soccer team has players from other countries like Canada, Germany, Wales, and France.

   _____

   _____

2. Soccer players need to have strong legs to do many things. They have to run fast and for a long time; they have to move the ball with their feet and kick it to their teammates or in the goal; and they have to use their legs to block the ball or take it from the other team.

   _____

   _____

3. Some famous soccer players have other jobs like coaching teams, advertising products, and even acting in movies.

   _____

   _____

2 ▶ Listen to the excerpts from Listening One. Use *e.g.* or *ex.* to take notes on the examples you hear. Then compare your notes with a partner.

1. _____

   _____

2. _____

   _____

⬆ Go to **MyEnglishLab** for more note-taking practice.

COMPREHENSION

1 ▶ Listen to the entire radio show. Create a chart like the one below to take notes. Try to use *e.g.* or *ex.* before examples in your notes.

TAKE NOTES America Talks	
Main Ideas	**Details**

2 Decide if each statement is *T* (true) or *F* (false). Correct the false statements. Use your notes to help you.

_____ 1. Most American sports fans watched the World Cup.

_____ 2. Bob thinks Americans prefer sports with high scores.

_____ 3. Americans like sports that always have a winner.

_____ 4. America has two traditional sports.

_____ 5. Drew thinks that the U.S. needs an American soccer superstar.

> **USE YOUR NOTES**
>
> Compare your notes with a partner's. How can you improve your notes next time?

LISTENING SKILL

Identifying Signal Words for Reasons and Results

A good listener understands signal words and phrases. These are important words and phrases that help listeners to understand what kind of information they are going to hear next. Some signal words introduce reasons. They tell us why. Some signal words introduce results. They tell us the effect of something else. When you hear the signal words for reasons and results, it will help you to understand what the speaker is going to say next.

Signal Words and Phrases for Reasons	
because + (reason)	*I love soccer **because** it's exciting.*
because of + (reason)	*I love soccer **because of** the simple rules.*
NOTE: After *because,* we use a sentence with a subject and verb. After *because of,* we use a noun.	
Signal Words and Phrases for Results	
(reason) **That's why +** result	*Soccer is exciting. **That's why** I love it.*
(reason) **That's (a / the / one / another) reason (that) +** result	*Soccer is simple. **That's another reason (that)** I love it.*
NOTE: When people use these signal phrases to introduce a result, they always say the reason first.	

▶ Listen to this excerpt from the radio talk show and choose the correct answer to the question.

Example

In Bob's opinion, why isn't soccer popular in the U.S.?

a. The games are slow.

b. The scores are low.

Explanation

The correct answer is *b.* The scores are low.

Bob used ***because of*** to introduce his reason (the low scores). This signal phrase helped us notice Bob's reason.

▶ **Listen to the excerpts from the radio show. Pay attention to the signal words that introduce reasons and results. Circle the reason or result that each speaker gives and check (✓) the signal word or phrase you hear.**

Excerpt One

In Bob's opinion, why isn't soccer popular in the U.S.?

a. Americans don't like their team to lose.

b. Americans don't like games with tie scores.

What signal word or phrase did you hear?

☐ because

☐ because of

☐ That's why

☐ That's another reason why

Excerpt Two

Linda says that most Americans didn't grow up watching soccer. What's the result of this today?

a. Soccer isn't as popular as other sports in the U.S.

b. American soccer teams aren't on TV.

What signal word or phrase did you hear?

☐ because

☐ because of

☐ That's why

☐ That's another reason why

Excerpt Three

In Drew's opinion, why isn't soccer popular in the U.S.?

a. Americans don't love big soccer superstars.

b. There aren't any American superstar soccer players.

What signal word or phrase did you hear?

☐ because

☐ because of

☐ That's why

☐ That's another reason why

🔊 Go to **MyEnglishLab** for more skill practice.

ORGANIZE

Write the number of each sentence in the correct column. The first one has been done for you.

USE YOUR NOTES

APPLY Review your notes from Listening One and Two. Use the information in your notes to complete the lists.

1. People from all countries can understand the rules of soccer.

2. Soccer is an art.

3. Most adults in the U.S. never learned to play soccer well.

4. People can play soccer without a lot of expensive things.

5. Soccer doesn't have high scores.

6. Americans have other traditional sports.

7. Soccer sometimes ends in a tie.

8. There are no soccer superstars from the U.S.

9. Soccer brings people from many countries together.

10. People in the U.S. did not grow up watching soccer on TV.

WHY SOCCER IS POPULAR IN MOST COUNTRIES	WHY SOCCER IS NOT POPULAR IN THE U.S.
_1_	____
____	____
____	____
____	____
____	____
____	____

SYNTHESIZE

Role-play with a partner. Student A is from the U.K., and Student B is from the U.S. Student A, explain to Student B why soccer is a great sport. Student B, explain to Student A why many Americans don't like soccer. Use all the information from Organize. Each student should say at least five more lines to continue the conversation. Begin like this:

A: I heard that most Americans don't like soccer. Is that true?

B: Yes, it is.

A: Why? Soccer is so easy to understand.

B: Well, one reason is that . . .

A: . . .

B: . . .

🔵 Go to **MyEnglishLab** to check what you learned.

REVIEW

Work with a partner. Two answers are correct. Cross out the incorrect word or phrase. Then take turns reading the sentence aloud with the two correct answers. The first one has been done for you.

1. After their team won, the fans (*were very excited* / *had a party* / ~~*made a goal*~~).

    A: After their team won, the fans were very excited.

    B: After their team won, the fans had a party.

2. Real Madrid is my favorite team. (*I don't like them very much.* / *They're the best!* / *I love them.*)

3. No one is in front of the goal! The player can (*take it* / *kick the ball in* / *make a goal*).

4. Let's leave when this (*study* / *tennis* / *soccer*) match is over.

5. The goalie is the only (*player* / *team* / *person*) who can use his or her hands.

6. The score was (*14 to 2* / *three–nothing* / *almost finished*).

7. Don doesn't like ties because (*nobody wins* / *you don't know who is best* / *you can't watch those games*).

8. In basketball, a final score can be 84–76. It can never be 84–84. In basketball, the scores are (*not very important* / *higher than in soccer* / *never a tie*).

9. It's important to follow the rules in (*television* / *soccer* / *school*).

10. You play soccer and (*baseball* / *basketball* / *American football*) on a field.

EXPAND

1 Read sentences A, B, and C. Then choose the correct definition for each boldfaced word.

A. In sports, **athletes compete against** their **opponents** and try to **defeat** them.

1. **Athletes** are _____ .

    a. superstars   b. the players in sports

2. When you **compete against** a team, you _____ a game or sport with them.

    a. win   b. play

3. If you **defeat** the other team, you _____ the game.

    a. win   b. lose

4. Your **opponents** are the players on _____ team.

    a. the other   b. your

B. When basketball players **throw** the ball into the basket, they usually **score** two points.

   5. When you **throw** the ball, you put it in the air with your _____ .

      a. hand   b. foot

   6. If you **score** points, your team _____ them.

      a. loses   b. gets

C. In soccer, only the goalies can **catch** the ball. Their job is to **block** the other team's goal.

   7. When you **catch** a ball, you get it with your _____ .

      a. hands   b. feet

   8. When you **block** a goal, you _____ it.

      a. win   b. stop

Sweden vs. Korea in the 2018 World Cup,
Final score: Sweden 1, Korea 0.

Ukraine vs. Latvia at the 2019 Basketball World Cup in China.
Final score: Ukraine 82, Latvia 68

2 **Talk about the photos. What is happening in the two photos? Use the vocabulary from Expand (sentences A, B, and C) to explain what is happening. With a partner, write three sentences to share with the class.**

Example

In photo 1, Sweden is competing against Korea.

   1. _____

   2. _____

   3. _____

CREATE

Work in groups of three. Look at the list of activities.

- cheerleading
- poker

- eating contests
- gymnastics

- wrestling
- skateboarding

cheerleading

skateboarding

Discuss these questions. Use the vocabulary from Review and Expand.

1. Which ones are sports?

2. Are all these activities sports? Why or why not?

When you finish, form new groups and have another conversation.

You may begin like this:

Example

A: I think a sport is a game with two teams, a ball, and a goal.

B: I disagree. Skateboarding and cheerleading don't have a goal.

C: Is cheerleading a sport? Do they compete against anyone?

B: Sure! There are large cheerleading competitions in the U.S. every year.

Go to the **Pearson Practice English App** or **MyEnglishLab** for more vocabulary practice.

1 Look at the sentences and answer the questions.

JANE: The world is getting **smaller**.

MARTA: Soccer is **simpler**—and it's also **more exciting** to watch **than** American football.

BOB: I think Americans like sports with **higher** scores.

LINDA: I think the main reason soccer is **less popular** here is that we just didn't grow up with it.

DREW: David Beckham made Americans **more interested** in soccer.

1. Which adjectives end with **-er**? _____ , _____ , and _____

   How many syllables do they have? (before **-er** is added) _____ or _____

2. Which adjectives have *more* or *less* in front of them (and no **-er**)? _____ , _____ , and _____

   How many syllables do they have? _____

Using Comparative Adjectives

1. Use the comparative form of adjectives + *than* to compare two people, things, or places.	*Soccer is **faster** than baseball.*
	*Soccer is **more popular** than American football.*
If there is a noun after the adjective, use:	
a(n)** + comparative adj. + noun + **than	*Soccer is **a more popular sport than** baseball.*
If there are two comparative adjectives connected by **and**, use **than** after the second adjective.	*Soccer is **faster** and **more popular than** baseball.*
Sometimes, it's *not necessary* to mention the second thing in the comparison because it's very clear. In this case, you can omit **than**.	*The world is **smaller**. (= than in the past)*
2. If an adjective has **one syllable** (e.g., small, big, low, high, fast), add **-er** to the adjective.	*Baseball games are **longer than** soccer matches.*
3. If an adjective has:	
two syllables and ends with -e (e.g., *simple*) add **-r** to the adjective.	*The rules of soccer are **simpler than** the rules of American football.*
two syllables and ends with -y (e.g., *easy, lucky*) change the **y** to **i** and add **-er** to the adjective.	*The rules of soccer are **easier than** the rules of American football.*
4. For all other **two-syllable adjectives**, and for **adjectives with three or more syllables**, add **more** or **less** before the adjective.	*Soccer is **more exciting than** baseball.*
	*Soccer is **less popular** in the U.S. **than** in all other countries.*
5. The adjectives **good** and **bad** have irregular comparative forms:	
good – better than	*This year, my team is **better than** your team.*
bad – worse than	*Last year, my team was **worse than** your team.*

2 **Read the two articles. Complete the sentences. Use the comparative form of the adjective in parentheses. In some blanks, you do not need to use *than*. The first one has been done for you.**

Is Soccer Becoming More Popular in the U.S.?

Most Americans love baseball, football, and basketball. Soccer is still

_____less popular than_____ these traditional American sports. However, soccer is
     1. (popular)

slowly becoming _____ in the U.S. Many Americans are
                         2. (popular)

immigrants[1] from other countries. Most of these immigrants, who are now American

citizens, grew up with soccer in their home countries, and they still love it. They play

soccer and they watch international matches on

TV. That's one reason why Americans are

becoming _____ in the
                 3. (interested)

sport. In 2014, around 4.3 million Americans

watched each World Cup match. This number

is 50% _____ the number of Americans who watched World
          4. (high)

Cup matches in 2010.   This shows that many Americans are

_____ about soccer now, especially when the U.S. is playing
          5. (excited)

in the World Cup!

[1] **immigrants:** people who leave their native country to live in a new country

U.S. Soccer's First Female Superstar

Mia Hamm was the first woman soccer superstar in U.S. history. When she was young, she was always

very good at sports. She was a _____ athlete _____ most of the boys
        6. (good)

her age. Mia loved to compete against other kids, especially boys who were _____ and
        7. (old)

_____ she was. This made her a _____ athlete. But when she got
  8. (fast)   **9. (strong)**

_____, it was _____ for her to play traditional sports like baseball or
  10. (old)   **11. (difficult)**

football. In most American high schools, those sports were only for boys. At that time, women's soccer

was new in the U.S., so it was _____ for an American girl to play soccer than other
        12. (easy)

American sports. Mia played soccer in high school, and she joined the U.S. women's national soccer team

when she was only 15 years old. She was _____ all of the other women on the team. At
        13. (young)

university, Mia was the "Player of the Year" for three years because she was _____ all
        14. (successful)

her teammates.

In 1991, when she was 19, Mia competed in her first World Cup, in China. The U.S. played against

teams from Sweden and Brazil. Those teams were always _____ the American team, but
        15. (strong)

with Mia Hamm, the Americans defeated Sweden (3–2) and Brazil (5–0). Then the U.S. played

against Japan. This match was _____ the first two, and the U.S. won 3–0.
        16. (easy)

The next match against Taiwan was _____ the match against Japan, and
        17. (exciting)

the U.S. won with a _____ score (7–0). Then they played in the
        18. (high)

semi-finals against Germany. The German team was _____
        19. (strong)

all of the other opponents, but the U.S. team defeated them 5–2. In the

final match, the U.S. competed against Norway, and again, the U.S. team

won the match, but the score was _____ (2–1).
        20. (close)

Mia Hamm—
American women's
soccer champion

Mia Hamm played soccer for the U.S. team for 17 years. She competed in

four World Cups and three Olympics. Mia Hamm scored a total of 158

international goals. That was more than any male or female soccer player in

the world. Mia wanted young girls to become _____ in sports.
        21. (interested)

After winning a gold medal in the Olympics, Mia said, "I hope all you young girls

see your[selves] up there [standing with the winners]. We were just like you." She wanted

them to know that every young girl can be a winner. Because of Mia Hamm and her

teammates, many young American women began to love soccer and sports.

3 APPLY **Think of two of your favorite athletes. Compare them with a partner. Remember to use comparative adjectives. Use the topics and adjectives below or your own ideas.**

Topics		Adjectives			
challenges	scoring record	difficult	fast	interested	strong
injuries	skills	easy	good	old	successful
pay	sport	excited	high	popular	young
popularity	training				

Go to the **Pearson Practice English App** or **MyEnglishLab** for more grammar practice. Check what you learned in **MyEnglishLab**.

PRONUNCIATION

Using Contrastive Stress

Sometimes, we want to correct someone's idea or show that our opinion is different or the opposite of someone else's. To do this, we stress the word that shows the contrast (the opposite information) more than the other stressed words in the sentence. This is called *contrastive stress*.

When we use contrastive stress, we say the word louder, longer, and with a higher pitch or note.

▶ **Listen to how the words sound with normal stress (underlined words) and contrastive stress (boldfaced words) and read the explanation.**

Example

DAD: Maya, get your soccer ball.

MAYA: I **have** it. But I can't find my **water bottle.**

Explanation

In the first sentence, Dad puts normal stress on his daughter's name, the main verb, and the object. In Maya's response, she uses contrastive stress on ***have*** and on ***water bottle***. Maya is correcting her dad and contrasting two things: She has her ***soccer*** ball, but she doesn't have her ***water bottle.***

1 ▶ **Listen to the conversations. Then listen again and repeat each line. Be sure to pronounce the underlined words with regular stress and the boldfaced words with contrastive stress. Then practice with a partner. Take turns reading the lines for A and B.**

1. **A:** Sammy made one goal.

   B: No, he made **three** goals.

2. **A:** I'm tired of baseball.

   B: So watch the **soccer** match today.

3. **A:** I **watch** soccer, but I don't **play** it.

   B: I am the opposite. I **play** it, but I don't **watch** it!

4. **A:** Soccer is very popular in my country.

   B: Yeah, but in the U.S., **football** is more popular.

5. **A:** Are you looking for basketball shoes?

   B: No, I need to buy **running** shoes.

2 Work with a partner. Student A, read the first question aloud. Be careful to pronounce the boldfaced words with extra stress. Student B, cover the questions with a piece of paper. Listen carefully for the stress in the question. Choose the response that has the correct contrastive stress, and then read the response to your partner. Make sure to use contrastive stress. Change roles after Question 2.

Student A Questions

1. In your country, do kids start playing school sports in **primary** school?

Student B Answers

a. No, kids start **playing** school sports in high school.
b. No, kids start playing school sports in **high school**.

2. Isn't **baseball** the most popular sport where you live?

a. No, **soccer** is the most popular sport.
b. No, soccer is the **most** popular sport.

(*Switch roles.*)

3. Did you play **tennis** when you were a child?

(*Switch roles.*)

a. No. When I was a child, I played **basketball**.
b. No. When I was a **child**, I played basketball and soccer.

4. Are you playing any sports **these days**?

a. No, I don't have enough **time** to play sports.
b. No, I don't have enough time to play **sports**.

3 Work with a partner. First, read the conversations together and circle the words that have contrastive stress (louder, longer, and higher pitch). Then take turns performing the conversations. Each student should play both roles. Use contrastive stress.

1. **A:** You like watching sports on TV, right?

   B: No, I don't like watching sports on TV. I like watching sports at a stadium.

   A: Me, too! Let's go see a game sometime.

2. **A:** These days, more schools should have sports teams.

   B: That's right! All kids need to play sports, not just a few kids.

3. **A:** Want to play the new soccer video game?

   B: I don't like soccer video games. I like golfing video games.

   A: OK. I have one of those, too.

4. **A:** It is really common for a country's team to have players from all over the world.

   B: Yes, but in the World Cup, players usually play for their home countries, not for another country.

Expressing Results

In speaking, you can explain a result with "That's why" or "That's the reason why."

You can also say "So that's why" or "So that's the reason why."

Examples

American football has a lot of rules. That's why it's hard to understand.

Many Americans originally came from countries where soccer is very popular, so that's one reason why soccer is becoming more popular in the U.S.

1 **Below are some statements about American football. Take turns with a partner. Read one statement from Column A, and one possible result of the statement from Column B. Use one of the phrases from the box.**

That's why . . .	So that's why . . .
That's the reason why . . .	So that's the reason why . . .
That's one reason why . . .	So that's one reason why . . .
That's another reason why . . .	So that's another reason why . . .

A

1. American football is very violent.[2]

2. Many immigrant teenagers aren't interested in American football.

3. Soccer is becoming more popular than American football in U.S. high schools.

4. American football teams play only 16 games a year.

B

_____ a. Some people don't like to watch it on TV

_____ b. Many parents are afraid that their children will get hurt if they play.

_____ c. American football fans always want to see every game.

_____ d. Many parents don't allow their kids to play it.

_____ e. Many high school football teams can't find enough players for a team.

_____ f. Some professional football players have died.

---

[2] **American football is very violent:** Football players hurt each other physically.

2 Nicole found a list of Winter Olympic sports in the newspaper. She made notes about what she wants to watch on TV and what she doesn't want to watch.

Look at the list. With a partner, discuss which sports she is going to watch and which sports she isn't going to watch. Explain her reasons. Use the phrases from the box in Exercise 1. Then share some of your reasons with another pair of students.

The Winter Olympic Games are coming!

Events will include:

✓ snowboarding — exciting!
want to see Chloe Kim!

✓ speed skating — fast and exciting

NO! downhill skiing — too scary!
don't like to see crashes

NO! ice hockey — players always fight!

✓ bobsled — makes me laugh!

NO! cross-country skiing — not interesting

snowboarding

downhill skiing

speed skating

bobsled

cross-country skiing

ice hockey

Examples

Snowboarding is exciting. That's one reason why Nicole is going to watch it.

Nicole wants to see Chloe Kim. **That's why** she's going to watch snowboarding.

1. _____
2. _____
3. _____
4. _____
5. _____
6. _____

Go to **MyEnglishLab** for more skill practice and to check what you learned.

Around the world, famous athletes often appear in TV commercials[3]. They endorse[4] products, such as cars, clothes, and healthy food and vitamins. If a famous athlete says that he or she uses a product, the company that makes it thinks that many people will buy it.

You work for a company in your country that is selling a new energy drink. They are looking for a very famous athlete to make a TV commercial for them. Your company asked you to research and find an athlete for the commercial. You will do a short presentation about why your athlete is a better choice than other athletes.

an energy drink

---

[3] **TV commercial:** an advertisement for a product that you can see while you watch TV
[4] **endorse:** to express support for or approval of something

PREPARE

1 Form three groups. Each group is responsible for researching and presenting information about one athlete. Read the information about your athlete on pages 206–207.

2 Read the information about the other athletes. With your group, answer this question: Why is your athlete a better choice than the others to endorse this product? Make sure to take notes. Think about the athlete's:

- sport
- team (strong or weak)
- personality
- personal life
- age
- years of experience
- popularity
- awards or prizes

3 APPLY Use the vocabulary, grammar, pronunciation, and speaking skills from the unit. Use the checklist to help you.

- ☐ **Vocabulary:** Look at the list of vocabulary on page 201. Which words can you use to describe your athlete in your presentation? Choose at least six words and add them to your notes.

- ☐ **Grammar:** Look at the notes you wrote with your group. Did you use comparative adjectives to explain why your athlete is better than others? Try to add this grammar where it is possible.

- ☐ **Pronunciation:** Think about your comparative sentences. Are you using contrastive stress to show how your player is better? Practice pronouncing the sentences with your group.

- ☐ **Speaking Skill:** Decide which sentences should begin with "That's why" or "That's the reason (that)" and which should begin with "That's [one / another / a second, etc.] reason (that)." Practice saying the sentences aloud.

PRACTICE

Take turns with one partner from your group.

STUDENT A: Practice making the short presentation about your athlete.

STUDENT B: Listen. Is your partner using the new language correctly? Does your partner need to change anything?

PRESENT

1 Form new groups of three, with one person from each original group. Give the short presentations about your athletes. When you finish, compare the athletes to each other and decide which athlete to choose for the TV commercial.

2 Report to the class which athlete your group chose and explain why. Compare your decisions with those of your classmates.

ALTERNATIVE SPEAKING TOPICS

APPLY Discuss one of these topics in small groups. Use the vocabulary, grammar, pronunciation, and speaking skills you learned in the unit.

1. Many people say that basketball and soccer are similar games. Do you agree? Compare these two sports. How are they similar? How are they different? Which one do you prefer, and why?

2. What sports are popular in the country where you grew up? Did you play any of these sports? If yes, which ones? Were you a good athlete? If you didn't play any sports, why not? How did you spend your free time?

3. "It's more difficult to stay on top than to get there."—Mia Hamm
   What does this mean? Do you agree with her opinion? Why or why not?

CHECK WHAT YOU'VE LEARNED

Check (✔) the outcomes you've met and vocabulary you've learned. Put an X next to the skills and vocabulary you still need to practice.

Learning Outcomes

☐ Infer the meaning of comparisons
☐ Take notes with *e.g.* and *ex.*
☐ Identify signal words for reasons and results
☐ Use comparative adjectives
☐ Use contrastive stress
☐ Express results

Vocabulary

☐ fans
☐ favorite
☐ field
☐ higher
☐ kick
☐ lose
☐ low
☐ match

☐ players
☐ rules
☐ score (*n.*)
☐ simple
☐ team AWL
☐ tie
☐ win

○ Go to **MyEnglishLab** to watch a video about sports for non-jocks, access the Unit Project, and take the Unit 8 Achievement Test.

STUDENT ACTIVITIES

STUDENT A	TIMES	
1. The hours of the video about Ojibwe people (verbs: *begin*, *end*)	2:00 P.M.	3:00 P.M.
2. The hours of the Ojibwe Museum store (verbs: *open*, *close*)	11:00 A.M.	5:00 P.M.
3. The hours of the bus to the dream catcher store		
4. The hours of George Wolf's storytelling		

UNIT 4: Final Speaking Task

Vice Presidents: Read the example questions below. Think about other questions you can ask about saving time, saving money, exercising, staying healthy, moving around the office, communicating easily with other employees, and anything else you think is important.

Examples

Are there ways for the employees to have fun at work?

How many cafeterias or restaurants are there?

Is there a way for employees to feel relaxed at work?

After you ask all your questions, ask the designers: *Is there anything else you want to tell us about your plan?*

Office designers of Plan A: Read your ideas for the new office. Decide which five ideas are the most important for creativity. Take short notes to explain why your choices are the most important.

an indoor rock-climbing wall

ten cafeterias (open from 5 A.M. to midnight)

a basketball court

a 24-hour coffee bar with free coffee

skateboards to move around the office

big red rubber exercise balls around the office

glass walls between the offices inside

a hair salon

a video game room

a sushi bar

a massage room with free massages

funny posters on the walls

Office designers of Plan B: Read your ideas for the new office. Decide which five ideas are the most important for creativity. Take short notes to explain why your choices are the most important.

glass walls between the offices inside

Razor® scooters

electric train sets

balloons with happy faces all around the office

a meditation room

a game room with video games, foosball, air hockey, and a billiards table

a dog play area (dogs only, no cats)

whiteboards on the walls—employees can write any ideas they have on the walls, and other employees can add their ideas

a doctor's office

a four-star restaurant

two lap-swimming pools

an exercise room with free sports training

1 Prepare a profile for your risk-taker. Answer these questions:

1. What is your name?

2. Where are you from?

3. How old are you?

4. What are you famous for? Think about the risks you take.

5. Why do you take these risks? Think about the following reasons:

- to feel a challenge
- to set a new record
- to entertain people
- to become famous
- to continue a family tradition
- to prove something (what?)

6. What is your greatest success? What is your greatest failure?

7. What are your future plans?

2 Look at the photos of "you" taking risks. Take notes on how you will describe them.

1 Prepare a profile for your risk-taker. Answer these questions:

1. What is your name?

2. Where are you from?

3. How old are you?

4. What are you famous for? Think about the risks you take.

5. Why do you take these risks? Think about the following reasons:

   - to feel a challenge
   - to set a new record
   - to entertain people
   - to become famous
   - to continue a family tradition
   - to prove something (what?)

6. What is your greatest success? What is your greatest failure?

7. What are your future plans?

2 Look at the photos of "you" taking risks. Take notes on how you will describe them.

UNIT 3: Pronunciation

STUDENT B	TIMES	
1. The hours of the video about Ojibwe people		
2. The hours of the Ojibwe Museum store		
3. The hours of the bus to the dream catcher store (verbs: *leave, arrive*)	1:00 P.M.	2:00 P.M.
4. The hours of George Wolf's storytelling (verbs: *start, end*)	3:00 P.M.	4:00 P.M.

UNIT 8: Final Speaking Task
Group A

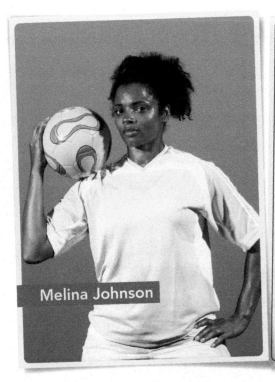

Melina Johnson

Age: 25

Sport: soccer

Team: Tennessee Cougars (U.S. women's professional soccer league)

Personality: outgoing, fun, interesting

Years of experience: 18 (started playing competitively at age 7, began professional career at age 21)

Popularity: She is popular among young female athletes but is not well known to others.

Skills: She plays as a forward and is very good at scoring goals. She is a great team player. Her teammates think she is a good leader. She wins many games for her team because she scores so many goals.

Awards: Most Valuable Player (MVP) 2017

(continued on next page)

Group B

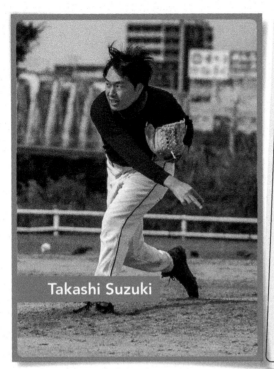

Takashi Suzuki

Age: 32

Sport: baseball

Team: Kyoto Comets

Personality: serious, bossy, arrogant

Years of experience: 20 (started playing baseball in middle school, began professional career at age 22)

Popularity: He is very popular and famous because he is a great pitcher, but people don't think he is very nice.

Skills: He is a great pitcher but is not good at hitting the ball. His teammates admire and respect him, but he is not good at playing on a team. He wins almost every game for his team.

Awards: He got a big award in Japan for being a great pitcher.

Group C

Marco Russo

Age: 21

Sport: downhill skiing (slalom)

Team: Italy Ski Team for the Olympics

Personality: modest, humble, friendly, kind

Years of experience: 15 (started skiing when he was only 4 years old and began his professional career at age 14)

Popularity: He is well known because he started skiing so young, but he's not very popular among people who don't play or watch winter sports. People like to cheer for him even if they don't know him because he is very nice and friendly.

Skills: He is a very fast skier. He exercises regularly and is very strong. He has more muscles than many other skiers.

Awards: He won an Olympic gold medal.

EXPAND VOCABULARY

UNIT 1
Multi-word Units
save (space, time, money, energy)
spend (time, money)
waste (space, time, money, energy)

UNIT 2
Multi-word Units
I can take it or leave it.
I don't like it (at all).
I hate it.
I like it.
I like it a lot.
I like it very much.
I love it.
It's my favorite (kind of art).
(It's OK, but) I'm not crazy about it.

UNIT 3
Vocabulary
collector
recycle

Multi-word Units
clutter up
get rid of something
give something away
hold onto something

UNIT 4
Vocabulary
exercise
relax AWL
perks

Multi-word Units
do sports
have fun
reduce stress AWL
stay healthy
stressed out

UNIT 5
Vocabulary
common
confident
power

Multi-word Units
deal with

UNIT 6
Vocabulary
amazed
amazing
bored
boring
challenging AWL
determined
disappointed
disappointing
excited
exciting

frightened
frightening
interested
interesting
scared
surprised
surprising
tired
tiring
worried

UNIT 7
Vocabulary
independent
self-confident
selfish
spoiled

Multi-word Units
close friends
get along well with

UNIT 8
Vocabulary
athletes
block
catch
defeat
opponents
throw
score (v.)

Multi-word Units
compete against

ACADEMIC WORD LIST VOCABULARY AWL

Words with an * are target vocabulary in the unit. The remainder of the words appear in context in the reading texts.

affect (*v.*)

appreciate*

challenge* (*n.*)

challenging* (*adj.*)

comment (*n.*)

computer

conclude

creative*

creativity*

culture

definitely

energy*

finally

goal*

intelligent

issue*

job

mature* (*adj.*)

professional

relax*

relaxation

specific*

status

stress* (*n.*)

style* (*n.*)

team

technology*

temporary

traditional*

GRAMMAR BOOK REFERENCES

NorthStar: Listening and Speaking Level 1, Fourth Edition	*Focus on Grammar, Level 1, Fourth Edition*	*Azar's Basic English Grammar, Fourth Edition*
Unit 1 Present and past tense of *Be*	**Unit 3** Present of *Be*: Statements **Unit 5** Present of *Be*: *Yes / No* Questions, Questions with *Who* and *What* **Part III** *Be*: Past	**Chapter 1** Using *Be* **Chapter 3** Using the Simple Present: 3-1, 3-8, 3-9, 3-10, 3-11 **Chapter 8** Expressing Past Time, Part 1: 8-1, 8-2, 8-3
Unit 2 Simple present	**Unit 10** Simple Present: Statements **Unit 11** Simple Present: *Yes / No* Questions **Unit 12** Simple Present: *Wh-* Questions	**Chapter 3** Using the Simple Present: 3-1, 3-4, 3-5, 3-6, 3-8, 3-9, 3-10, 3-11
Unit 3 Simple present with Adverbs of frequency	**Unit 13** Simple Present with Adverbs of frequency	**Chapter 3** Using the Simple Present: 3-2, 3-3
Unit 4 *There is / There are / There was / There were*	**Unit 1** *There is / There are*	**Chapter 5** Talking About the Present: 5–4, 5–5
Unit 5 Simple past	**Part 8** Simple Past	**Chapter 8** Expressing Past Time, Part 1 **Chapter 9** Expressing Past Time, Part 2: 9-1, 9-2, 9-3, 9-4, 9-5, 9-6
Unit 6 Present progressive	**Unit 16** Present Progressive: Statements **Unit 17** Simple Present: *Yes / No* Questions **Unit 18** Present Progressive: *Wh-* Questions	**Chapter 4** Using the Present Progressive
Unit 7 *Be going to* for the future	**Part 10** Future with *Be going to*	**Chapter 10** Expressing Future Time, Part 1: 10–1
Unit 8 Comparative adjectives	**Unit 15** Comparative Adjectives	**Chapter 15** Making Comparisons: 15-1

AUDIO SCRIPT

Listening One, Page 5, Preview

REPORTER: Hi, and welcome to our show, "Tiny House, Happy Life." So, what is a tiny house? Is it just a small house? Well, no. A tiny house is very, very small—about the same size as a trailer or a bus! There are lots of different kinds of tiny houses, and today, we're going to visit a tiny house near Boston that is really unusual. It belongs to Adam and Jenny. Let's go!

JENNY AND ADAM: Hi! / Come in!

REPORTER: Hi, thanks!

JENNY: Welcome!

REPORTER: So, this is an old school bus!

ADAM: Yes, and now it's our tiny house.

REPORTER: What an unusual idea! Can you tell me more about how you decided to live in a bus?

Page 5, Listen

RECORDING: You are watching Beautiful Homes TV.

REPORTER: Hi, and welcome to our show, "Tiny House, Happy Life." So, what is a tiny house? Is it just a small house? Well, no. A tiny house is very, very small—about the same size as a trailer or a bus! There are lots of different kinds of tiny houses, and today, we're going to visit a tiny house near Boston that is really unusual. It belongs to Adam and Jenny. Let's go!

JENNY AND ADAM: Hi! / Come in!

REPORTER: Hi, thanks!

JENNY: Welcome!

REPORTER: So, this is an old school bus!

ADAM: Yes, and now it's our tiny house.

REPORTER: What an unusual idea! Can you tell me more about how you decided to live in a bus?

JENNY: Yeah, everyone asks us that question! Well, we loved Boston, but our apartment was small . . .

ADAM: Come on, Jen, small?

JENNY: OK, it was very small! And the rent was very expensive. We spent almost all our money every month just to pay the rent!

ADAM: And one day, we saw a really interesting video on YouTube about tiny houses. And then, about a week later, Jenny and I saw this old school bus on the street, and Jenny said, "That's it! That's our tiny house!" And it's crazy, but that same day, we bought this bus!

REPORTER: Wow, I'm surprised! You did it so quickly!

ADAM: I know, we were surprised, too! But we needed to change our lives, and we both thought a tiny house was a good idea, so . . . here we are!

REPORTER: This is really beautiful!

JENNY AND ADAM: Thanks! / Thank you.

REPORTER: But it is really small!

JENNY: Yeah, so in a tiny house, you need some unusual ideas about where to put everything, like your bed and your clothes . . . because your house is so . . . tiny!

REPORTER: Yeah . . . ummm . . . actually, I don't see a bed—where is it?

JENNY: OK—look up.

REPORTER: That's great! I'd love to know more about how it works!

ADAM: OK! Our bed is on a little elevator. At night it comes down, and in the morning it goes up again.

REPORTER: That's really an unusual way to save space!

ADAM: Uh-huh! OK, now look at the floor.

REPORTER: That's incredible! The floor opens!

ADAM: Yup! And that's where we put our shoes.

REPORTER: Do you really have enough space for everything?

JENNY: Yes, we do, but that's a very important question. When you live in a tiny house, there isn't enough space for everything you have, so you can only have the things you really need. And when you only have the things you need, your life is very simple. Like, it's easy to find everything in the house . . .

ADAM: . . . and it only takes 20 minutes to clean . . .

JENNY: . . . so we have more time to be with our family and friends and do other things we love.

ADAM: And it's easy to travel because our home is a bus!

JENNY: And—the best thing is—now we're not worried about money all the time.

REPORTER: Why is that?

JENNY: Well, because the bus costs less than the rent on our apartment in Boston for four months, so we're saving money. And also, when we lived in the city, we just always bought a lot of things.

ADAM: Uhh . . . especially you!

JENNY: OK, that's true. I spent a lot of time shopping for new things like clothes, and things for the house . . . But we really didn't need most of the things we had.

JENNY: And we're so happy! We really love our simple life!

REPORTER: Jenny, Adam, thanks so much for showing us your tiny house, and explaining why a simple life is so great!

JENNY AND ADAM: You're welcome! / Thanks for coming.

Page 7, Make Inferences

Example

ADAM: And then, about a week later, Jenny and I saw this old school bus on the street, and Jenny said, "That's it! That's our tiny house!" And it's crazy, but that same day, we bought this bus!

Excerpt One

REPORTER: Wow, I'm surprised! You did it so quickly!

ADAM: I know, we were surprised, too!

Excerpt Two

REPORTER: But it is really small!

JENNY: Yeah, so in a tiny house, you need some unusual ideas about where to put everything, like your bed and your clothes . . . because your house is so . . . tiny!

Excerpt Three

JENNY: When you live in a tiny house, there isn't enough space for everything you have, so you can only have the things you really need.

Pages 9–10, Note-taking Skill

Exercise 1
Excerpt One

REPORTER: Hi, and welcome to our show, "Tiny House, Happy Life." So, what is a tiny house? Is it just a small house? Well, no. A tiny house is very, very small—about the same size as a trailer or a bus!

Excerpt Two

JENNY: And when you only have the things you need, your life is very simple. Like, it's easy to find everything in the house . . .

ADAM: . . . and it only takes 20 minutes to clean . . .

Excerpt Three

HOST: Is living in a treehouse perfect? Of course not. It's very difficult to have water and electricity. And if the weather is too cold or too hot, it can be very uncomfortable. Some people have heat or air conditioning, but this is very expensive.

Listening Two, Page 11, Comprehension

HOST: Are you tired of life in the city—all the people and the cars? Do you want to change your life? Maybe you should live in a treehouse! That's right, treehouses are not just for children anymore. Today, people are living in treehouses.

Why do people want to live in a treehouse? Most of them love nature, and they want to feel a connection to it. In a treehouse, they can go to sleep listening to the sounds of the trees, and wake up in the morning with the birds singing. The view from a treehouse is always beautiful, and living in the trees is quiet and peaceful.

This is Masahiro Sato. He makes treehouses for people in Japan.

MASAHIRO SATO: Life today is full of technology. People love their computers and cell phones. But many of these people are not happy. Why? Because they don't have a connection to nature. People need a connection to trees, not technology, and treehouses are the answer."

HOST: Is living in a treehouse perfect? Of course not. It's very difficult to have water and electricity. And if the weather is too cold or too hot, it can be very uncomfortable. Some people have heat or air conditioning, but this is very expensive. And of course, treehouses are too small, and they are often far away from supermarkets and other stores.

But . . . many people all over the world still want to live in treehouses!

Most treehouses are "tiny houses"—small and simple—so some young people want to live in treehouses because they just want to have a simple life. Treehouses also help them save money because building or buying a treehouse is much less expensive than the rent for an apartment in the city. And today, some older people are also living in treehouses, but they are not all living a simple life! Many of their treehouses are big and very comfortable. They often have water and electricity, and some even have Wi-Fi!

Some people don't live in their treehouses full-time, so they rent them online when they aren't using them. Staying in a treehouse is a wonderful way for city people to leave their busy lives for a few days or weeks. They can enjoy the peace and quiet of living in nature.

And now there are even hotels in the trees. You can find treehouse hotels all over the world: in China, India, Mexico, Japan, Sweden, and many other countries. So the next time you want to take a vacation, think about staying in a treehouse! You may want to stay forever!

Page 12, Listening Skill

Exercise 1

ADAM: And it's easy to travel because our home is a bus!

JENNY: And the best thing is now we're not worried about money all the time.

Example 1

HOST: In a treehouse, they can go to sleep listening to the sounds of the trees and wake up in the morning with the birds singing. The view from a treehouse is always beautiful, and living in the trees is quiet and peaceful.

Example 2

JENNY: Yeah, everyone asks us that question! Well, we loved Boston, but our apartment was small . . .

ADAM: Come on, Jen, small?

JENNY: OK, it was very small! And the rent was very expensive. We spent almost all our money every month just to pay the rent!

Exercise 2
Excerpt One

HOST: Is living in a treehouse perfect? Of course not. It's very difficult to have water and electricity. And if the weather is too cold or too hot, it can be very uncomfortable. Some people have heat or air conditioning, but this is very expensive. And of course, treehouses are too small, and they are often far away from supermarkets and other stores.

Excerpt Two

HOST: Most treehouses are "tiny houses"—small and simple—so some young people want to live in treehouses because they just want to have a simple life. Treehouses also help them save money because building or buying a treehouse is much less expensive than the rent for an apartment in the city. And today, some older people are also living in treehouses, but they are not all living a simple life! Many of their treehouses are big and very comfortable. They often have water and electricity, and some even have Wi-Fi!

UNIT 2: Making Unusual Art

Listening One, Page 31, Listen

MUSEUM GUIDE: Hi, welcome to the museum.

MAGAZINE WRITER: Thanks. I'm very interested in Mia Pearlman's art.

GUIDE: Well, let me tell you a little about her.

WRITER: OK.

GUIDE: Mia is very interested in the world we live in. And she was always interested in the world - even when she was a little girl.

WRITER: Really? What do you mean?

GUIDE: Well, for example, when little girls play with dolls, like Barbie dolls, they usually make up stories about them, right?

WRITER: Sure.

GUIDE: But when Mia played with her dolls, she didn't do that. She was only interested in making the place where Barbie lived.

WRITER: You mean, like a Barbie house?

GUIDE: No, it was bigger than a house. It was a really big space—like a "Barbie world."

WRITER: That's very unusual!

GUIDE: Yes, Mia is an unusual person! Even when she was a child, she understood: The world is very big, and people are just a very small part of it.

WRITER: So, is that why her sculptures are so big?

GUIDE: Yes. Each sculpture is like a little "world."

WRITER: A lot of Mia's sculptures look like things we see in nature—like clouds, or the wind—like different kinds of weather . . .

GUIDE: Yes! Because her art is about the things in the world that are bigger than us, things that people don't control—like nature, the weather, even war . . .

WRITER: Mmm hmm . . .

GUIDE: So when people look at Mia's sculpture, she wants them to feel like they're inside something very big, and they're a small part of it—just like they're a small part of the world.

WRITER: Oh . . . .

GUIDE: Let's look at one of Mia's sculptures. This sculpture is called *Inrush*.

WRITER: It's beautiful.

GUIDE: OK, look up—do you see that window?

WRITER: Uh-huh . . .

GUIDE: The window is closed, but the sculpture looks like clouds and wind that are "rushing in" through the window, moving very quickly into this room.

WRITER: Yes, I see . . .

GUIDE: And the sunlight from outside really comes through the window, so it's part of the sculpture, too. It gives the sculpture light.

WRITER: So, the sculpture is like a part of nature inside the museum.

GUIDE: Yes, and when you stand near the sculpture, you feel like you're a part of it, too—so you feel like a part of nature.

WRITER: I do . . . I feel like I'm standing inside a cloud . . .

GUIDE: Mia wants people to feel things that they can't feel in the real world . . . That's why she makes art.

WRITER: Interesting! I have some specific questions about how Mia makes these sculptures.

GUIDE: Sure. What would you like to know?

WRITER: Well, when Mia begins a new sculpture, how does she decide what kinds of lines to draw?

GUIDE: Mia says that she doesn't really decide this. She just draws what she feels at that moment.

WRITER: Oh . . . And how many pieces of paper does she cut?

GUIDE: For each sculpture, she usually cuts thirty to eighty pieces.

WRITER: Wow. And, what's going to happen to this sculpture when this show ends? Is it going to a different museum?

GUIDE: No, when this show ends, her sculpture ends, too.

WRITER: What do you mean?

GUIDE: Well, Mia comes to the museum, and she takes down all the pieces of paper. And she never makes this specific sculpture again.

WRITER: But why? Her sculptures are so beautiful! I don't understand . . .

GUIDE: I know. But Mia thinks sculptures are just like dances, or theater, or music concerts. You enjoy them, but they don't last forever. And that's life, too—everything has an end. That's another thing Mia wants her art to show.

Pages 32–33, Make Inferences

Example

GUIDE: Mia is very interested in the world we live in. And she was always interested in the world—even when she was a little girl.

WRITER: Really? What do you mean?

GUIDE: Well, for example, when little girls play with dolls, like Barbie dolls, they usually make up stories about them, right?

WRITER: Sure.

GUIDE: But when Mia played with her dolls, she didn't do that. She was only interested in making the place where Barbie lived.

WRITER: You mean, like a Barbie house?

GUIDE: No, it was bigger than a house. It was a really big space—like a "Barbie world."

WRITER: That's very unusual!

Excerpt One

WRITER: And, what's going to happen to this sculpture when this show ends? Is it going to a different museum?

GUIDE: No, when this show ends, her sculpture ends too.

WRITER: What do you mean?

Excerpt Two

GUIDE: Well, Mia comes to the museum, and she takes down all the pieces of paper. And she never makes this specific sculpture again.

WRITER: But why? Her sculptures are so beautiful! I don't understand . . .

Page 35, Note-taking Skill

Exercise 1

WOMAN: The women in Gee's Bend make a lot of quilts. To make each quilt, we put many pieces of cloth together. Since we make so many quilts, when the quilts get old, we don't keep them. We just throw them away, and we make a new one. I had one very old quilt, and I didn't want it anymore, so I took it outside, and I put it near the garbage behind my house.

Exercise 2

WOMAN: And then one day, a man came to Gee's Bend, and he saw my old quilt. He said, "Look at that beautiful quilt!"

I thought he was crazy. I said, "Here, you can have it."

He asked me, "Do you have any more quilts like this?"

So we went inside my house, and I showed him all my quilts. He paid me $2,000 for three of my quilts! Two thousand dollars?! How could my old quilts be so expensive? I thought they were old and dirty, but he said they were art. Then he bought a lot of quilts from different women in Gee's Bend, and he put them in a museum! Can you believe that? It's true.

Listening Two, Page 36, Comprehension

HOST: Gee's Bend, a small, poor town in Alabama, is making big news in the art world. The big news is quilts—beautiful covers for the bed to keep people warm at night. Now these quilts are in museums; these quilts are works of art. They look like paintings by modern artists. The women in Gee's Bend didn't think their quilts were art. They just made the quilts to stay warm. But these women work just like artists. They decide how to put all the pieces together, always in new and different ways. The quilts are really beautiful—and unusual. Why? Because the people in Gee's Bend don't have much money. They can't buy expensive material. So they make their quilts with material from old clothes, like old jeans and shirts.

ELDERLY WOMAN 1: In Gee's Bend, we don't throw any clothes away—oh no! We use everything in our quilts.

HOST: One woman made a quilt with her husband's old work clothes. They were the only things she had to remember him.

ELDERLY WOMAN 2: After he died, I took all his shirts and pants, and I made a quilt with them to keep him near me. I can't believe that quilt's in a museum now. A museum! Those clothes were old. My husband wore them outside, working on the farm, our potato farm.

MIDDLE-AGED WOMAN: I was 17 when my father died, and my Mama said, "Come here and help me cut up all your Daddy's old clothes." I remember they had all these different blue and brown colors: dark colors from inside the pockets, and light colors from the outside. Those clothes were so old, but she made them look beautiful in that quilt.

ELDERLY WOMAN 1: To make a quilt, you cut the material into pieces, and then you put them all on the floor. You put the pieces this way and that. You see how the colors look together. Then you take another piece, and another. You don't have a plan, really. That's why we call some of these "Crazy Quilts." You just keep adding and changing the pieces until they all look good together.

Then, the women—your sisters, daughters, granddaughters—we all help to put the pieces together and make the quilt. Most evenings, we sit together and sew the quilt and we sing, and we talk . . .

HOST: In Gee's Bend, the older women teach the younger women to make quilts, and they teach them about their family.

ELDERLY WOMAN 2: My great-grandmother came from Africa. She made a quilt with all the colors of Africa. And when I was very little, every day she said, "Come on now, sit down and eat your lunch on this quilt. Let me tell you my story. Listen to the story of my life."

HOST: Grandmothers teaching granddaughters, mothers teaching daughters—working together for years. In Gee's Bend, a very poor town, the art is rich.

Pages 37–38, Listening Skill

Pages 37–38

Example

HOST: . . . these women work just like artists. They decide how to put all the pieces together, always in new and different ways.

Exercise 2
Excerpt One

HOST: The quilts are really beautiful—and unusual. Why? Because the people in Gee's Bend don't have much money. They can't buy expensive material. So they make their quilts with material from old clothes.

Excerpt Two

HOST: So they make their quilts with material from old clothes, like old jeans and shirts . . . One woman made a quilt with her husband's old work clothes.

Excerpt Three

HOST: In Gee's Bend, the older women teach the younger women to make quilts, and they teach them about their family.

ELDERLY WOMAN 2: My great-grandmother came from Africa. She made a quilt with all the colors of Africa. And when I was very little, every day she said, "Come on now, sit down and eat your lunch on this quilt. Let me tell you my story. Listen to the story of my life."

UNIT 3: Special Possessions

Listening One, Page 55, Preview

GEORGE WOLF: To make a dream catcher, we first use parts of trees and plants to make a circle. It shows how the sun travels across the sky. Next, we make a web with a hole in the center. Also, there is a little feather in the center. The meaning of the feather is "breath" or "air."

Page 56, Listen

PROFESSOR: Class, today we have a special guest, Mr. George Wolf of the Ojibwe Nation. Please welcome Mr. Wolf.

GEORGE WOLF: Hello, class. Today, I am happy to tell you the story of dream catchers. This is a story from my Ojibwe people . . . Imagine a time long, long ago. All our people lived together and enjoyed telling our traditional stories about Spider Woman—the one who gave life to the world. In our stories, we talked about her beautiful web. Every morning, she made her web to catch the sun for us. Then we started moving to other parts of North America. As we moved far away, it became difficult for Spider Woman to take care of us all. To help Spider Woman, all of our mothers, sisters, and grandmothers started making dream catchers for sleeping babies.

We still make dream catchers today. To make a dream catcher, we first use parts of trees and plants to make a circle. It shows how the sun travels across the sky. Next, we make a web with a hole in the center.

The dream catcher is very important. The web stops bad dreams from entering the mind of the sleeping baby. Only good dreams pass through the hole in the center. This protects the baby—keeping out bad dreams, letting in the good dreams. Also, there is a little feather in the center. The meaning of the feather is "breath" or "air." As the little feather moves in the air, the baby watches it and feels happy. The baby enjoys good, healthy air.

Now remember, the baby will grow. He or she will not stay a baby forever. This is just like the dream catcher! The dream catcher is temporary—it is made of trees and plants, and it does not last.

But of course, old traditional ways always change. Today, you can find many styles of dream catchers, with so many beautiful colors and feathers. These dream catchers are made of modern material. Many people use them and give them as gifts. They believe that the dream catcher will stop bad dreams. The good dreams, the important dreams—all of these come to you through the little hole in the center. In this way, the dream catcher is good for your mind. It will help you to feel happy and peaceful.

And of course, in the 21st century, you can always shop for dream catchers online. There is one website that says dream catchers are good gifts for friends. It says that when you give a dream catcher to a friend, other people will start asking, "Where did you get that beautiful dream catcher?" And your friend will tell the story of you and your friendship, and the story of you giving the dream catcher as a gift. Do you see how beautiful this is? The dream catcher helps your friend to remember you, to appreciate your love and friendship.

To conclude, I want to say that traditional life is very important to Native Americans. Our young people still learn about our culture today. They understand that dream catchers are important to us. Today, you sometimes see very big dream catchers in

stores and online. These are popular, but they are not traditional. The traditional size is small—just four or five inches across. Also, you sometimes see dream catchers in people's cars. Maybe people think they are good luck for driving. But no, the dream catcher is not for your car. The traditional dream catcher goes over your bed, in the place where you sleep and dream.

Thank you so much for listening today! I wish you all beautiful dreams!

Page 58, Make Inferences

Example

GEORGE WOLF: The dream catcher is very important. The web stops bad dreams from entering the mind of the sleeping baby. Only good dreams pass through the hole in the center. This protects the baby—keeping out bad dreams, letting in the good dreams.

Excerpt One

GEORGE WOLF: The good dreams, the important dreams—all of these come to you through the little hole in the center. In this way, the dream catcher is good for your mind. It will help you to feel happy and peaceful.

Excerpt Two

GEORGE WOLF: . . . your friend will tell the story of you and your friendship, and the story of you giving the dream catcher as a gift. Do you see how beautiful this is?

Excerpt Three

GEORGE WOLF: . . . you sometimes see dream catchers in people's cars. Maybe people think they are good luck for driving. But no, the dream catcher is not for your car. The traditional dream catcher goes over your bed . . .

Page 60, Note-taking Skill

Exercise 1

STUDENT: Today, I want to talk about a cool tradition—the four-leaf clover. This is a little green plant with four leaves. It's a tradition to believe a four-leaf clover is special—why? One reason is that a four-leaf clover is hard to find. There are 5,000 clovers with three leaves for every one clover with four leaves. 5,000 three-leaf clovers for one four-leaf clover. Maybe that's why some people think that a four-leaf clover is a special plant. Finding a four-leaf clover is hard, so some people think that finding one can make you happy. So, what does a four-leaf clover look like? Well, of course, there are four green leaves. Each one is round, like a ball. To draw a four-leaf clover, you first draw the four round leaves, and then you draw a line going down. This line is the stem—the part of a plant that the leaves grow from. It's easy to draw—just a stem and four leaves. The interesting part is the meaning of leaves. The traditional belief is that each leaf has meaning. For example, one leaf means love, and another leaf means hope. And a clover with five leaves is really special—leaf number five means money!

Listening Two, Page 61, Comprehension

SARA: Is it OK if I put my books over here? How about my computer?

AMBER: That's fine.

SARA: Look! There's someone outside with a big teddy bear! I mean, it's really big. I can't believe it!

AMBER: Where?

SARA: Outside. She's getting out of the car with her parents. She's coming this way!

AMBER: I see her now. I think the bear is cute! Here—let me help you with that computer . . .

LAUREN: Bye, Mom. Bye, Dad. I'll be OK. I'll call you . . . Hello? Anybody here?

SARA: Come in.

LAUREN: Hi. I'm Lauren.

SARA: I'm Sara, and this is Amber.

AMBER: Wow, that's a big bear. And now he's in college with you!

LAUREN: *She's* in college with me. This is Lucy—my special bear. She goes everywhere with me.

AMBER: That's cool.

LAUREN: Yeah. Lucy has a lot of sentimental value. She was my grandmother's bear for a long time. Then my grandmother gave her

to my mom, and my mom passed her down to me!

SARA: I guess that's pretty cool—for a stuffed animal.

LAUREN: Lucy isn't just a stuffed animal. She's a part of my life--and part of my family, too. What about you? Don't you have any special possessions?

AMBER: Not really. I'm not a pack rat. I never keep old things. Old things really aren't that important to me. How about you, Sara?

SARA: I don't know. I don't think about it much. But I do have something special. See this dream catcher? I'm going to hang it right over my bed to help me catch good dreams.

LAUREN: Really? It catches good dreams?

SARA: Yes—it's a Native American tradition. It stops the bad dreams. It only lets the good dreams come into your mind. Isn't it beautiful?

LAUREN: Yes, it is. Is it a good luck charm? Does it help you pass tests?

SARA: No, I use my lucky pen for that. When I take notes with my lucky pen, I usually get As! What about you—do you ask the big bear for help with your tests?

LAUREN: No. I just use my big brain for that . . . no help from Lucy on tests!

Page 62, Listening Skill

Exercise 1

SPEAKER A: Look at this. I found a four-leaf clover.

SPEAKER B: Look at this. I found a four-leaf clover!

Example

LAUREN: Lucy has a lot of sentimental value. She was my grandmother's bear for a long time. Then my grandmother gave her to my mom, and my mom passed her down to me!

Exercise 2

Excerpt One

AMBER: I'm not a pack rat. I never keep old things.

Excerpt Two

AMBER: I see her now. I think the bear is cute!

SARA: I use my lucky pen for that. When I take notes with my lucky pen, I usually get A's!

UNIT 4: Creativity in Business

Listening One, Page 80, Preview

PROFESSOR CHANDLER: KK, could you tell everyone how you got the idea to make Wristies?

KK GREGORY: Sure. Um . . . As I said, I was 10 years old, and it was winter, and I was playing outside in the snow. I was wearing warm clothes and warm gloves, but my wrists were really cold! And that's when I had the idea. I just thought of it. So I went home, and I found some warm material. I put it around my wrists, and I made a little hole for my thumb. And that's how I made the first pair of Wristies.

PROFESSOR CHANDLER: That's so interesting. Are there any questions? Yes, Nathan?

STUDENT: Yeah, um . . . how did you decide to start a business?

KK GREGORY: Well, at first, I didn't think about starting a business at all. I mean, I was only 10! I just made a lot of Wristies in different colors, and I gave them to my friends. They all wore them every day and loved them, and I was happy! But then my friends said, "You know, you can sell these things!" And I thought, "Hmm . . . that could be exciting!" So, I asked my mother about it, and she thought it was a great idea. And then she helped me to start my company.

Page 80, Listen

PROFESSOR CHANDLER: OK, everyone, let's get started. Today, our guest speaker is KK Gregory. KK is a successful business owner, and she's only seventeen years old. Her company makes Wristies. KK?

KK GREGORY: Hi, . . . umm . . . It's really exciting to be here, in a business school class, because I'm still in high school! I'm 17 now, but when I started my company, I was 10.

STUDENTS: That's unbelievable! Wow! So young . . .

KK GREGORY: Really! It's true . . . See? These are Wristies. They're long gloves, but they have no fingers. So they keep your hands and your wrists warm and dry, but you can move your fingers easily. You can wear them outside, for sports or work. But you can also wear them inside, in a cold house or office. There are really a lot of places that you can wear them.

PROFESSOR CHANDLER: That's great. KK, could you tell everyone how you got the idea to make Wristies?

KK GREGORY: Sure. Um . . . As I said, I was 10 years old, and it was winter, and I was playing outside in the snow. I was wearing warm clothes and warm gloves, but my wrists were really cold! And that's when I had the idea. I just thought of it. So I went home, and I found some warm material. I put it around my wrists, and I made a little hole for my thumb. And that's how I made the first pair of Wristies.

PROFESSOR CHANDLER: That's so interesting. Are there any questions? Yes, Nathan?

STUDENT 1: Yeah, um . . . how did you decide to start a business?

KK GREGORY: Well, at first, I didn't think about starting a business at all. I mean, I was only 10! I just made a lot of Wristies in different colors, and I gave them to my friends. They all wore them every day and loved them, and I was happy! But then my friends said, "You know, you can sell these things!" And I thought, "Hmm . . . that could be exciting!" So, I asked my mother about it, and she thought it was a great idea. And then she helped me to start my company.

PROFESSOR CHANDLER: Really . . . Did your mother have any business experience?

KK GREGORY: No! My mother didn't know anything about business, and of course I didn't either. But we talked to a lot of people, and we asked a lot of questions; we got a lot of advice, and we learned a lot. There were a few problems in the beginning, but most of the time, we had fun!

STUDENT 2: KK, where can people buy Wristies?

KK Gregory: Oh, a lot of department stores and clothing stores sell them, and there's also a website. And one time, I went on a TV shopping show. I was really nervous, but it was so exciting—I sold six thousand pairs of Wristies in six minutes!

Students: Wow! Six thousand pairs. . . . That's amazing!

KK Gregory: Yeah, it was! And I had a great time!

Professor Chandler: OK, there are just a few minutes left. Is there one more question? Yes? Marla?

Student 3: KK, do you have any advice for us?

KK Gregory: Advice? Well, there are a lot of things, but I guess the most important thing is to be creative. You know, don't be afraid to try something new.

Professor Chandler: I think that's great advice, KK. Ms. KK Gregory—thank you so much for speaking to us today. And good luck!

KK Gregory: Thank you.

Pages 83–84, Make Inferences

Excerpt One

KK: I'm seventeen now, but when I started my company, I was ten.

Excerpt Two

KK: They're long gloves, but they have no fingers.

Excerpt Three

KK: You can wear them outside, for sports or work. But you can also wear them inside, in a cold house or office.

Excerpt Four

KK: I was wearing warm clothes and warm gloves, but my wrists were really cold!

Pages 85–86, Note-taking Skill

Exercise 2

1. The Joyful Company is a successful advertising company.

2. What does it mean to be creative? When you are creative, you think in new ways.

3. Creativity classes are not art classes or writing classes; they're training classes for employees.

4. In creativity classes, some important advice that teachers give to employees is to relax. When people relax, they can think better.

Listening Two, Pages 86–87, Comprehension

Professor Chandler: OK, everybody . . . what can we learn from KK Gregory? First, she came up with a new idea. She made something that SHE needed and OTHER people needed, too. Second, she listened to other people. When her friends said, "You can sell these Wristies," she listened to them. And when she decided to start a business, she went to people with business experience, and she asked them for advice. That's important. You have to listen to people. And third, KK wasn't afraid to try something completely new. She didn't know anything about business, but she wasn't afraid to start her own company. You see, sometimes children can do great things because they aren't afraid to try, and they aren't afraid to make mistakes. And you know what our problem is? We're not children anymore, so we are afraid. We're afraid to do new things and creative things because we're afraid to make mistakes! In school, at our jobs, making mistakes is bad, right?

Students: Yeah, sure, right . . .

Professor Chandler: OK, so then what happens? We don't want to make mistakes, so we stop being creative. We forget that great ideas sometimes come from mistakes! But—and this is very important—we can learn how to be creative again. We can increase our creativity if we can remember how children feel. That's what I want to teach you. Now, how do we do it? Well, today we're going to do it with a relaxation exercise.

Students: What? A relaxation exercise? Huh? Really?

Professor Chandler: So let's begin. OK, now, everybody close your eyes . . . Everybody! Come on . . . Try to relax . . . Relax. Now, think about when you were a child . . .

Maybe you were 7, or 10, or 11 . . . Think about a time that you did something new . . . You tried to do something for the first time . . . and you weren't afraid . . . You did it . . . and it made you feel good . . . Try to remember that good feeling . . . Take your time . . . Just think . . . When you remember something, you can open your eyes, and then tell your story to another student. When you're finished, we'll discuss your stories together.

Pages 87–88, Listening Skill

Exercise 2

PROFESSOR CHANDLER: OK, everybody . . . what can we learn from KK Gregory? First, she came up with a new idea. She made something that SHE needed and OTHER people needed, too. Second, she listened to other people. When her friends said, "You can sell these Wristies," she listened to them. And when she decided to start a business, she went to people with business experience, and she asked them for advice. That's important. You have to listen to people. And third, KK wasn't afraid to try something completely new. She didn't know anything about business, but she wasn't afraid to start her own company.

UNIT 5: Understanding Fears and Phobias

Listening One, page 105, Preview

DOCTOR JONES: A phobia is a very strong fear. When you have a phobia, your body sometimes shakes and your heart beats very fast. You feel like you are in danger, but really there is no danger.

Page 106, Listen

DOCTOR JONES: I'm Doctor Jones and this is a show about real life and the human mind. This morning we're going to talk about phobias. A phobia is a very strong fear. When you have a phobia, your body sometimes shakes and your heart beats very fast. You feel like you are in danger, but really there is no danger. For example, I know one person with arachnophobia, the fear of spiders. She can't even look at a picture of a spider. Now, a picture can't

hurt you. We all know that. But a phobia means having a very strong fear—when there is really no danger. A phobia is very strong, and it changes your life. Believe me, a phobia is a very serious issue.

DOCTOR JONES: Good morning! Here's our first caller: Anna, from New York. Hello, Anna.

ANNA: Doctor Jones, hello! Thanks so much for taking my call. I have a phobia story for you.

DOCTOR JONES: Please go ahead. We're listening.

ANNA: Well, first of all, I really agree with you—a phobia is a very serious issue. Here's my story: I always wanted to go to Paris. So, I worked really hard and saved a lot of money. Finally, I went to Paris, and I was so happy. I went to the Eiffel Tower . . . You know, it was the dream of my life. I was so excited when I started to climb up the tower. But after a few minutes, I started to feel very scared. I didn't know where I was. And I was confused. Where was the top? Where was the bottom? I just didn't know. So I started running down the stairs really fast. I was so scared—I had to get out. There were lots of kids on the stairs, kids on a class trip or something. But I didn't care. I just ran past them! I had to get out. I felt like I was going to die in there.

DOCTOR JONES: It sounds like you had claustrophobia: the fear of small spaces. Was that your first experience with a phobia?

ANNA: Yes. And that was just the beginning. Then it got worse. After I came home, I couldn't take elevators or drive my car.

DOCTOR JONES: Yes, because those are both small, closed spaces.

ANNA: For a long time, I couldn't do so many things.

DOCTOR JONES: What kinds of things?

ANNA: Well, some of my good friends live in tall apartment buildings, and I was afraid to take the elevator. I always walked up the stairs—and it took forever! And when I looked for a new job, I could only work in low buildings, not high ones. And I couldn't drive my car, so I couldn't travel easily.

DOCTOR JONES: I see . . . So, there were a lot of changes in your life . . .

ANNA: Yeah, and not good ones. But I'm better now.

DOCTOR JONES: What helped you?

ANNA: Different things—going to doctors. They helped me. And reading books. I read about twenty books a week because I really want to understand my phobias.

DOCTOR JONES: And how's your life today?

ANNA: It's still not very easy, but it's better. I'm a lot better with elevators.

DOCTOR JONES: Any advice for people with elevator phobias?

ANNA: Yes—don't take a job in a high building—not even for a million dollars! I'm just kidding. I guess my advice is: Don't be angry with yourself. Lots of people have phobias—you're not the only one. And it's not your fault.

DOCTOR JONES: That's right, Anna. I completely agree. Thanks so much for calling today . . . and good luck!

Page 108, Make Inferences

Example

ANNA: I had to get out . . . I felt like I was going to die in there.

Excerpt One

ANNA: I always walked up the stairs—and it took forever!

Excerpt Two

ANNA: Different things—going to doctors. They helped me. And reading books. I read about twenty books a week because I really want to understand my phobias.

Excerpt Three

ANNA: Yes—don't take a job in a high building—not even for a million dollars!

Page 110, Note-taking Skill

Exercise 1

PSYCHOLOGIST: Come on, Allen. You can do it. Think of all the other things you do well: your job, your sports, your music. You're very good at everything you do . . . Believe in yourself!

Listening Two, pages 110–111, Comprehension

PSYCHOLOGIST: Come on, Allen. You can do it. We talked about this. You know what to do.

ALLEN: I know. I know what to do, but I just can't do it.

PSYCHOLOGIST: Now what is it, Allen? What exactly are you scared of?

ALLEN: I don't know. I just hate crossing the bridge. I know there is no reason to be afraid—but I just don't want to do it!

PSYCHOLOGIST: Come on, Allen. You can do it. Think of all the other things you do well: your job, your sports, your music. You're very good at everything you do. You can do this, too. Remember what the book said? Believe in yourself!

ALLEN: Too many trucks.

PSYCHOLOGIST: What did you say?

ALLEN: I'm scared of the trucks! The trucks are going to hit me!

PSYCHOLOGIST: They're not going to hit you, Allen. Calm down. Don't look at the trucks. Just look at the road.

ALLEN: I can't! This bridge is so high!

PSYCHOLOGIST: Don't think about that, Allen. Just look at the road. Look straight ahead.

ALLEN: Oh no, we're on the bridge! I hate driving—it scares me.

PSYCHOLOGIST: Keep going, Allen. Look straight ahead. You're doing fine. Keep going. There! You did it! You crossed the bridge!

ALLEN: *We* crossed the bridge. I can't do it by myself. What's wrong with me? Why am I so afraid of a bridge? Why aren't the books helping me? Why can't you help me?

PSYCHOLOGIST: I am helping you, Allen. The books are helping, too. You're going to cross this bridge by yourself. You will. Now keep going . . .

Page 112, Listening Skill

Example

ALLEN: I'm scared of the trucks! The trucks are going to hit me!

PSYCHOLOGIST: They're not going to hit you, Allen. Calm down.

Exercise 2
Excerpt One

PSYCHOLOGIST: You're doing fine. Keep going. There! You did it! You crossed the bridge!

ALLEN: *We* crossed the bridge. I can't do it by myself.

Excerpt Two

ALLEN: Why am I so afraid of a bridge? Why aren't the books helping me? Why can't you help me?

PSYCHOLOGIST: I am helping you, Allen. The books are helping, too You're going to cross this bridge by yourself. You will. Now keep going . . .

UNIT 6: Risks and Challenges

Listening One, Page 130, Preview

SUE: Hello again. I'm Sue Fujimura.

JIM: And I'm Jim Goodman.

SUE: And we're speaking to you from a boat, somewhere between Cuba and Key West, Florida. As everyone knows, Diana Nyad is trying for the fourth time to swim from Cuba to Florida. And after 51 hours in the ocean, she is still swimming, but things are not going very well right now.

Page 131, Listen

SUE: Hello again. I'm Sue Fujimura.

JIM: And I'm Jim Goodman.

SUE: And we're speaking to you from a boat, somewhere between Cuba and Key West, Florida. As everyone knows, Diana Nyad is trying for the fourth time to swim from Cuba to Florida. And after 51 hours in the ocean, she is still swimming, but things are not going very well right now.

JIM: Yes, as you can hear, it's raining very hard and it's very windy!

SUE: Unfortunately, the wind is pushing Diana very far off her course, and that means she will have to swim much longer to get to Florida.

JIM: She also has jellyfish bites all over her body, and they're making her feel very sick.

SUE: Yes, she's swimming slowly now, and her body is shaking, and . . . is she having problems breathing?

JIM: I think she is. That's also because of the jellyfish. Jellyfish are very dangerous. You know, most swimmers give up if they get a few jellyfish bites, or if the weather is as . . . as terrible as it is right now. But, just look at Diana! How does she do it?!

SUE: I know! She really is amazing. You know, long-distance swimming is so difficult, even in good conditions.

JIM: That's very true. Diana called it "the loneliest sport in the world." I mean, there are a few people on the boat that is following her, but she is swimming in the ocean alone. She has to move her body the same way again and again for so many hours and days. That is really hard—and boring!

SUE: It sure is. So I want to tell people how Diana pushes herself to keep going after so many hours and days of swimming. Diana doesn't only train her body, she also trains her mind. Diana knows how to clear her mind, so when she's swimming, she doesn't think about anything.

JIM: How does she do that?

SUE: She does a kind of meditation. When Diana is swimming, she counts from one to 1,000 in four different languages: English, French, Spanish, and German. She does that over and over. She also knows a lot of songs. When she finishes counting, she sings those songs in her mind, sometimes one or two thousand times. Can you imagine that? But Diana says that when she counts and sings, she can't think about anything else. And when her mind is clear, she can keep swimming for a long time.

JIM: Y'know, that's interesting, because scientists say that for long-distance sports, training the mind is more important than training the body. That's probably why Diana said that long-distance swimming "is not a young person's game."

SUE: Right. Older people can train their minds more easily. So even when Diana's having a lot of problems, like now, she can keep swimming. She doesn't let the problems stop her.

JIM: To Diana, problems are just challenges, and she likes challenges!

SUE: That's right. People also say that Diana Nyad has no fear. I mean, there are a lot of sharks in this ocean, but she is swimming without a shark cage to protect her! No shark cage! Who does that?!

JIM: You're right! She really isn't afraid of anything! And she's so determined! I mean, she's 62 years old, and she's trying to set a new long-distance swimming record for the fourth time! How many people are that determined to do anything?

SUE: I think we can agree that Diana Nyad is much more than an amazing swimmer. Y'know, a lot of people say that because of Diana's example, they chose new goals in their own lives and pushed themselves to reach them.

JIM: Yes, I think many people have learned a lot from Diana, especially older people. She really shows people that it's never too late to have a goal.

SUE: Oh no. . . . Jim, look . . . Diana is swimming over to her boat.

JIM: She's talking to her coach and doctor.

SUE: Oh no! They're pulling her out of the water. I hope she's OK . . . We'll be back in just a moment with the latest information on Diana Nyad.

Pages 132–133, Make Inferences

Example 1

JIM: You know, most swimmers give up if they get a few jellyfish bites, or if the weather is as . . . as terrible as it is right now. But, just look at Diana! How does she do it?!

SUE: I know. She really is amazing.

Example 2

SUE: So I want to tell people how Diana pushes herself to keep going after so many hours and days of swimming. Diana doesn't only train her body, she also trains her mind. Diana knows how to clear her mind, so when she's swimming, she doesn't think about anything.

JIM: How does she do that?

SUE: She does a kind of meditation.

Excerpt One

SUE: She does a kind of meditation. When Diana is swimming, she counts from one to 1,000 in four different languages: English, French, Spanish, and German. She does that over and over. She also knows a lot of songs. When she finishes counting, she sings those songs in her mind, sometimes one or two thousand times. Can you imagine that?

Excerpt Two

JIM: You're right! She really isn't afraid of anything! And she's so determined! I mean, she's 62 years old, and she's trying to set a new long-distance swimming record for the fourth time! How many people are that determined to do anything?

Excerpt Three

SUE: Yes, she's swimming slowly now, and her body is shaking, and . . . is she having problems breathing?

Pages 135–136, Note-taking Skill

Example 1

SUE: Unfortunately, the wind is pushing Diana very far off her course. And that means she will have to swim much longer to get to Florida.

Example 2

JIM: She also has jellyfish bites all over her body, and they're making her feel very sick.

SUE: Yes, she is swimming slowly now, and her body is shaking, and . . . . is she having problems breathing?

JIM: I think she is. That's also because of the jellyfish.

SUE: It sure is. So I want to tell people how Diana pushes herself to keep going after so many hours and days of swimming. Diana doesn't only train her body, she also trains her mind. Diana knows how to clear her mind, so when she's swimming, she doesn't think about anything.

JIM: How does she do that?

SUE: She does a kind of meditation. When Diana is swimming, she counts from one to 1000 in four different languages: English, French, Spanish, and German. She does that over and over. She also knows a lot of songs. When she finishes counting, she sings those songs in her mind, sometimes one or two thousand times. Can you imagine that? But Diana says that when she counts and sings, she can't think about anything else. And when her mind is clear, she can keep swimming for a long time.

Excerpt Two

JIM: To Diana, problems are just challenges, and she likes challenges!

SUE: That's right. People also say that Diana Nyad has no fear. I mean, there are a lot of sharks in this ocean, but she is swimming without a shark cage to protect her! No shark cage! Who does that?!

JIM: You're right! She really isn't afraid of anything! And she's so determined! I mean, she's 62 years old, and she's trying to set a new long-distance swimming record for the fourth time! How many people are that determined to do anything?

SUE: I think we can agree that Diana Nyad is much more than an amazing swimmer. Y'know, a lot of people say that because of Diana's example, they chose new goals in their own lives and pushed themselves to reach them.

JIM: Yes, I think many people have learned a lot from Diana, especially older people. She really shows people that it's never too late to have a goal.

Listening Two, Pages 136–137, Comprehension

INTERVIEWER: Hi, Jeremy. Thanks for taking some time to meet with me.

JEREMY: That's OK.

INTERVIEWER: So, tell me . . . why did you decide to go on Outward Journeys this summer?

JEREMY: Well, I wanted to have some new experiences and learn how to do some new things. Those were my main goals.

INTERVIEWER: And why were those goals important to you? Do you know?

JEREMY: Umm . . . yeah, I think it's because I'm fourteen years old, but I'm the youngest kid in my family, so everyone thinks I'm the "baby." So I wanted to prove that I'm not.

INTERVIEWER: You wanted to prove that to your family?

JEREMY: Yeah, and to myself, too.

INTERVIEWER: And do you feel like you're proving that now?

JEREMY: Yeah, definitely. I'm doing a lot of new things, and it feels great.

INTERVIEWER: Really? But don't you sleep outside at night and walk in the mountains with a heavy backpack? Isn't that hard for you?

JEREMY: Yeah, it *is* hard, but that's why I joined Outward Journeys. I wanted to have new challenges. And . . . doing challenging things is really exciting!

INTERVIEWER: Uh huh, I see . . . So, what kinds of things do you do?

JEREMY: Well, a few days ago we went whitewater rafting, and yesterday we went rock climbing up this really big mountain . . .

INTERVIEWER: Wow, did you know how to do those things before you came here?

JEREMY: No, and I also didn't think I could do those things, especially the rock climbing.

INTERVIEWER: Weren't you afraid?

JEREMY: Yeah, I was super afraid! When I saw that mountain, I said, "There's *no way* I can do that!" It looked really scary . . .

INTERVIEWER: Well—sure! Didn't all the kids feel the same way?

JEREMY: I guess so . . . Anyway, after I did it, I felt like, "Wow—I really climbed that mountain!" It felt amazing! That's the really cool thing about Outward Journeys. You learn that you can do a lot of things even if you're afraid.

INTERVIEWER: So, it sounds like you're discovering some new things about yourself.

JEREMY: Yeah. I feel much more confident. I'm not really afraid to do anything hard, because rock climbing up that mountain was the hardest thing I ever did in my life! Our group leaders say that most people are really strong inside, but they just don't know it.

INTERVIEWER: I see, so when you do these difficult things, like rock climbing, you can discover how strong you really are.

JEREMY: Right. And that's really exciting!

INTERVIEWER: I can understand that. But aren't some of the things you're doing a little dangerous? Aren't you all a little young to take such big risks?

JEREMY: No, our group leaders teach us how to do everything, and especially how to be very careful. So we *are* doing some difficult things, but it's really not dangerous. We always feel safe.

INTERVIEWER: Well, you do sound like you've become a very confident young man!

JEREMY: Thank you.

INTERVIEWER: OK, then, Jeremy, thank you, and enjoy the rest of your experience.

JEREMY: Thanks, I will! (Hey guys . . . Wait up!)

Pages 138–139, Listening Skill

Exercise 1

JEREMY: I'm doing a lot of new things, and it feels great.

INTERVIEWER: Really? But don't you sleep outside at night and walk in the mountains with a heavy backpack?

Example

INTERVIEWER: I see, so when you do these difficult things, like rock climbing, you can discover how strong you really are.

JEREMY: Right. And that's really exciting!

INTERVIEWER: But aren't some of the things you're doing a little dangerous? Aren't you all a little young to take such big risks?

Exercise 2

Excerpt One

JEREMY: Umm . . . yeah, I think it's because I'm fourteen years old, but I'm the youngest kid in my family, so everyone thinks I'm the "baby." . . . So I wanted to prove that I'm not.

INTERVIEWER: And do you feel like you're proving that now?

Excerpt Two

JEREMY: I also didn't think I could do those things, especially the rock climbing.

INTERVIEWER: Weren't you afraid?

Excerpt Three

INTERVIEWER: But aren't some of the things you're doing a little dangerous?

Excerpt Four

JEREMY: Yeah! I was super afraid! When I saw that mountain, I said, "There is *no way* I can do that!" It looked really scary . . .

INTERVIEWER: Well—sure! Didn't all the kids feel the same way?

UNIT 7: Only Child—Lonely Child?

Listening One, page 156, Preview

MARIA SANCHEZ: Hello! Welcome to *Changing Families*. I'm Maria Sanchez, and today we're going to talk about only children. In the past, people thought that an only child was a lonely child. But now, more and more parents all over the world are deciding to have just one child, especially in big cities. Today, we are going to meet two families with only children.

Page 157, Listen

MARIA SANCHEZ: Hello! Welcome to *Changing Families*. I'm Maria Sanchez, and today we're going to talk about only children. In the past, people thought that an only child was a lonely child. But now, more and more families all over the world are deciding to have just one child, especially in big cities.

Today, we are going to meet two families with only children. First, we're going to talk with Marion and Mark Carter, from Chicago, Illinois. Hello!

MARK AND MARION: Hi. / Hi, Maria.

MARIA: Welcome! Please tell us—Why did you decide to have just one child?

MARK: Well, um . . . we were both thirty-six when we got married . . .

MARIA: Uh-huh.

MARION: . . . and then, when we had Tonia, our daughter, I was thirty-eight. Tonia is so wonderful, and we love her more than anything. But . . . well, it isn't easy to raise a young child at our age.

MARK: That's for sure. We're always tired!

MARIA: I think many young parents feel the same way!

MARK: Mmm . . . Maybe . . . Anyway, at some point, we just decided that we couldn't take care of Tonia and a new baby.

MARION: Yeah. We decided that we were happy with our little family, and that one child was enough for us.

MARIA: Uh-huh. And how does Tonia feel about your family? Is she ever lonely?

MARION: Um . . . I don't think so, because we spend a lot of time with her, and she has lots of friends.

MARK: That's for sure! She's very popular!

MARIA: Really! You know, that's interesting because I read that only children are often more popular—and also more intelligent—than children with siblings.

MARK: Yes, that *is* interesting!

MARIA: Isn't it? It's really something to think about. Another thing to think about is the world population problem. By the year 2050, there are going to be more than 9 billion people in the world, and we don't know if we're going to have enough food and water for everyone. So some people feel that it's not responsible to have more than one child. They say that everyone needs to think about the future of the world, not just about their own family. Mark, Marion, did you think about that issue, too?

MARK: Well, of course we know about the population problem in the world, and we think it's a very serious issue, but I'd say that our decision was really a personal one.

MARIA: I understand. OK, thank you, Mark and Marion. And now, let's say hello to Tom and Jenna Mori from New York City.

TOM AND JENNA: Hi, Maria! / Hi.

MARIA: Now, Tom and Jenna, you also made a decision to have only one child.

TOM: Yes, that's right . . .

MARIA: Can you tell us why?

TOM: Well, it was a difficult decision for us . . .

JENNA: Yes, very difficult . . .

TOM: . . . because Jenna and I really love kids. When we got married, we wanted to have two or three children.

MARIA: Oh?

JENNA: But we're both teachers, and I'm sure you know teachers don't make a lot of money!

MARIA: That's true. Most teachers aren't rich!

JENNA: Well, before we had a child, money wasn't really so important to us.

MARIA: That's interesting . . .

JENNA: But now . . . well, when you have a child, it's different. We want our son Jay to have a good life—you know—to go to a good school, take piano lessons, travel . . . And those things are very expensive!

MARIA: You're right about that!

TOM: Yeah, and we know we can't afford all of those things for two children. So we decided to have only one child, so we can give him the best.

MARIA: I understand. But do you think Jay wants a sibling? Does he ever feel lonely?

TOM: Jay?! Never!

JENNA: Oh, no. He's always so busy with his friends.

TOM: Yeah, and with his sports and his music, too.

MARIA: Well, that's wonderful. Tom and Jenna Mori—thanks for talking with us.

Tom and Jenna: Our pleasure. Thank you!

Maria: OK, next, I'm going to talk to the kids! Don't go away!

Pages 158–159, Make Inferences

Example

Mark: Anyway, at some point, we just decided that we couldn't take care of Tonia and a new baby.

Excerpt One

Marion: . . . when we had Tonia, our daughter, I was thirty-eight. Tonia is so wonderful, and we love her more than anything. But . . . well, it isn't easy to raise a young child at our age.

Mark: That's for sure. We're always tired!

Excerpt Two

Marion: Um . . . I don't think so, because we spend a lot of time with her, and she has lots of friends.

Mark: That's for sure! She's very popular!

Maria: Really! You know, that's interesting because I read that only children are often more popular—and also more intelligent— than children with siblings.

Mark: Yes, that *is* interesting!

Maria: Isn't it? It's really something to think about.

Excerpt Three

Jenna: Well, before we had a child, money wasn't really so important to us.

Maria: That's interesting . . .

Jenna: But now . . . well, when you have a child, it's different. We want our son Jay to have a good life—you know—to go to a good school, take piano lessons, travel . . . And those things are very expensive!

Pages 160–161, Note-taking Skill

Exercise 1

Maria: I'm Maria Sanchez, and today we're going to talk about only children. In the past, people thought that an only child was a lonely child. But now, more and more families all over the world are deciding to have just one child, especially in big cities.

Today, we are going to meet two families with only children.

Exercise 2

Maria: It's really something to think about. Another thing to think about is the world population problem. By the year 2050, there are going to be more than 9 billion people in the world, and we don't know if we're going to have enough food and water for everyone. So some people feel that it's not responsible to have more than one child. They say that everyone needs to think about the future of the world, not just about their own family. Mark, Marion, did you think about that issue, too?

Listening Two, Pages 161–162, Comprehension

Maria Sanchez: Hello, and welcome back. So, what do kids think about being an only child? Let's find out right now! I'm going to speak to Marion and Mark's daughter, Tonia, and to Tom and Jenna's son, Jay. Hi, Tonia.

Tonia: Hi.

Maria: How old are you, sweetheart?

Tonia: Eight.

Maria: Eight. And Jay, you are . . . ?

Jay: I'm twelve.

Maria: OK. Now Tonia, you're the only child in your family, right?

Tonia: Uh-huh.

Maria: And is that OK with you?

Tonia: No! I hate it . . .

Maria: Really . . . Why?

Tonia: Because I want a sister.

Tonia: All my friends have brothers and sisters. I'm the only kid in my class who doesn't have one!

Maria: Oh, I see . . . Umm . . . did you ever talk to your parents about it?

Tonia: Yeah, I talked to my mom.

Maria: And what did she say?

Tonia: She said, "I am so busy with you and with my job. We are not going to have another child."

Maria: And how did you feel then?

TONIA: I was sad.

MARIA: But can you understand your parents' decision?

TONIA: Yeah . . .

MARIA: Well, that's good.

TONIA: But I still want a sister!

MARIA: Well, here's a little girl who knows what she wants! Thank you, Tonia. And Jay, how about you? Do you feel the same way?

JAY: No, not at all. I like my family this way.

MARIA: Mm hmm . . . But do you ever feel lonely?

JAY: No, I never feel lonely. I feel . . . special! My parents do a lot of things with me, and we always have fun together. And they also give me a lot of opportunities that kids in some big families don't have.

MARIA: What kinds of opportunities?

JAY: Well, the best thing is that we travel a lot, all over the world. Like, last summer, we went to Asia for a month. And this winter, we're going to go skiing in Europe.

MARIA: Wow, that's exciting!

JAY: Yeah, and I think we can do all of these things because it's just the three of us.

MARIA: You mean, because your parents can afford it?

JAY: Yeah, uh-huh . . .

MARIA: But do you ever feel different from your friends?

JAY: Mm . . . no, not in a bad way. I mean, every family is different, right?

MARIA: Yes, that's true.

JAY: So maybe I'm a little different because I enjoy doing things alone.

MARIA: That *is* a little unusual for someone your age.

JAY: Well, my parents taught me how to enjoy doing things by myself. I don't act like a baby and cry because I don't have a sibling to do things with.

MARIA: What a mature young man you are!

JAY: Thank you.

MARIA: Thank you, Jay, and thanks to you, too, Tonia.

TONIA AND JAY: You're welcome.

MARIA: Well, there you have it—two children, and two very different opinions about being an only child. Thanks for watching!

Page 163, Listening Skill
Exercise 1

MARION: We decided that we were happy with our little family, and that one child was enough for us.

Exercise 2
Excerpt One

MARIA: Thank you, Jay, and thanks to you, too, Tonia.

TONIA AND JAY: You're welcome.

MARIA: Well, there you have it—

Excerpt Two

MARIA: Wow, that's exciting!

JAY: Yeah, and I think we can do all of these things because it's just the three of us.

Excerpt Three

MARIA: Mm hmm . . . But do you ever feel lonely?

JAY: No, I never feel lonely.

Excerpt Four

JAY: So maybe I'm a little different because I enjoy doing things alone.

MARIA: That *is* a little unusual for someone your age.

UNIT 8: Soccer: The Beautiful Game

Listening One, Page 181, Preview

M: Goooal! It's a goal! Gooooal!

JANE: That is the sound of soccer, the world's favorite sport. Of course, soccer is still not very popular in the U.S. But with the internet and satellite TV, the world is getting smaller, and, today, Americans see that people all over the world really love this game! To understand why people outside the U.S. love soccer so much, we went to Paolinho's Pizza Restaurant in Minneapolis, Minnesota, to watch the first match of World Cup soccer.

Listening One, page 181, Listen

M: Goooal! It's a goal! Gooooal!

JANE: That is the sound of soccer, the world's favorite sport. Of course, soccer is still not very popular in the U.S. But with the internet and satellite TV, the world is getting smaller, and, today, Americans can see that people all over the world really love this game! To understand why people outside the U.S. love soccer so much, we went to Paolinho's Pizza Restaurant in Minneapolis, Minnesota, to watch the first match of World Cup soccer.

JANE: Hello. What is your name, and where are you from?

GILBERTO: I'm Gilberto, and I am from Brazil.

JANE: Why do you like soccer, Gilberto?

GILBERTO: Why? Ha! That is not even a question in Brazil. Soccer is our life. It is an art. It's like music. Does anyone ever ask you, "Why do you like music?"

JANE: Well, no. . . .

GILBERTO: Well, soccer is the same. You know Pele, the famous Brazilian soccer player?

JANE: Sure, he . . .

GILBERTO: He called soccer "The Beautiful Game." Why? Because when the ball flies through the air, it's beautiful, and when the player jumps into the air, it's like he's flying—like a bird or a dancer. And when he heads the ball or kicks it across the field into the goal, it is simple and beautiful. It is perfect. It is like a . . .

JANE: Thank you, Gilberto. And what about you, sir? What's your name and where are you from?

ERNESTO: I'm Ernesto from Mexico City.

JANE: And why do you like soccer, Ernesto?

ERNESTO: I don't *like* soccer—I *love* soccer! And look at all these people here—they all love it, too.

JANE: Yes, but why?

ERNESTO: Because soccer is like an international language. I come here to watch soccer with these soccer fans from all over the world. For example, I don't know this guy's name here. What's your name?

ANDERS: Anders.

ERNESTO: Yes, Anders—he's from Germany. And I don't really know him, but today we both want the team from Mexico to win. You see, I'm Mexican, he's German, but we both love soccer. It's like there are really only two countries: the country that loves soccer and the country that doesn't understand.

ANDERS: That's the United States—the country that doesn't understand!

JANE: Well, we're trying! That's why I'm talking to you today! Anders, Ernesto said you're from Germany?

ANDERS: Yes, and this is my girlfriend, Marta. She's from Spain.

JANE: Hi, Marta.

MARTA: Hello.

JANE: What do you like about soccer?

ANDERS: Soccer is a sport for everyone. You don't need a lot of special things to play it— you just need a ball and a goal. So everyone can play soccer.

MARTA: Yes, and also, everyone can understand soccer—not like American football. You have to read books to understand all of the rules in American football! Soccer is simpler—and it's also more exciting to watch.

JANE: So there are a few reasons that people love soccer. If you still don't understand, go and watch a match at a restaurant like Paolinho's. You might become a fan! With *The Sports File*, this is Jane Tuttle.

Pages 183–184, Make Inferences

Example

JANE: Why do you like soccer, Gilberto?

GILBERTO: Why? Ha! That is not even a question in Brazil. Soccer is our life. It is an art. It's like music. Does anyone ever ask you, "Why do you like music?"

Excerpt One

GILBERTO: You know Pele, the famous Brazilian soccer player?

JANE: Sure, he . . .

Gilberto: He called soccer "The Beautiful Game." Why? Because when the ball flies through the air, it's beautiful, and when the player jumps into the air, it's like he's flying—like a bird or a dancer.

Excerpt Two

Jane: And why do you like soccer, Ernesto?

Ernesto: I don't *like* soccer—I *love* soccer! And look at all these people here—they all love it, too.

Jane: Yes, but why?

Ernesto: Because soccer is like an international language. I come here to watch soccer with these soccer fans from all over the world.

Excerpt Three

Marta: Yes, and also, everyone can understand soccer—not like American football. You have to read books to understand all of the rules in American football!

Pages 185–186, Note-taking Skill

Exercise 2

Excerpt One

Ernesto: Because soccer is like an international language. I come here to watch soccer with these soccer fans from all over the world. For example, I don't know this guy's name here. What's your name?

Anders: Anders.

Ernesto: Yes, Anders—he's from Germany. And I don't really know him, but today we both want the team from Mexico to win. You see, I'm Mexican, he's German, but we both love soccer.

Excerpt Two

Jane: What do you like about soccer?

Anders: Soccer is a sport for everyone. You don't need a lot of special things to play it—you just need a ball and a goal. So everyone can play soccer.

Listening Two, Pages 186–187, Comprehension

Commentator: Welcome to *America Talks.* This morning, we're taking calls from sports fans to hear your opinions about soccer: Why isn't soccer more popular in the United States? During the last World Cup, around 3.4 billion people all over the world watched matches on television. That's almost half of the world population! But many Americans, even big sports fans, didn't even know that the World Cup was happening. How can Americans *not* be interested in a sport that the rest of the world loves—a sport that is so international? Well, for one thing, the U.S. team didn't even qualify for the World Cup in 2018! They didn't make it into the tournament. So, a lot of Americans felt they didn't have a team to root for. You could also argue that the American team hasn't been as successful at winning matches as other countries' teams, and that affects the sport's popularity. Anyway, let's hear what our listeners have to say. Our first caller is Bob from Kearny, New Jersey. Welcome to the show, Bob.

Bob: Hi. Thanks for taking my call.

Commentator: Bob, why isn't soccer popular in this country?

Bob: Well, I think it's mostly because of the low scores.

Commentator: Uh-huh . . .

Bob: You can have a great soccer match, but the final score can be zero to one. I think Americans like sports with higher scores.

Commentator: Interesting. And speaking of scores, people also say that ties are a problem for sports fans in the U.S. Americans really like one team to win and one team to lose.

Bob: Yeah, that's definitely another reason that soccer isn't very popular here.

Commentator: Thanks for the call, Bob. Next, we have Linda from Rochester, New York on the line. Hello, Linda.

Linda: Hi. I think soccer is less popular here because we didn't know about any professional soccer teams growing up. Also, a lot of soccer matches were on international TV with teams from other countries. It wasn't easy to watch these matches when we were growing up.

Baseball and basketball were definitely more popular. And football.

Commentator: So you think the problem is just that soccer is not a traditional sport in this country?

Linda: Yeah. Our traditional sports in the U.S. are baseball, football, and basketball. And if you watch all three of those sports, you're pretty busy. We don't really need another sport.

Commentator: Thanks for your comments, Linda. We have one more call, from Drew in Seattle, Washington. Drew, why do you think soccer isn't more popular here in the U.S.?

Drew: Hi. Americans love superstars. But we haven't had any real big American soccer stars yet. That's why soccer isn't more popular here. I mean, Pele played in the U.S. in 1975, but he's from Brazil, and that was a really long time ago. I think David Beckham made Americans more interested in soccer. He *was* a superstar, and so was his wife, Victoria. I think they helped soccer in the U.S. a lot.

Commentator: Yes, I agree.

Drew: But they're from England. These days, Cristiano Ronaldo from Portugal seems to be getting closer to that superstar status, but I think he's still unfamiliar to a lot of Americans. If you ask me, we need an American superstar. Then soccer will become more popular, for sure!

Commentator: OK, thanks for your call, Drew. And that's it for today's show. Tune in again tomorrow for *America Talks*.

Pages 187–188, Listening Skill

Example

Bob: Hi. Thanks for taking my call.

Commentator: Bob, why isn't soccer popular in this country?

Bob: Well, I think it's mostly because of the low scores.

Commentator: Uh-huh . . .

Excerpt One

Commentator: Interesting. And speaking of scores, people also say that ties are a problem for sports fans in the U.S. Americans really like one team to win and one team to lose.

Bob: Yeah, that's definitely another reason that soccer isn't very popular here.

Excerpt Two

Linda: Hi. I think soccer is less popular here because we didn't know about any professional soccer teams growing up. Also, a lot of soccer matches were on international TV with teams from other countries. It wasn't easy to watch these matches when we were growing up.

Excerpt Three

Drew: Hi. Americans love superstars. But we haven't had any really big American soccer stars yet. That's why soccer isn't more popular here.

THE PHONETIC ALPHABET

Consonant Symbols			
/b/	be	/t/	to
/d/	do	/v/	van
/f/	father	/w/	will
/g/	get	/y/	yes
/h/	he	/z/	zoo, busy
/k/	keep, can	/θ/	thanks
/l/	let	/ð/	then
/m/	may	/ʃ/	she
/n/	no	/ʒ/	vision, Asia
/p/	pen	/tʃ/	child
/r/	rain	/dʒ/	join
/s/	so, circle	/ŋ/	long

Vowel Symbols			
/α/	far, hot	/iy/	we, mean, feet
/ɛ/	met, said	/ey/	day, late, rain
/ɔ/	tall, bought	/ow/	go, low, coat
/ə/	son, under	/uw/	too, blue
/æ/	cat	/ay/	time, buy
/ɪ/	ship	/aw/	house, now
/ʊ/	good, could, put	/oy/	boy, coin

CREDITS

NOTES